The Top UK Perfume and Toilet Preparations Manufacturers

Profiles of the leading 900 companies

John D Blackburn

Editor

dp

First Edition

Summer 2019

ISBN-13: 978-1-912736-28-7

ISBN-10: 1-912736-28-4

All rights reserved. No part of this publication may be reproduced, distributed, or transmitted in any form or by any means, including photocopying, recording, or other electronic or mechanical methods, without our prior written permission, except in the case of brief quotations embodied in critical reviews and certain other non-commercial uses permitted by copyright law. For permission requests, please write to us.

Copyright © 2019 Dellam Publishing Limited

Printed in 8pt Nimbus Sans L

Designed by URW++ Design and Development GmbH

Dellam Publishing Limited

2 Heath Drive, Sutton, Surrey, SM2 5RP

Fax: 020 8770 7478   email: enquiries@dellam.com

SAN: 0177881   EAN/GLN: 5030670177882

Table of Contents

1 Acknowledgements iv

2 Introduction v

3 Total Assets League Table 1

- As a measure of size, total assets is preferable to turnover which is influenced by profit margins and whether companies are capital or labour intensive.

4 Age of Companies 7

- Each company is ranked by its date of incorporation. Newcomers are defined as those registered since 2017.

5 Geographic Distribution 15

- Each company is classed by county .

6 Company Profiles 23

- Full company name, date incorporated, net worth, total assets, registered office, activities, shareholders and parent company, directors (with date of birth, nationality and occupation) and number of employees (if available).

7 Index of Directorships 79

- Alphabetical list of directors showing their directorships. If several directors have identical names then their date of birth is shown.

8 Standard Industrial Classification 99

- These codes are used to classify businesses by the type of economic activity in which they are engaged.

9 *finis* 107

Acknowledgements

This is a long and detailed publication containing thousands of facts and figures. It is only to be expected, despite continuous and repeated editing and checking, that errors may occur. In such cases, once we are aware of any, we publish a correction on our website.

Readers are encouraged to check regularly at www.dellam.com/books for any corrections and updates.

Although we take extreme care to ensure accuracy and being up-to-date, we cannot accept responsibility for any errors or omissions.

Contains public sector information licensed under Open Government Licence v3.0. from The Charity Commission (England and Wales) and The Charity Commission for Northern Ireland. © Crown Copyright and database right (2018).

Contains information from the Scottish Charity Register supplied by the Office of the Scottish Charity Regulator and licensed under the Open Government Licence v.2.0. © Crown Copyright and database right (2018).

Contains OS data © Crown copyright and database right (2018)

Contains Royal Mail data © Royal Mail copyright and database right (2018)

Contains National Statistics data © Crown copyright and database right (2018)

Contains Office for National Statistics © Crown copyright and database right (2018)

Maps based on those produced by the Office for National Statistics Geography GIS & Mapping Unit (2012 and 2018).

Contains HM Land Registry data © Crown copyright and database right (2018).

Contains Parliamentary information licensed under the Open Parliament Licence v3.0.

House of Commons Library Briefing Papers licensed under the Open Parliament Licence v3.0.

Contains Food Standards Agency data © Crown copyright and database right (2018).

Contains Eurostat data, 1995-2018, copyright European Commission by the Decision of 12 December 2011.

Maps based on produced by ONS Geography GIS & Mapping Unit.

Contains Companies House data supplied under section 47 and 50 of the Copyright, Designs and Patents Act 1988 and Schedule 1 of the Database Regulations (SI 1997/3032).

We appreciate your interest in our publications, and your comments and suggestions are always welcome. Please contact us at enquiries@dellam.com.

Introduction

This study looks at all companies registered in the United Kingdom where they identify themselves as manufacturers of perfume and toilet preparations.

This study includes companies that are dormant or non-trading some of which might be latent while others may operate under their owners' names but incorporate to protect the business name. In addition, all newly incorporated companies are included. The study will exclude those companies that do not specifically identify themselves as manufacturers of perfume and toilet preparations.

The aim of this study is to provide an overview of the key movers and shakers in the UK manufacture of perfume and toilet preparations sector. Only key data has been isolated, particularly the company's net worth and total assets, but also its full name, date incorporated, registered office, other activities, shareholders, directors (with date of birth, occupation and nationality) and number of employees.

Two indicators of size are used: net worth and total assets. These are preferable to turnover which is influenced by profit margins and whether the companies are capital or labour intensive.

In the years 2016, 2017 and 2018, new company incorporations in the manufacture of perfume and toilet preparations sector were 72, 158 and 256 respectively.

In 2017, in this manufacturing sector, there were 575 VAT or PAYE based companies employing 14,837 people with total turnover of £2.426 billion.

Product price inflation for years 2010-2018 was 100.0, 101.1, 100.4, 100.7, 101.6, 102.6, 102.1, 100.9 and 112.7.

The Cosmetic, Toiletry & Perfumery Association (CTPA) represents all companies involved in making, supplying and selling cosmetic and personal care products. It represents 80% of the market.

The market size is £ 9.769 billion (retail sales) and employs 200,000 people.

The breakdown is as follows: skin care £2.3 billion; toiletries £2.3 billion; perfumes and fragrances £1.8 billion; hair care £1.7 billion and make-up £1.6 billion.

Exports are £3.94 billion (2016) while imports were £4.28 billion. Exports to EU was 65%.

Cosmetics Europe is the European trade association for the cosmetics and personal care industry.

Valued at €77.6 billion at retail sales price in 2017, the European cosmetics and personal care market is the largest in the world. The largest national markets are Germany (€13.6 billion), France (€11.3 billion), the UK (€11.1 billion), Italy (€10.1 billion) and Spain (€6.8 billion).

The sector brings at least €29 billion in added value to the EU economy annually. €11 billion is contributed directly by the manufacture of cosmetic products and €18 billion indirectly through the supply chain.

Standard cataloguing guidelines for company names in the profile section have been used, but there will be occurrences when the name may not be strictly alphabetical. A certain licence was adopted where it was felt that strictly alphabetical could lead to improper cataloguing. Some company names have been shortened in the league tables for aesthetic reasons.

John D Blackburn
Editor

This page is intentionally left blank

Total Assets League Table

Company	Value	Company	Value
Robert McBride Ltd	£170,578,000	Potter & Moore (Devon) Ltd	£3,267,000
Lush Ltd.	£133,899,000	Miller Harris Limited	£3,230,946
Coty Manufacturing UK Limited	£107,977,000	M.S. George Limited	£3,202,793
CPL Aromas Limited	£93,899,000	Firmenich Holdings (UK) Limited	£3,062,000
BCM Limited	£90,600,000	Ferndale Pharmaceuticals Limited	£2,920,641
CPL Aromas (Holdings) Limited	£81,190,000	John Gosnell & Company, Limited	£2,833,054
Meiyume (UK) Limited	£75,902,000	Heaven Scent Incense Limited	£2,646,548
Gillette U.K. Limited	£63,434,000	Arco England Limited	£2,549,470
Islestarr Holdings Limited	£61,629,924	Arcania Apothecary Ltd	£2,481,689
Elemis Limited	£61,136,348	Phoenix Fragrances Limited	£2,415,650
Swallowfield PLC	£60,490,000	In Line Health and Beauty Limited	£2,264,920
Molton Brown Limited	£55,077,000	Jarvis Cosmetic Developments Ltd.	£2,257,317
Lush Manufacturing Limited	£53,155,000	Sabel Cosmetics Limited	£2,253,220
Fragrance Oils (International) Limited	£48,507,260	S.R.S. Aromatics Limited	£2,054,031
Firmenich UK Limited	£45,554,000	Mavala (U.K.) Limited	£2,004,162
Kao (UK) Limited	£42,610,000	Universal Toiletries Corporation Limited	£1,933,357
Liz Earle Beauty Co. Limited	£38,463,136	Groomers Limited	£1,879,278
Barony Universal Products PLC	£35,509,000	Blazergold Limited	£1,806,500
Ungerer Limited	£35,211,000	International Toiletries & Cosmetics Limited	£1,768,367
Acheson & Acheson Limited	£34,998,828	Geo. F. Trumper (Perfumer and Products) Limited	£1,759,021
Emerald Kalama Chemical Limited	£34,191,000	A. & E. Connock (Perfumery & Cosmetics) Limited	£1,537,840
Dr. Organic Limited	£26,357,000	United Beauty Products Limited	£1,487,894
Professional Beauty Systems (Holdings) Limited	£26,159,012	La Riche Limited	£1,470,524
Fragrance Oils (Purchasing) Limited	£25,254,370	R.P.C. Midlands Ltd	£1,362,793
Mibelle Ltd	£24,631,000	The Beautiful Mind Series Limited	£1,329,002
Neal's Yard (Natural Remedies) Limited	£24,280,000	Teknord Limited	£1,266,151
Professional Beauty Systems Limited	£22,932,808	Wrimes Cosmetics Ltd	£1,250,000
Baylis & Harding Public Limited Company	£21,126,496	Designer Fragrances Limited	£1,230,000
Evans Vanodine International PLC	£20,189,306	Susan Molyneux Cosmetics Limited	£1,220,875
Thiscompany Limited	£20,047,952	Chuckling Goat Limited	£1,173,789
Creightons PLC	£16,646,000	Fragrances and Cosmetics Limited	£1,109,992
Fillcare Limited	£15,329,000	Faces Cosmetics Limited	£1,066,000
Potter & Moore Innovations Limited	£14,846,000	Eve Taylor (London) Limited	£1,049,308
KPSS (UK) Limited	£14,330,000	Morgan's Pomade Company Limited	£1,031,126
Robertet (U.K.) Limited	£9,973,241	Zodiac International (London) Limited	£966,878
Solab Group Limited	£9,265,814	Christina May Limited	£964,391
Combe International Limited	£8,769,294	Fashion Fragrances & Cosmetics UK Ltd	£959,217
Pierre Fabre Limited	£7,420,965	K.K. Toiletries Limited	£954,436
Aroma Trading Limited	£6,605,720	Fikkerts Limited	£905,822
L.E.C.(L'pool) Limited	£5,224,663	Nicholas James (UK) Limited	£884,281
Clover Chemicals Limited	£4,944,551	TWC Products Limited	£854,136
Sachets Limited	£4,853,222	Dreamweave Products Ltd	£832,350
Elsan Limited	£4,644,513	Quality Analysis Limited	£817,683
First Natural Limited	£4,327,044	Fragrances UK Limited	£712,273
Freshorize Ltd	£4,209,926	Stantondown Limited	£686,153
Superfine Manufacturing Limited	£4,200,140	KD Trading (UK) Limited	£670,729
First Natural Brands Ltd	£3,952,657	MAC Professional Haircare Limited	£643,953
The Somerset Toiletry Company Limited	£3,623,954	McCallum Manufacturing Limited	£636,003
Surefil Beauty Products Limited	£3,569,123	T & H Marketing Limited	£633,155
Itaconix (U.K.) Limited	£3,310,000	Bahoma Limited	£625,243

The Top UK Perfume and Toilet Preparations Manufacturers

Excel (GS) Limited	£607,348	Doris Michaels Cosmetics Ltd	£148,860
Natural Looks Trading Limited	£568,690	Inspired Health & Beauty Products Limited	£145,502
Fragrant Earth International Limited	£548,683	Karaama Fragrances Ltd	£145,319
Laboratory Facilities Limited	£538,890	JLP Cosmetics Ltd	£140,019
Butterbur and Sage Limited	£519,549	Odejo Limited	£136,965
Waterman Corporate Enterprises Limited	£514,087	Cool Gell Limited	£134,916
Hair Systems Europe Limited	£487,853	Archem (N.I.) Ltd	£133,839
Ayurveda Pura Ltd	£480,253	Q-Pack Limited	£126,611
Paddy's Bathroom Limited	£433,263	Ahwaz Ltd	£120,800
Travik Chemicals (UK) Limited	£380,966	Aventual Ltd	£120,318
R.M. Investments Limited	£378,048	IQ-Area Ltd	£120,256
The Wildsmith Collection Limited	£373,484	Perfume By Design Ltd.	£112,444
Cosmetics a la Carte Limited	£368,897	Elequra Limited	£111,570
Penny Price Aromatherapy Ltd	£340,260	Gallivant Perfumes Limited	£110,328
Pure Lakes Skincare Limited	£334,800	This Wode Company Ltd	£105,103
Caldey Island Estate Company Limited	£334,766	Essentially Yours Limited	£103,849
Mayfair Perfumes Limited	£326,083	Herc Ltd.	£97,450
Mitchell and Peach Limited	£320,669	Eden Classics Limited	£93,934
Nectar International Limited	£304,139	Christian Lincoln Enterprise Limited	£87,042
Natural Aromatics Limited	£303,900	83 Associates Limited	£85,680
The Highland Soap Co. Limited	£294,882	Gracetree Ltd	£84,566
Maison Ex Nihilo UK Limited	£294,310	4160 Tuesdays Limited	£83,889
Geltec Limited	£293,570	Scrubbingtons Limited	£81,078
Jean Christian Perfumes Limited	£289,970	Arriva Fragrances Limited	£80,790
Get Lucky Inc Ltd	£289,543	Experimental Perfume Club Ltd	£78,891
Project Renegades Ltd	£252,270	Belinda Brown Limited	£75,958
Ottimo Supplies Limited	£248,284	Solar Cosmetics International Limited	£75,176
Wilde Beauty Limited	£245,762	Queen Cosmetics Limited	£75,123
Double Take Limited	£243,557	TH / Edition Ltd	£75,004
Drom International UK Limited	£237,067	Body & Face St. Cyrus Limited	£74,285
Dr Jackson Ltd	£228,257	Gagnon Essentials Limited	£73,490
Sensa Personal Care Limited	£213,727	Paradoxical Solutions Limited	£71,358
Aim8 Limited	£212,584	THC Effect Ltd	£70,024
Continental Fragrances Limited	£210,816	Silyn Products Ltd	£68,264
Iam By Nature Ltd.	£210,488	Oleo Bodycare Limited	£67,785
South West Aesthetics Ltd	£204,073	AD Fragrances Ltd	£67,324
Parfums Bleu Limited	£202,656	JWO Beauty Limited	£67,061
Satellite Industries GB Limited	£202,499	Lobal Ltd	£66,354
Protect Biosciences Ltd	£185,285	B.S. Eurochem Limited	£65,019
Swaziboy Limited	£184,132	Indult Paris Ltd	£64,351
The Perfume Studio Limited	£180,242	The Fitzrovia Centre Ltd	£64,339
Possibility of London Ltd	£170,395	Purdie's of Argyll Ltd	£60,500
Kinski Limited	£165,901	Essancy Limited	£57,332
Zidac Laboratories Ltd	£164,028	Charles Jordi Limited	£56,947
Lyn Michel Limited	£162,924	Daniel Field Purity Project Ltd	£55,624
Spiezia Organics Limited	£157,594	Twelve Beauty Ltd	£55,560
Herbfarmacy Ltd	£153,836	Shaw & Company Business Ltd	£53,656
Phytacol Limited	£152,552	Washworks Bodycare Limited	£51,509
Natural Products Factory Ltd	£151,404	Nature Spirits Limited	£50,438
Un Air D'Antan Limited	£149,946	Andre Boyard Perfumes Limited	£49,878

Company	Value	Company	Value
Organatural Ltd	£49,558	Legendes Products Ltd	£20,397
One Green Lab Ltd	£48,653	Ostens Limited	£19,999
A.S Apothecary Limited	£48,281	Providence Ventures Limited	£19,950
Haych Cosmetics Limited	£45,429	Jove London Ltd	£19,128
Inovair Limited	£45,422	Lauren Stone Limited	£19,037
Gotvox Limited	£43,273	Veloskin Limited	£18,452
Jamal London Ltd	£43,049	Stormfree Holdings Ltd	£18,302
Verde London Ltd.	£42,392	By Kathryn Ltd	£18,061
Corincraft Limited	£40,536	De La Baie Arctic Skincare Ltd	£18,054
Thomas Kosmala Parfums Ltd	£39,284	BL Cosmetics Limited	£17,223
Elibec Limited	£38,447	Royale Essance Ltd	£17,215
Fumarette Ltd	£37,706	Kingdom Scotland Limited	£17,190
AC Packing Ltd	£37,692	Image Hub Limited	£15,937
Sloane Home Ltd	£37,320	Bearface Industries Limited	£15,496
Ainsel Limited	£36,975	Persephone Bio Ltd	£14,864
Shinso Skin Care Limited	£36,413	Spirit of The Isle Ltd.	£14,584
Activbod Limited	£35,182	Sultan Pasha Artisanal Perfumery Ltd	£14,455
Holistic Plant Technologies Ltd	£35,000	Marine Beauty Care Limited	£14,255
NTM (UK) Limited	£34,835	Barbara Scott Aromatics Ltd	£14,162
Braw Beard Oils Ltd	£33,188	Myroo Ltd	£14,070
Natural Science Aromas Ltd	£32,471	Happy Products Limited	£13,962
Storey Enterprises Limited	£31,525	Soapy Skin Limited	£13,866
The Natural Soap Company Limited	£30,984	Ninni Ltd	£13,681
Creative Perfumers London Ltd	£30,943	Elemental Beauty Limited	£13,635
Pot of Gold Cosmetics Limited	£30,438	La-Eva Limited	£13,625
Sears UK Ltd	£29,318	The Skin Specialist Limited	£13,293
Universal Chemicals Limited	£29,102	Earth Mother Soul Sister Limited	£13,186
Yverman Ltd	£28,803	Rodette International Limited	£13,062
The Natural Deodorant Co Limited	£28,566	Alice in Perfume Limited	£13,039
Beever Retail Limited	£28,492	Contour and More London Limited	£12,749
Art de Parfum Ltd.	£26,687	Black Cat Manufacturing Ltd	£12,627
Inari Skincare Ltd	£26,594	Toddle Born Wild Limited	£12,600
Magma London Ltd	£26,567	Papillon Perfumery Ltd	£12,387
Lola's Apothecary Ltd	£26,210	Midha Limited	£12,139
Aqua Natural Limited	£25,703	Body Reform Limited	£10,001
Scent from Ireland Ltd	£25,519	Essential Spirit Limited	£9,652
Nihad A Rawi Limited	£25,355	Razias London Ltd	£9,450
Renu Consultancy Ltd	£24,019	Bex London Ltd	£9,376
Mechmark Ltd	£23,833	Its All About The Skin Limited	£9,305
New Vistas Avant Garde Limited	£23,797	La Maison Hedonique Limited	£9,167
Lakeland Fragrances Limited	£23,101	Mbikudi Ltd	£9,015
Elmbronze Limited	£23,031	Esensi Skincare Ltd	£8,845
Ebex International Limited	£22,904	Auli London Ltd	£8,526
Yess Essentials Limited	£22,355	Savillequinn Pty Ltd.	£8,138
Beard Oil Company Limited	£21,930	Buachi Limited	£8,073
Paromachem Limited	£21,302	Owen Drew Luxury Candles Limited	£8,014
Naticuma Limited	£21,090	Fragrance Selection (UK) Limited	£7,931
Sensora Limited	£20,800	Tsaka Limited	£7,395
Sensapeel Ltd	£20,597	Balance By Nora Limited	£7,332
Mulondon Limited	£20,401	Natural Skincare London Limited	£7,210

The Top UK Perfume and Toilet Preparations Manufacturers

Company	Value	Company	Value
Prispens Limited	£6,390	Lathersmith Ltd	£929
Mr Vanguard Limited	£6,227	Drops of Humanity Ltd	£895
Claes Heavenly Therapies and Aromas Ltd	£5,837	Mary Jean Limited	£832
30 Minute Tan Limited	£5,788	MK Design & Art Direction Ltd	£770
Aswad P.S.S Ltd	£5,630	Flo Ventures Ltd	£747
Costradis Limited	£5,135	Wild & Organic Bioactive Essentials Limited	£742
Eastwing Grooming Co. Limited	£5,025	The 7 Virtues Beauty Ltd	£742
L'Ocean Limited	£5,005	Black Gem Cosmetics Ltd	£710
Ecopel Corporation Limited	£4,736	Old Park Farm Estate Limited	£707
Mono Naturoils Ltd	£4,660	Skyn Deep Ltd	£685
Maya Njie Perfumes Limited	£4,652	Madalyn and Rose Ltd	£599
Noblechart Cosmetic Ltd	£4,333	Freestyle Beauty Products Limited	£598
Almond & Avocado Ltd	£4,083	HE FE Ltd	£586
Sheabynature Ltd	£4,000	Beard Nature Limited	£519
Gellure Ltd	£3,797	Concept: Skin Limited	£497
General Flavours & Fragrances Ltd	£3,750	Hypha Cosmetics Ltd	£400
Neighbourhood Botanicals Ltd	£3,600	Fragrance du Bois (UK) Limited	£383
Sandine Zartaux Holding Ltd	£3,544	The Soap Souk Ltd	£370
Purplelilac Ltd	£3,328	Kingsmill Cosmetic Preparations Limited	£364
Hod Perfumes Limited	£3,205	Nadeane Letisha Ltd	£263
Aura Organics Limited	£2,923	Arizona Botaniq Limited	£200
Thomas Laurie Naturals Limited	£2,692	Dermafood Limited	£191
Nadarra Cosmetics Ltd	£2,483	Pepsyn Limited	£175
Purely Skincare Limited	£2,450	Vetivert & Co Ltd	£146
Savage Alchemy Limited	£2,436	Carrie Wilson Limited	£131
La Parfumerie Anglaise Limited	£2,421	Sharrier Beauty Incorporated Limited	£100
Scentz of Smell Ltd	£2,391	Lovefro Ltd.	£100
Honesty Skincare Limited	£2,373	J Deboy & Co Limited	£100
Purepure Limited	£2,330	Culpeper Limited	£100
Village Barber Skin Products Ltd	£2,279	Lip Sync Beauty Limited	£100
The Divine Hag Ltd	£2,187	Pure English Cosmetics Limited	£100
Madre Skincare Limited	£2,030	Jubilee Capital (UK) Ltd	£100
Cheshire Fragrances Limited	£1,931	Our Modern Lives Ltd	£100
Beauty Handmade Limited	£1,844	Balmpots Limited	£92
The Model Handmade Limited	£1,778	Simply Ewe Limited	£69
Aromatherapy Infusions Ltd	£1,721	Askett & English Ltd	£50
Kisens Ltd	£1,701	The L A Partnership Limited	£48
Science for Skin Ltd.	£1,660	Leum Skin Care Ltd	£35
Foad Wax Limited	£1,516	RMBeauty Limited	£25
Incoplex Limited	£1,498	Cocobubble Ltd	£24
Sikania Ltd	£1,447	Essential Gent Ltd	£24
Lucidlure Ltd	£1,160	Glamour Natural Cosmetics Ltd	£6
Amaranthine Beauty Ltd	£1,099	Everlasting Youth Limited	£5
Ray Alteraifi Limited	£1,004	Cyclax Limited	£2
Sipro (UK) Ltd	£1,002	G and B Beauty Products Ltd	£2
Designer Shaik Limited	£1,000	Cinsce Ltd	£1
LJSP Ltd	£1,000	Mayen Velvaere Limited	£1
O Sable France Ltd	£989	Naturali360 Limited	£1

This page is intentionally left blank

Age of Companies

1920-1929
Firmenich Holdings (UK) Ltd
Robert McBride Ltd
Geo. F. Trumper (Perfumer and Products)

1930-1939
Firmenich Wellingborough (UK) Ltd
Gillette U.K. Limited
John Gosnell & Co Ltd
Morgan's Pomade Co Ltd

1940-1949
Coty Manufacturing UK Limited
Laboratory Facilities Limited
Queen Cosmetics Limited

1950-1959 [5]
Evans Vanodine International PLC
KPSS (UK) Limited
Meiyume (UK) Limited
Ethel Roberts Limited
Ungerer Limited

1960-1969 [6]
Continental Fragrances Limited
Elsan Limited
Fragrance Oils (Purchasing) Ltd
H.E. Stringer (Perfurmery) Ltd
Superfine Manufacturing Ltd
Eve Taylor (London) Limited

1970-1979 [16]
Baylis & Harding PLC
CPL Aromas Limited
Caldey Island Estate Co Ltd
Combe International Limited
A. & E. Connock (Perfumery & Cosmetics)
Cosmetics a la Carte Limited
Creightons PLC
Pierre Fabre Limited
Fragrance Oils (International) Ltd
M.S. George Limited
Jarvis Cosmetic Developments Ltd.
Kingsmill Cosmetic Preparations Ltd
L.E.C.(L'pool) Limited
Mavala (U.K.) Limited
Northern Aromatics (Sales) Ltd
Robertet (U.K.) Limited

1980-1989 [28]
Abendana Enterprises Limited
Aqua Natural Limited
Arriva Fragrances Limited
Atlas Group Limited
Butterbur and Sage Limited
Elemis Limited
Fillcare Limited
First Natural Brands Ltd
General Flavours & Fragrances Ltd
Nicholas James (UK) Limited
Kensa Chemicals Limited
La Riche Limited
McCallum Manufacturing Limited
Molton Brown Limited
Susan Molyneux Cosmetics Ltd
Neal's Yard (Natural Remedies) Ltd
Ottimo Supplies Limited
Phoenix Fragrances Limited
Professional Beauty Systems Ltd

Quality Analysis Limited
R.M. Investments Limited
S.R.S.Aromatics Limited
Sachets Limited
Stantondown Limited
Surefil Beauty Products Ltd
Swallowfield PLC
Universal Chemicals Limited
Yellow Can Co Ltd

1990-1994 [16]
Acheson & Acheson Limited
Aroma Trading Limited
BCM Limited
Body & Face St. Cyrus Limited
Clover Chemicals Limited
Cyclax Limited
Elmbronze Limited
Fikkerts Limited
Firmenich UK Limited
Lush Ltd.
Make-Up Art Cosmetics (U.K.) Ltd
Miller Harris Limited
Parfums Bleu Limited
Zandra Rhodes Fragrances Ltd
Satellite Industries GB Ltd
Verde London Ltd.

1995 [7]
Drom International UK Limited
Liz Earle Beauty Co. Limited
Everlasting Youth Limited
L A Partnership Limited
Lakeland Fragrances Limited
Rodette International Limited
Sub Tropic Limited

1996
Aromaherb Limited
Pepsyn Limited
Solar Cosmetics International Ltd

1997 [9]
Ajmal Perfume (UK) Limited
Charles Jordi Limited
Heaven Scent Incense Limited
In Line Health and Beauty Ltd
Jean Christian Perfumes Ltd
K.K. Toiletries Limited
Lush Manufacturing Limited
Q-Pack Limited
Sabel Cosmetics Limited

1998
Ebex International Limited
Hair Systems Europe Limited
International Toiletries & Cosmetics
Perfume By Design Ltd.

1999 [14]
Barony Universal Products PLC
Blazergold Limited
CPL Aromas (Holdings) Limited
Cool Gell Limited
Corincraft Limited
Essentially Yours Limited
Excel (GS) Limited
Fragrances and Cosmetics Ltd
Freestyle Beauty Products Ltd

Mayfair Perfumes Limited
Somerset Toiletry Co Ltd
Teknord Limited
Universal Toiletries Corporation Ltd
Zodiac International (London) Ltd

2000 [10]
Arcania Apothecary Ltd
BL Cosmetics Limited
Designer Shaik Limited
Essential Spirit Limited
Groomers Limited
Christina May Limited
Natural Looks Trading Limited
Natural Soap Co Ltd
Nature Spirits Limited
T & H Marketing Limited

2001 [5]
Designer Fragrances Limited
Emerald Kalama Chemical Ltd
Marine Beauty Care Limited
Nectar International Limited
Yess Essentials Limited

2002 [8]
Andre Boyard Perfumes Limited
Freshorize Ltd
Iam By Nature Ltd.
Inovair Limited
Kao (UK) Limited
L.A Life Limited
Midha Limited
Perfume Studio Limited

2003 [12]
Archem (N.I.) Ltd
Ayurveda Pura Ltd
B.S. Eurochem Limited
Beever Retail Limited
Dermapharm Skincare Limited
Ferndale Pharmaceuticals Ltd
G and B Beauty Products Ltd
Doris Michaels Cosmetics Ltd
Penny Price Aromatherapy Ltd
Potter & Moore Innovations Ltd
Spiezia Organics Limited
Winterpark Paris Parfums Ltd

2004
Face Boutique Limited
Legendes Products Ltd
Pot of Gold Cosmetics Limited
Strathpeffer Spa Soap Co Ltd

2005 [5]
Itaconix (U.K.) Limited
Mibelle Ltd
Old Park Farm Estate Limited
United Beauty Products Limited
WT Limited

The Top UK Perfume and Toilet Preparations Manufacturers

2006 [11]
Bahoma Limited
Body Reform Limited
Earth Mother Soul Sister Ltd
Eden Classics Limited
Faces Cosmetics Limited
First Natural Limited
Gagnon Essentials Limited
Herc Ltd.
Highland Soap Co. Limited
Organatural Ltd
Professional Beauty Systems (Holdings)

2007 [9]
Calibria Ltd
Dr. Organic Limited
Elemental Beauty Limited
Fragrant Earth International Ltd
New Vistas Avant Garde Limited
Paromachem Limited
R.P.C. Midlands Ltd
Wild & Organic Bioactive Essentials
Yin Yang Natural Sciences Ltd

2008 [7]
Arco England Limited
Dr Jackson Ltd
L'Ocean Limited
MAC Professional Haircare Ltd
Mary Jean Limited
Paddy's Bathroom Limited
Sears UK Ltd

2009 [16]
Beautiful Mind Series Limited
Belinda Brown Limited
Escentric Molecules Limited
Essancy Limited
Daniel Field Purity Project Ltd
Flo Ventures Ltd
Jaye O'Boye & Co Ltd
Oleo Bodycare Limited
Phytacol Limited
Protect Biosciences Ltd
Providence Ventures Limited
Purplelilac Ltd
Renbow Haircare Limited
ThatCo Ltd
ThisCo Ltd
Yverman Ltd

January-June 2010 [5]
Almond & Avocado Ltd
Elibec Limited
Gracetree Ltd
Mitchell and Peach Limited
Triblaz Limited

July-December 2010
Fragrances UK Limited
Heavenly Fragrance (UK) Ltd
Skin Specialist Limited
Travik Chemicals (UK) Limited

January-June 2011 [9]
Aim8 Limited
Askett & English Ltd
Bex London Ltd
By Kathryn Ltd
Foad Wax Limited
Madre Skincare Limited
Natural Skincare London Ltd
Shinso Skin Care Limited
Wilde Beauty Limited

July-December 2011 [15]
De La Baie Arctic Skincare Ltd
Dermafood Limited
Elequra Limited
Fragrance du Bois (UK) Limited
Islestarr Holdings Limited
Kaira Luchi Ltd
Kinski Limited
Lola's Apothecary Ltd
Lovefro Ltd.
Mama Mio Distribution Limited
Natural Products Factory Ltd
Papillon Perfumery Ltd
Paradoxical Solutions Limited
Renu Consultancy Ltd
Sharrier Beauty Incorporated Ltd

January-March 2012
Concept: Skin Limited
Dreamweave Products Ltd
Fumarette Ltd
Nihad A Rawi Limited

April-June 2012 [5]
4160 Tuesdays Limited
Fragrance Selection (UK) Ltd
Perfair Limited
Silyn Products Ltd
Solab Group Limited

July-September 2012
Gellure Ltd
Herrmann + Herrmann Limited
Jamal London Ltd
Waterman Corporate Enterprises Ltd

October-December 2012
Dermamaitre Ltd.
Herbfarmacy Ltd
NTM (UK) Limited

January-March 2013 [7]
7 Virtues Beauty Ltd
Dilecta Cosmetics Limited
Lathersmith Ltd
Ninni Ltd
Sensapeel Ltd
Spirit of The Isle Ltd.
Swaziboy Limited

April-June 2013 [7]
Beauty Essentials (Scotland) Ltd
Beauty Exchange Limited
Carrie Wilson Limited
Cocoa Twist Limited
Premier Specialties Europe Ltd
Soapy Skin Limited
Washworks Bodycare Limited

July-September 2013 [9]
Braw Beard Oils Ltd
Creative Perfumers London Ltd
Designer IP (2) Ltd
My Life But Greener Limited
Neville Cut and Shave Limited
Sensa Personal Care Limited
Shaw & Company Business Ltd
Sipro (UK) Ltd
Stormfree Holdings Ltd

October-December 2013 [10]
Athena Cosmetics Limited
Balance By Nora Limited
Beauty 4 Me Ltd
Berachah Consulting Limited
Eyegenius Ltd
Lobal Ltd
Sloane Home Ltd
Storey Enterprises Limited
Urban Nymph Limited
Village Barber Skin Products Ltd

January-March 2014 [9]
Alice in Perfume Limited
Good Skin Care Co Ltd
Hod Perfumes Limited
House of Sanders Limited
Pure Lakes Skincare Limited
Sensora Limited
TH / Edition Ltd
Umma Therapy Ltd.
XDC Limited

April-June 2014 [12]
Aroma Cosmetics Laboratory Ltd
Buachi Limited
Chuckling Goat Limited
Image Hub Limited
KD Trading (UK) Limited
Thomas Kosmala Parfums Ltd
Lana-Rae Ltd Ltd
Leum Skin Care Ltd
Natural Science Aromas Ltd
THC Effect Ltd
This Wode Co Ltd
Wrimes Cosmetics Ltd

July-September 2014 [14]
AD Fragrances Ltd
Activbod Limited
Ainsel Limited
Aspire Eden Ltd
Gotvox Limited
Inari Skincare Ltd
Indult Paris Ltd
Maison Ex Nihilo UK Limited
Meadow Farm Friends Ltd
Noblechart Cosmetic Ltd
O Sable France Ltd
Odejo Limited
Persephone Bio Ltd
Scrubbingtons Limited

October-December 2014 [11]
Affinity Organics Limited
Bonita Lou Ltd
Female Balance Shop Limited
Field Fresh Skincare Ltd
Geltec Limited
HMMT Holdings Ltd.
Inspired Health & Beauty Products
Magma London Ltd
Lyn Michel Limited
Sandine Zartaux Holding Ltd
Skin Defence Limited

January 2015
Aventual Ltd
Happy Products Limited
One Green Lab Ltd

February 2015 [5]
Bearface Industries Limited
Black Cat Manufacturing Ltd
IQ-Area Ltd
Royale Essance Ltd
Twelve Beauty Ltd

March 2015
Natural Deodorant Co Limited

April 2015
Beard Oil Co Ltd
Hampshire Cosmetics Limited
Mechmark Ltd
Naticuma Limited

May 2015 [6]
83 Associates Limited
Art de Parfum Ltd.
Double Take Limited
Honesty Skincare Limited
Hypothesis One Ltd
Scots Mist Ltd

June 2015
Christian Lincoln Enterprise Ltd
Science for Skin Ltd.

July 2015 [6]
A.S Apothecary Limited
Ray Alteraifi Limited
Dareen London Ltd.
J Deboy & Co Limited
M.C Skin Truth Ltd
Madalyn and Rose Ltd

August 2015 [5]
Bigben Healthcare Limited
Costradis Limited
Hypha Cosmetics Ltd
Mulondon Limited
Possibility of London Ltd

September 2015
Its All About The Skin Limited

October 2015
Drops of Humanity Ltd
Get Lucky Inc Ltd
Vinculum Ltd

November 2015 [6]
Aromatherapy Infusions Ltd
Cinsce Ltd
Eleuthere Ltd
Green Jiva Ltd
Holistic Plant Technologies Ltd
Nadeane Letisha Ltd

December 2015 [6]
30 Minute Tan Limited
Aura Organics Limited
Ishga Ltd
JWO Beauty Limited
Lucidlure Ltd
Pandorra Ltd.

January 2016
Culpeper Limited
HE FE Ltd
Jogb Limited
Project Renegades Ltd

February 2016 [6]
Eifelcorp Consumer Care Ltd
Fitzrovia Centre Ltd
Kingdom Scotland Limited
Natural Aromatics Limited
Potter & Moore (Devon) Ltd
Swiss Pharma Dynamic Ltd

March 2016 [5]
Ecopel Corporation Limited
Lip Sync Beauty Limited
Mayen Velvaere Limited
Mbikudi Ltd
Mono Naturoils Ltd

April 2016 [10]
Adunni Ori Limited
Black Gem Cosmetics Ltd
Cheshire Fragrances Limited
Essential Gent Ltd
Gallivant Perfumes Limited
Jove London Ltd
Neighbourhood Botanicals Ltd
TWC Products Limited
Tsaka Limited
Wildsmith Collection Limited

May 2016
Aexents Ltd
Myroo Ltd
Organic Youth Limited
Veloskin Limited

June 2016 [9]
Glamoessence Ltd
HBNatura Ltd
Incoplex Limited
JLP Cosmetics Ltd
La Parfumerie Anglaise Limited
Maya Njie Perfumes Limited
RMBeauty Limited
Razias London Ltd
Lauren Stone Limited

July 2016
Cybele UK Ltd
Ombotas Limited
Scent from Ireland Ltd
Soap Cellar Limited

August 2016
Experimental Perfume Club Ltd
LJSP Ltd
Raw Supremo Ltd
Toddle Born Wild Limited

September 2016 [6]
Auli London Ltd
Owen Drew Luxury Candles Ltd
La-Eva Limited
Monreale Limited
Nobell Group Ltd
Purely Skincare Limited

October 2016 [6]
Ahwaz Ltd
Arizona Botaniq Limited
Fashion Fragrances & Cosmetics UK Ltd
Moyy Limited
Phyto Pharm Limited
Phyto Pharma Limited

November 2016 [8]
AC Packing Ltd
Above Beyond Group Ltd
Balmpots Limited
Hi Energy Healing Limited
J2NR Ltd
Kisens Ltd
Nadarra Cosmetics Ltd
Ring in Ring Ltd

December 2016 [6]
Arrivatech Limited
Aswad P.S.S Ltd
Buddy Direct Ltd
Haych Cosmetics Limited
Lucidly Ltd
Organic Alchemist Ltd

January 2017 [11]
Amaranthine Beauty Ltd
Contour and More London Ltd
Divine Hag Ltd
Just Skincare Limited
Midnight Apothecary Limited
Nature's Embrace Limited
Pur-D Natural Skin Care Ltd
Purdie's of Argyll Ltd
Pure English Cosmetics Limited
Scent Pod Co Ltd
Sikania Ltd

February 2017 [12]
Beard Nature Limited
Glamour Natural Cosmetics Ltd
Hope and Rose Limited
La Maison Hedonique Limited
Naturali360 Limited
Ostens Limited
Potions & Possibilities Ltd
Prosody London Limited
Pure Fiji (EU) Limited
Scentz of Smell Ltd
Sharakkas United Kingdom Ltd
Zidac Laboratories Ltd

March 2017 [5]
Carzel Limited
Claes Heavenly Therapies and Aromas Ltd
Prispens Limited
Sheabynature Ltd
Vetivert & Co Ltd

April 2017 [10]
Aromatic Scents Ltd
Cocobubble Ltd
Eastwing Grooming Co. Limited
Glad Gent Ltd
Jubilee Capital (UK) Ltd
Poseidon Skincare Limited
SE & SA Limited
Barbara Scott Aromatics Ltd
Simply Ewe Limited
Simply Seaweed Limited

May 2017 [20]
BLVNCO Limited
Beauty Handmade Limited
Bixie Group Ltd
DBI Innovations Group Limited
Eco Labyrinth Limited
Esensi Skincare Ltd
Hamiltons of Canterbury Ltd
Karaama Fragrances Ltd
Lily Her Limited
Lucayan Limited
MK Design & Art Direction Ltd
Millicent and Snob Limited
Mr Vanguard Limited
Pierre Precieuse Parfum UK Ltd
Saltaire Soap Ltd
Sanofi International Biotech Co Ltd.
Sultan Pasha Artisanal Perfumery Ltd
Swanny's Ltd.
Tom's Garden Limited
Un Air D'Antan Limited

June 2017 [12]
Beard Armour Limited
Cambridge Genefit Technologies Ltd
Cosmetic Hooligans Ltd
Thomas Laurie Naturals Ltd
London Goddess Limited
Manhattan Group Ltd.
Model Handmade Limited
Muir Events Ltd
Purepure Limited
Rustic Blends Limited
Savillequinn Pty Ltd.
Zahrat Alqurashi Ltd

July 2017 [22]
Ava Corporations Ltd
Baum of London Limited
Beauty Core Limited
Elie Consumer Care Ltd
Elliott Nutrition Ltd
Felix Medical Group Ltd
Flynn Group of Companies Ltd
Hemo Bioscience Ltd
Hkka Limited
Holistica Skin Ltd
Julie's Natural Health Ltd
Man Mountain Beard Care Ltd
Marsh Organics Limited
Olfactive London Ltd
Our Modern Lives Ltd
Pretty Little Treat Company (Yorkshire)
Regis Personal Care Ltd
Riley & Sons Ltd
Salopian Ltd
Skinirvana Limited
Viraj Organics Ltd
Zaeda Alexia Limited

August 2017 [13]
Jenni Douglas Limited
Evocativ Limited
Greatest of All Time Soapworks Ltd
Agnes Jackson Limited
Jaemae Ltd
Kylah K Skincare Ltd
Ladd Cosmetics Ltd
Making Scents Ltd
Maskalin Ltd
Renewyou Cancertology UK Ltd
Skyn Deep Ltd
Soap Souk Ltd
Wist and Wonder Limited

September 2017 [23]
Awake Organics Ltd
Ayuroma Limited
Bear Head Grooming Products Ltd
Bedeaux Ltd
Benefit & Riley Healthcare Ltd
Body Thyme Limited
Brigantia Personal Care Ltd
CS Holistic Therapy Products Ltd
Clarins & Felix Healthcare Ltd
Coriungo Limited
Dach Cosmeceutics Limited
Elan Skincare Ltd
Forte Organics Ltd
Garnier & Hemo Healthcare Ltd
Honey Corn Limited
Lamer & Ava Healthcare Ltd
Nars & Elliott Healthcare Ltd
Revlon & Elie Healthcare Ltd
Rimmel & Flynn Healthcare Ltd
South West Aesthetics Ltd
Thomas Andy Ltd.
Three Organics Ltd
Tiger Lily Soapery Ltd

October 2017 [9]
B. Silki Naturally Ltd
Carefree Toiletries Limited
M.88 Fragrances Ltd
Maribella London Limited
Milo and James Limited
Nature B Limited
Project Cosmetics Limited
Squires and Trelawny Ltd
Tranquility Cosmetics Limited

November 2017 [11]
11:11 Limited
Advanced Aesthetics Training Academy
Alchemy Botanics Ltd
Ayurveda Wellness Ltd
Bill & Artisans Ltd
Hoc Parfum Ltd
Khushi Skincare Limited
Organic Stuff Limited
Psyche Com & Merch Ltd
Savon de V Ltd
Three Fizzy Pigs Ltd

December 2017 [10]
Aroma Amour Ltd
Aroma Body Treats Limited
Aromabar (Scotland) Ltd
Bath Candy Ltd
Castlefields Cosmetics Ltd.
Eden's Legends Limited
Emily Victoria Candles Limited
Ikaa Cosmetics Limited
Molecula Ltd
Since Six Ltd

January 2018 [21]
Anuvaayum Ltd
Aromatic Answers Ltd
Axwood Limited
Balm House Limited
Bathroom Cosmetics Ltd
Bell & Loxton Innovations Ltd
Blackbird and Rain Limited
EEM Botanicals Limited
Flowery Whiff Limited
Fragrance and Glamour Ltd
Fragrant Spa Limited
Fysifarm Limited
Hemp Garden Ltd
IAP Cosmetics International Ltd
Leviticus 19:27 Beard Co Ltd
Lukas Products Limited
Marinical Limited
Nova Extraction Ltd
Perfance Limited
Savage Alchemy Limited
Scents of Nature Ltd

February 2018 [31]
Ark Perfumeries Limited
Aube Laboratories Ltd
Avenge Skincare Limited
Biologico Cosmetics Limited
Bloom Remedies Ltd
Body Candy Ltd.
Boselli Europe Ltd
Busy Bees Cosmetics Limited
Carapoll Chemicals Ltd
Claycoco Limited
Cocoa Lime Limited
Eco Earth Limited
Elinor-UK Ltd
Glory Skin Ltd
Hart Enterprise Limited
Hoff Beards Limited
Ko. Essentials Ltd.
LTSC Ltd
LU Aromatherapy Ltd
Littlemore Candle Co Ltd
Nutracrest Ltd
Onlyou Limited
Pitt London Ltd
Relax Candle and Bath Co Ltd
Saints & Co London Ltd
Scrummy U Health Ltd
Skin Nectar Ltd
TAC Perfumes & Cosmetics (UK) Ltd
Thread and Co UK Limited
Uzu Ltd
Wrath Cosmetics Limited

March 2018 [17]
Bloom Aromatics Limited
Bloomtown Ltd
Chaud Solutions Limited
Department Health & Beauty Ltd
Divine Earth Ltd
Earth Aroma Limited
Happy Melon Skin Care Limited
House of Unique Parfum Limited
Juni Cosmetics Limited
Lum Lifestyle Ltd.
Joy Myfanwy Limited
Natural Sheaness Ltd
A W Oliver & Co Ltd
Oliver & Taylor Ltd
Tahmasso Limited
Urembo Naturally Ltd
Wonder and Wild Ltd

April 2018 [14]
Camblabs Ltd
Cutelovelee Limited
Good Mela Ltd
H H Formulations Ltd
Heidi J Naturals Limited
Sarah Ireland Perfumes Ltd
Koze Limited
Little Green Beehive Ltd
Mitchell London Limited
Osunti Limited
Pharmaco Group Limited
Skincare Laboratories Ltd
Soapberries Ltd
Tea & Therapy Ltd

May 2018 [19]
Al Oxford Ltd
Act of Kindness Organics Ltd
Artisane Aromatherapy Limited
Authenticus Ltd
Blank Factory Limited
Caley's of Exeter Ltd
Canco Candles Limited
D'Iusso Collection Ltd
Elinor Sophia Limited
Garden Perfumers Ltd
Gio Natura Ltd
I Love Myself Ltd
Kropp & Hem Ltd
Scence Ltd
Scent To Inspire Ltd
Soap Legacy Ltd
Spots & Stripes Products Ltd
TCJ Treatments Limited
Tresaigh Ltd

June 2018 [16]
4RM Ltd
Aroma Design Ltd
Artemis Oils Ltd
Care By Jords Ltd
Custom Skin Lab Limited
Farasha-Cosmetics Ltd
Gelspa Limited
Maskologist Ltd
Organic Fragrance Co Ltd
Otte Limited
Precious Clothing & Beauty Ltd
Rutherford Bambury Ltd
Sophrina Gos Limited
Terra Mater Ltd
Vaunt Limited
Virtue Botanicals Limited

July 2018 [19]
All Good Skincare Limited
Berry Inc Ltd
Cactus Skincare Limited
Charmpits Ltd
Clay Club Skincare Limited
Earthwhile Ltd
Elegant Boss Ltd
Frosts of London Limited
Icaro Sana Limited
Intradicted Ltd
Macks Wax Ltd
Majestic Company London Ltd
Mata Labs Cosmetics Ltd
Orton Limited
Ostera Limited
Ru Si Lacquers Global Ltd.
Squeaky Clean Queen Ltd
Valorem Bespoke Ltd
Wayus Limited

August 2018 [18]
Astarra Ltd
Banyan Skincare Ltd
Bleu D'Argan Skincare Limited
Chirps London Ltd
Fizzy Thistle Ltd
Haromatic Ltd
House of 18 Ltd
Kadiricosmetics Ltd
Kairn Holding Limited
Lex Roris Ltd
Paisley Soap Co Ltd
Sphere 7 Lab Ltd
Sunshapers Limited
Valencia Vanna Ltd.
Very Good Vegan Co Ltd
Wheesht Ltd
Whole International Limited
Wicked Vicky Co Ltd

September 2018 [19]
AA Group Holdings Ltd
Alkaiser Perfumes Ltd
Beauty Alliance International Ltd
Dermaplaning Pro Official Ltd
EMC Botanica Limited
Green Ladies N.I Ltd
Karamat Collection Ltd
Kyoka Pro Ltd
Lumine Beauty Ltd
Magpie's Ocean Ltd
Oyepitan and Okunniwa Limited
Plant Department Ltd
Polka Lab Limited
Sandwich Consultants Ltd
Splash Cosmetics Ltd
TheManeCo Ltd
Uncareditional Ltd
Unique Relaxation Specialist Ltd
Wickham Soap Co. Ltd

October 2018 [23]
A Natural Treat Limited
AS Manufacturing Ltd
Acarrier Limited
Convoy Fragrances Ltd
Daughters of Circe Ltd
East China Sourcing Ltd
Ecocrushuk Ltd
Es-Ssentially Yours Ltd
Foltex Hair Technology Limited
Icilda's Ltd
JST Exports (UK) Ltd
Kisu Skincare Ltd
L & A Natural Limited
Lick Labs Limited
Lofty Gardens Ltd
MLC Parfum & Oudh Ltd
Victoria March Skincare Ltd
Neurocosmetics Limited
Pure Ohana Limited
Soap People Ltd
Stunning Fragrance Ltd
Sundarak Ltd
Sweet Arabian Ltd

November 2018 [32]
AM Fragrances Limited
Adam Michaels Group Ltd
Ally Dog Co Ltd
Argos International Fragrances Ltd
Body Station Limited
Cosmos Cosmetics Limited
Credence Hair Venture Limited
Eabir Ltd
Eden in Valley Soapworks Ltd
Good By Nature Ltd
Grace & Hartland Ltd
Hairs & Graces Cosmetics Ltd
Hunk Grooming Ltd
Jorum of Scotland Limited
Kehal Ltd
Lese & Lista Ltd
Mrs Greens Hemp Remedies Ltd
Naturoganik Limited
Omprus Limited
Qualkem Ltd
Radiant Glow Beauty UK Ltd
Rasta Life Ltd
Saisha Marra Ltd.
Seilich Limited
Shea Natural Skincare Limited
Shifting London Ltd
Skinsence Ltd
Softme Beauty Ltd
Sonyah Adan Limited
Superfood Beauty Limited
Villa Sauod Ltd
Zelenci Natural Health Ltd

December 2018 [27]
Atmosy Ltd
Bespoke Natural Health Ltd
Bluhans Ltd
Luissa Burton Limited
Credo Felix Ltd
Ethical House Ltd
Evoiq International Ltd
Infinity Global Corporation & Investment - IGCI
Insensed Ltd
Inspired Diffusing Ltd

Irregular Cosmetics Co Ltd
Jardins D'Eden Ltd
Linden and Lime Limited
Liza.B. Glow Actives Ltd
MWK Cosmetics (UK) Ltd
Man Mask Ltd
Mast - Art Group Limited
Mayla Skincare Ltd
Onze Limited
Organic Basics Ltd
Reesoaps.co.uk Ltd
Salix Moon Apothecary Ltd
Soak Rochford Ltd
Trees of Beauty Ltd
UK Pandora Fairy Skin Beautiyfying Co.,
Ulu Botanicals Ltd
Zoe Lane Ltd

January 2019 [41]
5 Senses Healthcare Ltd
Alchemy Skin and Soul Ltd.
Anyki Ltd
Arbar Ltd
Atypical Cosmetics Ltd
B Luxury Scents Ltd
Bamboobar Online Ltd
CC Business Limited

Calmen Lifestyle Co Ltd
Dolphin Eco Ltd
Ekstaze London Limited
Fizzy Lizzy's Ltd
Fragrantia Limited
Freshly Whip'd Limited
G & G Skincare Ltd
Ginger & Vanilla Ltd
Green Mass Limited
Hanan Pacha Ltd
Icebox Brands EU Limited
Ink of Coco Skincare Ltd
Karma Cosmetics Co Ltd
Khali Min Limited
La Mu London Limited
Libhairation Ltd
Little House of Wild Ltd
Mint Julip Ltd
Mob Fragrances Ltd.
Modernista London Limited
Onyii's Cosmetics Ltd
Orikii Naturals Ltd
P & H Natural Skincare Ltd
Palm Bars Ltd
Paz By Nature Ltd
Platinum Beards Ltd
Pools of Cleopatra Limited
Prophylaxis Ltd

Rodriguez Corporation Ltd
Skin Intuition Ltd
Slavikk Ltd
So Skincare Limited
Wild Bathing Co Ltd

February 2019 [20]
Al-Jazeera Perfumes Ltd
Anyone Limited
Astroscent Ltd
Bubble-Bubble Ltd
Chapel House Skincare Limited
Ed N' Grace Ltd
Hands Organic Ltd
Luxurious Personal Care Ltd
Luxury Personal Care Ltd
Meek and Mild Essentials Ltd
Missy D Collection Limited
Neptune Perfume Ltd
Olire Ltd
Orion Independent Limited
Quint Essence Lab Ltd
Sansuraya Limited
Smelliz Ltd
Thebubblebar Ltd
Uyumbu Limited
E. Zabari Holdings UK Limited

This page is intentionally left blank

Geographic Distribution by County

Co Antrim [12]
Ayurveda Wellness Ltd
Elie Consumer Care Ltd
Elliott Nutrition Ltd
Felix Medical Group Ltd
Irregular Cosmetics Co Ltd
Lamer & Ava Healthcare Ltd
Nars & Elliott Healthcare Ltd
Regis Personal Care Ltd
Riley & Sons Ltd
Rimmel & Flynn Healthcare Ltd
Science for Skin Ltd.
Simply Seaweed Limited

Co Armagh
Ava Corporations Ltd

Co Down [8]
Archem (N.I.) Ltd
Beard Oil Co Ltd
Clarins & Felix Healthcare Ltd
Green Ladies N.I Ltd
Hemo Bioscience Ltd
Revlon & Elie Healthcare Ltd
Scent from Ireland Ltd
Wild Bathing Co Ltd

Co Fermanagh
Flynn Group of Companies Ltd

Co Londonderry
Garnier & Hemo Healthcare Ltd
Julie's Natural Health Ltd

Co Tyrone
Benefit & Riley Healthcare Ltd

Aberdeenshire
Arizona Botaniq Limited
Body & Face St. Cyrus Limited
Costradis Limited
M.88 Fragrances Ltd

Angus
Superfine Manufacturing Ltd

Argyll & Bute
Purdie's of Argyll Ltd

Ayrshire [5]
Barony Universal Products PLC
Beard Armour Limited
Elmbronze Limited
Fizzy Thistle Ltd
Mint Julip Ltd

Clackmannanshire
Sophrina Gos Limited

Dumfries-shire
Essential Spirit Limited

Highland
Highland Soap Co. Limited

Isle of Lewis
Ishga Ltd

Lanarkshire [15]
30 Minute Tan Limited
Atypical Cosmetics Ltd
Balmpots Limited
Dermafood Limited
Divine Hag Ltd
Essential Gent Ltd
Liza.B. Glow Actives Ltd
Lucidly Ltd
Marinical Limited
Mbikudi Ltd
Osunti Limited
Paisley Soap Co Ltd
Sanofi International Biotech Co Ltd.
Scots Mist Ltd
Uzu Ltd

Moray
Mary Jean Limited
Nature Spirits Limited

Renfrewshire [8]
Aromabar (Scotland) Ltd
Beauty Essentials (Scotland) Ltd
Beauty Exchange Limited
MWK Cosmetics (UK) Ltd
Professional Beauty Systems (Holdings)
Professional Beauty Systems Ltd
Renbow Haircare Limited
Terra Mater Ltd

Ross & Cromarty
Strathpeffer Spa Soap Co Ltd

Ross-shire
Dolphin Eco Ltd

Stirlingshire
Bear Head Grooming Products Ltd

Anglesey
Spirit of The Isle Ltd.

Bedfordshire [10]
Anuvaayum Ltd
Buddy Direct Ltd
Claes Heavenly Therapies and Aromas Ltd
Essancy Limited
Hair Systems Europe Limited
Happy Products Limited
Leviticus 19:27 Beard Co Ltd
Man Mask Ltd
Neptune Perfume Ltd
Royale Essance Ltd

Berkshire [13]
Alkaiser Perfumes Ltd
Avenge Skincare Limited
Dareen London Ltd.
Divine Earth Ltd
Groomers Limited
Inari Skincare Ltd
Lucayan Limited
Phyto Pharm Limited
Phyto Pharma Limited
Scents of Nature Ltd
Slavikk Ltd
TCJ Treatments Limited
Wayus Limited

Buckinghamshire [12]
Aroma Trading Limited
Arriva Fragrances Limited
Arrivatech Limited
Askett & English Ltd
Bahoma Limited
Chapel House Skincare Limited
Double Take Limited
Its All About The Skin Limited
Lobal Ltd
Premier Specialties Europe Ltd
So Skincare Limited
WT Limited

Cambridgeshire [13]
11:11 Limited
Contour and More London Ltd
Creightons PLC
Good Skin Care Co Ltd
L A Partnership Limited
L.A Life Limited
Legendes Products Ltd
Linden and Lime Limited
Potter & Moore (Devon) Ltd
Potter & Moore Innovations Ltd
Q-Pack Limited
Eve Taylor (London) Limited
Triblaz Limited

Cardiganshire
Chuckling Goat Limited

Carmarthenshire
Hemp Garden Ltd

Cheshire [18]
Aroma Amour Ltd
B Luxury Scents Ltd
Balance By Nora Limited
Charles Jordi Limited
Cheshire Fragrances Limited
Emerald Kalama Chemical Ltd
Emily Victoria Candles Limited
Holistica Skin Ltd
Organic Youth Limited
Ostera Limited
Paromachem Limited
Perfance Limited
Qualkem Ltd
Sachets Limited
Sensora Limited
Lauren Stone Limited
TheManeCo Ltd
Ungerer Limited

Cleveland
Scentz of Smell Ltd
THC Effect Ltd

Clwyd
Toddle Born Wild Limited

Co Durham [5]
Astarra Ltd
Chaud Solutions Limited
J2NR Ltd
Mechmark Ltd
Village Barber Skin Products Ltd

Cornwall [9]
Berachah Consulting Limited
Bloom Remedies Ltd
Bloomtown Ltd
Continental Fragrances Limited
Lick Labs Limited
Macks Wax Ltd
Scence Ltd
Spiezia Organics Limited
Tea & Therapy Ltd

Cumbria
Dilecta Cosmetics Limited
Lakeland Fragrances Limited
Victoria March Skincare Ltd
Pure Lakes Skincare Limited

Denbighshire
Polka Lab Limited

Derbyshire [6]
Banyan Skincare Ltd
Clover Chemicals Limited
Jubilee Capital (UK) Ltd
Organic Alchemist Ltd
Purely Skincare Limited
Satellite Industries GB Ltd

Devon [13]
Aroma Cosmetics Laboratory Ltd
BL Cosmetics Limited
Bell & Loxton Innovations Ltd
Caley's of Exeter Ltd
Charmpits Ltd
Ebex International Limited
Geltec Limited
Just Skincare Limited
Lola's Apothecary Ltd
Lukas Products Limited
Natural Looks Trading Limited
Prispens Limited
Soap Cellar Limited

Dorset [8]
Bubble-Bubble Ltd
Designer Shaik Limited
Lush Ltd.
Lush Manufacturing Limited
Neal's Yard (Natural Remedies) Ltd
Oleo Bodycare Limited
Barbara Scott Aromatics Ltd
T & H Marketing Limited

Essex [24]
Abendana Enterprises Limited
Aromaherb Limited
Artisane Aromatherapy Limited
CS Holistic Therapy Products Ltd
A. & E. Connock (Perfumery & Cosmetics)
J Deboy & Co Limited
Everlasting Youth Limited
Evoiq International Ltd
Herc Ltd.
House of Sanders Limited
Infinity Global Corporation & Investment - IGCI
Agnes Jackson Limited
Karma Cosmetics Co Ltd
La Riche Limited

Lip Sync Beauty Limited
Mono Naturoils Ltd
Natural Deodorant Co Limited
Natural Sheaness Ltd
Orikii Naturals Ltd
Quality Analysis Limited
Salix Moon Apothecary Ltd
Sansuraya Limited
Sharrier Beauty Incorporated Ltd
Shaw & Company Business Ltd

Flintshire
Gelspa Limited

Glamorgan [14]
Athena Cosmetics Limited
Body Reform Limited
Cocobubble Ltd
Dr. Organic Limited
Daniel Field Purity Project Ltd
Gellure Ltd
Inovair Limited
Christian Lincoln Enterprise Ltd
Renu Consultancy Ltd
Ru Si Lacquers Global Ltd.
Sloane Home Ltd
Sub Tropic Limited
UK Pandora Fairy Skin Beautiyfying Co.,
Universal Chemicals Limited

Gloucestershire [9]
Blackbird and Rain Limited
Clay Club Skincare Limited
Field Fresh Skincare Ltd
Get Lucky Inc Ltd
LTSC Ltd
Mitchell London Limited
Susan Molyneux Cosmetics Ltd
Oyepitan and Okunniwa Limited
Plant Department Ltd

Gwent
Cyclax Limited
Solar Cosmetics International Ltd

Hampshire [27]
Bamboobar Online Ltd
Bearface Industries Limited
Bluhans Ltd
Claycoco Limited
Dach Cosmeceutics Limited
De La Baie Arctic Skincare Ltd
Earth Aroma Limited
Eco Labyrinth Limited
Eleuthere Ltd
Fragrantia Limited
General Flavours & Fragrances Ltd
Glamour Natural Cosmetics Ltd
Gotvox Limited
Hampshire Cosmetics Limited
La-Eva Limited
O Sable France Ltd
Poseidon Skincare Limited
Sensa Personal Care Limited
Sikania Ltd
Skin Specialist Limited
Skinsence Ltd
Solab Group Limited
Tsaka Limited
Very Good Vegan Co Ltd

Wickham Soap Co. Ltd
Yverman Ltd
Zidac Laboratories Ltd

Herefordshire
Beauty 4 Me Ltd
Herbfarmacy Ltd
Radiant Glow Beauty UK Ltd

Hertfordshire [30]
Ainsel Limited
Alice in Perfume Limited
B. Silki Naturally Ltd
B.S. Eurochem Limited
BLVNCO Limited
Bixie Group Ltd
Jenni Douglas Limited
Ecopel Corporation Limited
Eden Classics Limited
Essentially Yours Limited
Flo Ventures Ltd
Foltex Hair Technology Limited
Fragrances and Cosmetics Ltd
Freestyle Beauty Products Ltd
Hands Organic Ltd
House of 18 Ltd
Icaro Sana Limited
London Goddess Limited
Luxurious Personal Care Ltd
Manhattan Group Ltd.
Marine Beauty Care Limited
Mayfair Perfumes Limited
Milo and James Limited
Olfactive London Ltd
Ombotas Limited
Onlyou Limited
Palm Bars Ltd
H.E. Stringer (Perfumery) Ltd
Universal Toiletries Corporation Ltd
Wrimes Cosmetics Ltd

Isle of Wight
Liz Earle Beauty Co. Limited

Kent [24]
Aroma Body Treats Limited
Ayurveda Pura Ltd
Beard Nature Limited
Blank Factory Limited
Calibria Ltd
Calmen Lifestyle Co Ltd
Concept: Skin Limited
Coty Manufacturing UK Limited
Inspired Diffusing Ltd
L & A Natural Limited
Doris Michaels Cosmetics Ltd
Mitchell and Peach Limited
Morgan's Pomade Co Ltd
Neurocosmetics Limited
Nutracrest Ltd
Perfume Studio Limited
Purplelilac Ltd
Razias London Ltd
Rodette International Limited
Sandwich Consultants Ltd
Shifting London Ltd
Splash Cosmetics Ltd
Unique Relaxation Specialist Ltd
Virtue Botanicals Limited

Lancashire [39]
Acheson & Acheson Limited
Adam Michaels Group Ltd
Aromatherapy Infusions Ltd
Aromatic Scents Ltd
Bathroom Cosmetics Ltd
Bigben Healthcare Limited
Black Cat Manufacturing Ltd
D'Iusso Collection Ltd
Dermaplaning Pro Official Ltd
Dreamweave Products Ltd
Drom International UK Limited
Eabir Ltd
Earth Mother Soul Sister Ltd
Evans Vanodine International PLC
Pierre Fabre Limited
Fragrance Oils (International) Ltd
Fragrance Oils (Purchasing) Ltd
Happy Melon Skin Care Limited
Haych Cosmetics Limited
Jardins D'Eden Ltd
Kyoka Pro Ltd
La Parfumerie Anglaise Limited
Lofty Gardens Ltd
MLC Parfum & Oudh Ltd
Mama Mio Distribution Limited
Maskalin Ltd
Robert McBride Ltd
Northern Aromatics (Sales) Ltd
A W Oliver & Co Ltd
Oliver & Taylor Ltd
Project Cosmetics Limited
Relax Candle and Bath Co Ltd
Smelliz Ltd
Soap Legacy Ltd
Soapy Skin Limited
Stunning Fragrance Ltd
Tom's Garden Limited
Tranquility Cosmetics Limited
Urembo Naturally Ltd

Leicestershire [6]
Aim8 Limited
Gio Natura Ltd
Jamal London Ltd
KD Trading (UK) Limited
Madre Skincare Limited
Penny Price Aromatherapy Ltd

Lincolnshire
Fragrances UK Limited
JLP Cosmetics Ltd
Marsh Organics Limited
Soak Rochford Ltd

London [269]
4160 Tuesdays Limited
4RM Ltd
7 Virtues Beauty Ltd
A Natural Treat Limited
AA Group Holdings Ltd
Act of Kindness Organics Ltd
Adunni Ori Limited
Aexents Ltd
Affinity Organics Limited
Ahwaz Ltd
Al-Jazeera Perfumes Ltd
Alchemy Botanics Ltd
Alchemy Skin and Soul Ltd.
Ally Dog Co Ltd

Almond & Avocado Ltd
Anyki Ltd
Arbar Ltd
Argos International Fragrances Ltd
Ark Perfumeries Limited
Art de Parfum Ltd.
Aspire Eden Ltd
Aswad P.S.S Ltd
Aube Laboratories Ltd
Auli London Ltd
Aura Organics Limited
Aventual Ltd
Axwood Limited
Ayuroma Limited
Balm House Limited
Beautiful Mind Series Limited
Beauty Handmade Limited
Berry Inc Ltd
Bespoke Natural Health Ltd
Bill & Artisans Ltd
Black Gem Cosmetics Ltd
Bleu D'Argan Skincare Limited
Bloom Aromatics Limited
Body Candy Ltd.
Body Station Limited
Boselli Europe Ltd
CC Business Limited
Camblabs Ltd
Cambridge Genefit Technologies Ltd
Carrie Wilson Limited
Chirps London Ltd
Cinsce Ltd
Cocoa Twist Limited
Convoy Fragrances Ltd
Cosmetics a la Carte Limited
Cosmos Cosmetics Limited
Creative Perfumers London Ltd
Culpeper Limited
Custom Skin Lab Limited
Cybele UK Ltd
DBI Innovations Group Limited
Daughters of Circe Ltd
Department Health & Beauty Ltd
Drops of Humanity Ltd
EEM Botanicals Limited
EMC Botanica Limited
East China Sourcing Ltd
Ecocrushuk Ltd
Ed N' Grace Ltd
Eden in Valley Soapworks Ltd
Ekstaze London Limited
Elan Skincare Ltd
Elegant Boss Ltd
Elequra Limited
Elinor-UK Ltd
Es-Ssentially Yours Ltd
Escentric Molecules Limited
Evocativ Limited
Experimental Perfume Club Ltd
Face Boutique Limited
Faces Cosmetics Limited
Farasha-Cosmetics Ltd
Fashion Fragrances & Cosmetics UK Ltd
Female Balance Shop Limited
Fitzrovia Centre Ltd
Fizzy Lizzy's Ltd
Forte Organics Ltd
Fragrant Spa Limited
Freshorize Ltd
Frosts of London Limited
Fumarette Ltd
Fysifarm Limited

G & G Skincare Ltd
G and B Beauty Products Ltd
Gagnon Essentials Limited
Gallivant Perfumes Limited
Garden Perfumers Ltd
Glad Gent Ltd
Glamoessence Ltd
Glory Skin Ltd
Good By Nature Ltd
Gracetree Ltd
Green Mass Limited
H H Formulations Ltd
HBNatura Ltd
HE FE Ltd
Hairs & Graces Cosmetics Ltd
Hanan Pacha Ltd
Heavenly Fragrance (UK) Ltd
Hkka Limited
Hoc Parfum Ltd
Holistic Plant Technologies Ltd
Honey Corn Limited
Hunk Grooming Ltd
Hypothesis One Ltd
IQ-Area Ltd
Iam By Nature Ltd.
Icebox Brands EU Limited
Icilda's Ltd
Ikaa Cosmetics Limited
Incoplex Limited
Indult Paris Ltd
Sarah Ireland Perfumes Ltd
Islestarr Holdings Limited
Itaconix (U.K.) Limited
JST Exports (UK) Ltd
JWO Beauty Limited
Jove London Ltd
KPSS (UK) Limited
Kaira Luchi Ltd
Kao (UK) Limited
Karamat Collection Ltd
Kehal Ltd
Khali Min Limited
Kinski Limited
Kisens Ltd
LJSP Ltd
La Maison Hedonique Limited
La Mu London Limited
Ladd Cosmetics Ltd
Lana-Rae Ltd Ltd
Lathersmith Ltd
Leum Skin Care Ltd
Lex Roris Ltd
Libhairation Ltd
Lum Lifestyle Ltd.
Lumine Beauty Ltd
Luxury Personal Care Ltd
M.C Skin Truth Ltd
MAC Professional Haircare Ltd
MK Design & Art Direction Ltd
Madalyn and Rose Ltd
Maison Ex Nihilo UK Limited
Majestic Company London Ltd
Make-Up Art Cosmetics (U.K.) Ltd
Maribella London Limited
Maskologist Ltd
Mast - Art Group Limited
Mata Labs Cosmetics Ltd
Mavala (U.K.) Limited
Mayen Velvaere Limited
Meek and Mild Essentials Ltd
Lyn Michel Limited
Midnight Apothecary Limited

Miller Harris Limited
Millicent and Snob Limited
Mob Fragrances Ltd.
Model Handmade Limited
Molecula Ltd
Molton Brown Limited
Monreale Limited
Moyy Limited
Mr Vanguard Limited
Muir Events Ltd
Mulondon Limited
Joy Myfanwy Limited
Naticuma Limited
Natural Skincare London Ltd
Naturali360 Limited
Nature B Limited
Nature's Embrace Limited
Nectar International Limited
Neighbourhood Botanicals Ltd
Neville Cut and Shave Limited
New Vistas Avant Garde Limited
Nihad A Rawi Limited
Maya Njie Perfumes Limited
Nobell Group Ltd
Noblechart Cosmetic Ltd
Nova Extraction Ltd
Jaye O'Boye & Co Ltd
Odejo Limited
Old Park Farm Estate Limited
Olire Ltd
Organic Basics Ltd
Organic Stuff Limited
Orion Independent Limited
Orton Limited
Ostens Limited
Otte Limited
Our Modern Lives Ltd
P & H Natural Skincare Ltd
Paddy's Bathroom Limited
Papillon Perfumery Ltd
Paz By Nature Ltd
Perfair Limited
Pharmaco Group Limited
Pitt London Ltd
Platinum Beards Ltd
Pools of Cleopatra Limited
Possibility of London Ltd
Precious Clothing & Beauty Ltd
Project Renegades Ltd
Prophylaxis Ltd
Prosody London Limited
Providence Ventures Limited
Psyche Com & Merch Ltd
Pure Fiji (EU) Limited
Pure Ohana Limited
Rasta Life Ltd
Rustic Blends Limited
SE & SA Limited
Saisha Marra Ltd.
Sandine Zartaux Holding Ltd
Savillequinn Pty Ltd.
Sears UK Ltd
Sharakkas United Kingdom Ltd
Shinso Skin Care Limited
Silyn Products Ltd
Since Six Ltd
Skin Nectar Ltd
Skincare Laboratories Ltd
Skyn Deep Ltd
Soapberries Ltd
Softme Beauty Ltd
Sonyah Adan Limited

Sphere 7 Lab Ltd
Squires and Trelawny Ltd
Sultan Pasha Artisanal Perfumery Ltd
Sundarak Ltd
Sunshapers Limited
Swaziboy Limited
Sweet Arabian Ltd
Swiss Pharma Dynamic Ltd
TAC Perfumes & Cosmetics (UK) Ltd
TH / Edition Ltd
TWC Products Limited
ThatCo Ltd
This Wode Co Ltd
ThisCo Ltd
Thomas Andy Ltd.
Thread and Co UK Limited
Three Organics Ltd
Trees of Beauty Ltd
Tresaigh Ltd
Geo. F. Trumper (Perfumer and Products)
Twelve Beauty Ltd
Ulu Botanicals Ltd
Umma Therapy Ltd.
Un Air D'Antan Limited
Uncareditional Ltd
United Beauty Products Limited
Uyumbu Limited
Vaunt Limited
Villa Sauod Ltd
Vinculum Ltd
Viraj Organics Ltd
Washworks Bodycare Limited
Wildsmith Collection Limited
Winterpark Paris Parfums Ltd
Wist and Wonder Limited
Yess Essentials Limited
E. Zabari Holdings UK Limited
Zelenci Natural Health Ltd
Zoe Lane Ltd

Lothian
Braw Beard Oils Ltd
Thomas Laurie Naturals Ltd
Seilich Limited

Merseyside [11]
AC Packing Ltd
Owen Drew Luxury Candles Ltd
Fragrance and Glamour Ltd
Hart Enterprise Limited
L.E.C.(L'pool) Limited
LU Aromatherapy Ltd
Laboratory Facilities Limited
Pur-D Natural Skin Care Ltd
Ethel Roberts Limited
Surefil Beauty Products Ltd
Whole International Limited

Middlesex [24]
Beauty Core Limited
Bonita Lou Ltd
Andre Boyard Perfumes Limited
Buachi Limited
Butterbur and Sage Limited
Cactus Skincare Limited
Designer IP (2) Ltd
Eyegenius Ltd
Firmenich Holdings (UK) Ltd
Firmenich UK Limited
Firmenich Wellingborough (UK) Ltd
Freshly Whip'd Limited

Hi Energy Healing Limited
House of Unique Parfum Limited
Lese & Lista Ltd
Mayla Skincare Ltd
Onze Limited
Pandorra Ltd.
Saints & Co London Ltd
Scrummy U Health Ltd
Sipro (UK) Ltd
Skin Intuition Ltd
Vetivert & Co Ltd
Zodiac International (London) Ltd

Midlothian [6]
Amaranthine Beauty Ltd
Biologico Cosmetics Limited
Credence Hair Venture Limited
Jorum of Scotland Limited
Kingdom Scotland Limited
Wheesht Ltd

Monmouthshire
Beauty Alliance International Ltd
Green Jiva Ltd
Insensed Ltd

Norfolk [8]
Juni Cosmetics Limited
NTM (UK) Limited
Natural Soap Co Ltd
Persephone Bio Ltd
Protect Biosciences Ltd
Sensapeel Ltd
Tiger Lily Soapery Ltd
Wild & Organic Bioactive Essentials

Northamptonshire [14]
Aqua Natural Limited
Awake Organics Ltd
CPL Aromas (Holdings) Limited
CPL Aromas Limited
Eifelcorp Consumer Care Ltd
Excel (GS) Limited
Good Mela Ltd
Intradicted Ltd
Jaemae Ltd
Little House of Wild Ltd
Phoenix Fragrances Limited
Raw Supremo Ltd
Rodriguez Corporation Ltd
Storey Enterprises Limited

Northumberland
Esensi Skincare Ltd

Nottinghamshire [11]
All Good Skincare Limited
BCM Limited
Baum of London Limited
Carapoll Chemicals Ltd
Credo Felix Ltd
Kropp & Hem Ltd
Nadeane Letisha Ltd
Lily Her Limited
Potions & Possibilities Ltd
Savage Alchemy Limited
Zaeda Alexia Limited

Oxfordshire [9]
Al Oxford Ltd
Aroma Design Ltd
Artemis Oils Ltd
Elinor Sophia Limited
Littlemore Candle Co Ltd
Natural Science Aromas Ltd
Organic Fragrance Co Ltd
Phytacol Limited
Scrubbingtons Limited

Pembrokeshire
Caldey Island Estate Co Ltd
Mrs Greens Hemp Remedies Ltd

Rhondda Cynon Taf
Fillcare Limited

Shropshire [6]
AD Fragrances Ltd
Cocoa Lime Limited
Elibec Limited
Greatest of All Time Soapworks Ltd
Haromatic Ltd
Salopian Ltd

Somerset [21]
Above Beyond Group Ltd
Arcania Apothecary Ltd
Astroscent Ltd
Atlas Group Limited
Designer Fragrances Limited
Dr Jackson Ltd
Elemis Limited
Fragrant Earth International Ltd
Grace & Hartland Ltd
Heidi J Naturals Limited
Image Hub Limited
Jean Christian Perfumes Ltd
Kairn Holding Limited
Kylah K Skincare Ltd
Meadow Farm Friends Ltd
Organatural Ltd
Savon de V Ltd
Scent To Inspire Ltd
Somerset Toiletry Co Ltd
Swallowfield PLC
Yellow Can Co Ltd

Staffordshire [5]
Fragrance du Bois (UK) Limited
IAP Cosmetics International Ltd
Magpie's Ocean Ltd
Reesoaps.co.uk Ltd
Shea Natural Skincare Limited

Suffolk [9]
Aromatic Answers Ltd
Body Thyme Limited
Busy Bees Cosmetics Limited
Herrmann + Herrmann Limited
Jarvis Cosmetic Developments Ltd.
Kingsmill Cosmetic Preparations Ltd
R.M. Investments Limited
S.R.S.Aromatics Limited
Travik Chemicals (UK) Limited

Surrey [30]
Ajmal Perfume (UK) Limited
By Kathryn Ltd
Carzel Limited
Combe International Limited
Coriungo Limited
Dermapharm Skincare Limited
Foad Wax Limited
M.S. George Limited
Gillette U.K. Limited
Hod Perfumes Limited
Hoff Beards Limited
Hope and Rose Limited
Hypha Cosmetics Ltd
I Love Myself Ltd
Jogb Limited
Karaama Fragrances Ltd
Magma London Ltd
Natural Products Factory Ltd
Ninni Ltd
Pepsyn Limited
Pierre Precieuse Parfum UK Ltd
Zandra Rhodes Fragrances Ltd
Ring in Ring Ltd
Robertet (U.K.) Limited
South West Aesthetics Ltd
Tahmasso Limited
Valorem Bespoke Ltd
Verde London Ltd.
Wonder and Wild Ltd
XDC Limited

Sussex [39]
83 Associates Limited
A.S Apothecary Limited
Ray Alteraifi Limited
Authenticus Ltd
Bedeaux Ltd
Bex London Ltd
Belinda Brown Limited
Corincraft Limited
Dermamaitre Ltd.
Eastwing Grooming Co. Limited
Elemental Beauty Limited
Elsan Limited
First Natural Brands Ltd
First Natural Limited
John Gosnell & Co Ltd
HMMT Holdings Ltd.
Hamiltons of Canterbury Ltd
Inspired Health & Beauty Products
International Toiletries & Cosmetics
K.K. Toiletries Limited
Thomas Kosmala Parfums Ltd
L'Ocean Limited
Christina May Limited
Modernista London Limited
Nadarra Cosmetics Ltd
Natural Aromatics Limited
Naturoganik Limited
One Green Lab Ltd
Perfume By Design Ltd.
Pure English Cosmetics Limited
Queen Cosmetics Limited
Quint Essence Lab Ltd
Renewyou Cancertology UK Ltd
Rutherford Bambury Ltd
Skin Defence Limited
Skinirvana Limited
Soap People Ltd
Squeaky Clean Queen Ltd
Yin Yang Natural Sciences Ltd

Tyne & Wear
Earthwhile Ltd
Ginger & Vanilla Ltd
Superfood Beauty Limited

Warwickshire [9]
Bath Candy Ltd
Eco Earth Limited
Eden's Legends Limited
Little Green Beehive Ltd
Lovefro Ltd.
My Life But Greener Limited
Soap Souk Ltd
Thebubblebar Ltd
Valencia Vanna Ltd.

West Midlands [23]
5 Senses Healthcare Ltd
AM Fragrances Limited
AS Manufacturing Ltd
Anyone Limited
Atmosy Ltd
Care By Jords Ltd
Carefree Toiletries Limited
Cosmetic Hooligans Ltd
Cutelovelee Limited
Fragrance Selection (UK) Ltd
Kisu Skincare Ltd
Koze Limited
Lucidlure Ltd
Missy D Collection Limited
Omprus Limited
Onyii's Cosmetics Ltd
Paradoxical Solutions Limited
Purepure Limited
R.P.C. Midlands Ltd
Scent Pod Co Ltd
Swanny's Ltd.
Three Fizzy Pigs Ltd
Wicked Vicky Co Ltd

Wiltshire [8]
Activbod Limited
Arco England Limited
Heaven Scent Incense Limited
Meiyume (UK) Limited
Simply Ewe Limited
Spots & Stripes Products Ltd
Stormfree Holdings Ltd
Wilde Beauty Limited

Worcestershire
Baylis & Harding PLC
Luissa Burton Limited
Canco Candles Limited

The Top UK Perfume and Toilet Preparations Manufacturers

Yorkshire [40]

Acarrier Limited
Advanced Aesthetics Training Academy
Beever Retail Limited
Blazergold Limited
Brigantia Personal Care Ltd
Castlefields Cosmetics Ltd.
Cool Gell Limited
Ethical House Ltd
Ferndale Pharmaceuticals Ltd
Fikkerts Limited
Flowery Whiff Limited
Honesty Skincare Limited
In Line Health and Beauty Ltd
Ink of Coco Skincare Ltd
Nicholas James (UK) Limited
Kadiricosmetics Ltd
Kensa Chemicals Limited
Khushi Skincare Limited
Ko. Essentials Ltd.
Making Scents Ltd
Man Mountain Beard Care Ltd
McCallum Manufacturing Limited
Mibelle Ltd
Midha Limited
Myroo Ltd
Ottimo Supplies Limited
Parfums Bleu Limited
Pot of Gold Cosmetics Limited
Pretty Little Treat Company (Yorkshire)
RMBeauty Limited
Sabel Cosmetics Limited
Saltaire Soap Ltd
Sheabynature Ltd
Stantondown Limited
Teknord Limited
Urban Nymph Limited
Veloskin Limited
Waterman Corporate Enterprises Ltd
Wrath Cosmetics Limited
Zahrat Alqurashi Ltd

This page is intentionally left blank

Company Profiles

11:11 Limited
Incorporated: 1 November 2017
Registered Office: 24 Sleford Close, Balsham, Cambridge, CB21 4DP
Shareholders: Heidi Gordon-Smith; Holly Anne Helt
Officers: Heidi Gordon-Smith [1981] Director; Holly Anne Helt [1964] Director [American]; Edward Alexander Sanson [1980] Director; Mark James Tanser [1968] Director

30 Minute Tan Limited
Incorporated: 1 December 2015
Net Worth: £48 *Total Assets:* £5,788
Registered Office: 21 Home Farm Court, Coatbridge, N Lanarks, ML5 1RW
Major Shareholder: Karen Wood
Officers: Karen Wood, Secretary; Karen Wood [1977] Director/Cosmetic Sales

4160 Tuesdays Limited
Incorporated: 28 May 2012 *Employees:* 6
Net Worth: £26,957 *Total Assets:* £83,889
Registered Office: Unit 8 Issigonis House, Cowley Road, London, W3 7UN
Shareholders: Nicholas Charles Randell; Sarah McCartney
Officers: Sarah McCartney [1960] Director/Consultant

4RM Ltd
Incorporated: 15 June 2018
Registered Office: 71-75 Shelton Street, London, WC2H 9JQ
Major Shareholder: Manjinder Virk
Officers: Ayazali Nazafi [1984] Director/Owner; Manjinder Virk [1987] Director

5 Senses Healthcare Ltd
Incorporated: 28 January 2019
Registered Office: 143 Monyhull Hall Road, Kings Norton, Birmingham, B30 3QG
Officers: Mandy Collins [1974] Director

The 7 Virtues Beauty Ltd
Incorporated: 20 February 2013
Net Worth: £262 *Total Assets:* £742
Registered Office: 10 Finsbury Square, London, EC2A 1AF
Major Shareholder: Barbara Ann Sarah Stegemann
Officers: Barbara Ann Sarah Stegemann [1969] Director [Canadian]

83 Associates Limited
Incorporated: 8 May 2015
Net Worth: £651 *Total Assets:* £85,680
Registered Office: Archer House, Britland Estate, Northbourne Road, Eastbourne, E Sussex, BN22 8PW
Major Shareholder: Augustine Anunta
Officers: Augustine Anunta [1983] Director

A Natural Treat Limited
Incorporated: 21 October 2018
Registered Office: 67-68 Hatton Garden, London, EC1N 8JY
Major Shareholder: Leigh-Marie Alcide
Officers: Leigh-Marie Alcide [1984] Director/Entrepreneur

A.S Apothecary Limited
Incorporated: 6 July 2015 *Employees:* 4
Net Worth: £7,298 *Total Assets:* £48,281
Registered Office: 163a The Old Forge, The High Street, Lewes, E Sussex, BN7 1XU
Major Shareholder: Amanda Jane Saurin
Officers: Amanda Jane Saurin [1964] Director

AA Group Holdings Ltd
Incorporated: 3 September 2018
Registered Office: 85 Great Portland Street, London, W1W 7LT
Major Shareholder: Adwoa Kuffour Akoto
Officers: Adwoa Kuffour Akoto [1990] Director/Entrepreneur

Abendana Enterprises Limited
Incorporated: 30 December 1981
Registered Office: Lambert Chapman, 3 Warners Mill, Silks Way, Braintree, Essex, CM7 3GB
Major Shareholder: Clive Lionel Bendon
Officers: Clive Lionel Bendon [1955] Director/Creative Perfumier

Above Beyond Group Ltd
Incorporated: 25 November 2016
Net Worth Deficit: £3,170
Registered Office: Spike Island, 133 Cumberland Road, Bristol, BS1 6UX
Officers: Caroline MacKenzie [1964] Director; Joe Jai Mallory-Skinner [1992] Director/Designer; Ava Regal [1955] Director; Gary Walsh [1961] Director

AC Packing Ltd
Incorporated: 22 November 2016 *Employees:* 2
Net Worth: £23,537 *Total Assets:* £37,692
Registered Office: 61 Rodney Street, Liverpool, L1 9ER
Major Shareholder: Neil Rice
Officers: Neil Rice, Secretary; Neil Rice [1980] Director/Manager

Acarrier Limited
Incorporated: 22 October 2018
Registered Office: 57 Market Street, Thornton, Bradford, BD13 3EN
Major Shareholder: Almas Khawar Ahmed
Officers: Dr Almas Khawar Ahmed [1986] Director/Pharmaceuticals

Acheson & Acheson Limited
Incorporated: 13 November 1992 *Employees:* 356
Net Worth: £19,989,940 *Total Assets:* £34,998,828
Registered Office: 5th Floor, Voyager House, Chicago Avenue, Manchester Airport, Manchester, M90 3DQ
Parent: The Hut IHC Limited
Officers: James Pochin, Secretary; John Andrew Gallemore [1969] Director; James Patrick Pochin [1976] Director

Act of Kindness Organics Ltd
Incorporated: 21 May 2018
Registered Office: 27 Old Gloucester Street, London, WC1N 3AX
Major Shareholder: Michele Carnes Ellis
Officers: Michele Carnes Ellis [1966] Director [American]

Activbod Limited
Incorporated: 7 July 2014 *Employees:* 2
Net Worth Deficit: £397,059 *Total Assets:* £35,182
Registered Office: Windover House, St Ann Street, Salisbury, Wilts, SP1 2DR
Major Shareholder: Lara Morgan
Officers: Lara Morgan [1967] Director

AD Fragrances Ltd
Incorporated: 20 August 2014
Previous: The Astbury Fragrances Ltd
Net Worth Deficit: £31,679 *Total Assets:* £67,324
Registered Office: 59 Cartway, Bridgnorth, Salop, WV16 4BG
Shareholders: Adrian Downing; Dean Richards
Officers: Adrian Downing [1968] Director; Dean Richards [1969] Director

Adam Michaels Group Ltd
Incorporated: 12 November 2018
Registered Office: 15 Drumhead Road, Chorley North Industrial Park, Chorley, Lancs, PR6 7BX
Officers: Soab Bhuta [1969] Director; Zuber Lulat [1979] Director; Shahid Malek [1970] Director; Nasim Akhtar Patel [1972] Director

Adunni Ori Limited
Incorporated: 18 April 2016
Registered Office: 7 Wilkes Close, London, NW7 1FP
Major Shareholder: Mobolaji Soremekun
Officers: Zaynab Adenrele Agoro [1997] Director/Cosmetics; Mobolaji Soremekun [1967] Director/Cosmetics

Advanced Aesthetics Training Academy Limited
Incorporated: 9 November 2017
Registered Office: 553-555 Attercliffe Road, Sheffield, S9 3RA
Major Shareholder: Vinisha Vinisha Ali
Officers: Vinisha Ali [1974] Director/Beautician

Aexents Ltd
Incorporated: 25 May 2016
Registered Office: 71-75 Shelton Street, Covent Garden, London, WC2H 9JQ
Major Shareholder: Phillip Jorge Henry
Officers: Phillip Jorge Henry [1982] Director [British/Jamaican]

Affinity Organics Limited
Incorporated: 11 November 2014
Net Worth Deficit: £3,630
Registered Office: 60 Windsor Avenue, London, SW19 2RR
Officers: Samuel Siklawi [1974] Director

Ahwaz Ltd
Incorporated: 10 October 2016
Net Worth: £60,568 *Total Assets:* £120,800
Registered Office: 20-22 Wenlock Road, London, N1 7GU
Major Shareholder: Fazel Hamidi
Officers: Fazel Hamidi [1988] Director

AI Oxford Ltd
Incorporated: 3 May 2018
Registered Office: The Oxford Science Park, Robert Robinson Avenue, The Magdalen Centre, Oxford, OX4 4GA
Major Shareholder: Allison Wild
Officers: Allison Wild [1962] Director/R&D Scientist

Aim8 Limited
Incorporated: 17 May 2011
Net Worth: £147,651 *Total Assets:* £212,584
Registered Office: 115 Vulcan Road, Leicester, LE5 3EE
Shareholders: Amir Ismail; Amir Ismail Memon
Officers: Amir Ismail [1980] Director/Retailer

Ainsel Limited
Incorporated: 18 August 2014
Net Worth: £25,424 *Total Assets:* £36,975
Registered Office: c/o Ascot Drummond, Devonshire House, Manor Way, Borehamwood, Herts, WD6 1QQ
Major Shareholder: Svetlana Prokhorova
Officers: Kirill Prokhorov, Secretary; Svetlana Prokhorova [1987] Director/CEO & Founder [Russian]

Ajmal Perfume (UK) Limited
Incorporated: 8 May 1997
Registered Office: 1st Floor, Crosspoint House, 28 Stafford Road, Wallington, Surrey, SM6 9AA
Parent: Fabson Import Export Ltd
Officers: Abdulla Amiruddin Ajmal, Secretary; Mohammed Amiruddin Ajmal [1953] Director [Indian]; Mohammed Sirajuddin Ajmal [1958] Director [Indian]; Mohammed Fakhruddin Ajmal [1954] Director [Indian]

Al-Jazeera Perfumes Ltd
Incorporated: 1 February 2019
Registered Office: Amine El-Bacha, 61 Mill Lane, London, NW6 1NB
Major Shareholder: Amine El-Bacha
Officers: Amine El-Bacha [1972] Director/Self Employed

Alchemy Botanics Ltd
Incorporated: 2 November 2017
Registered Office: 20-22 Wenlock Road, London, N1 7GU
Major Shareholder: Ngozi Plange
Officers: Ngozi Plange [1980] Director

Alchemy Skin and Soul Ltd.
Incorporated: 16 January 2019
Registered Office: 71-75 Shelton Street, Covent Garden, London, WC2H 9JQ
Major Shareholder: Natalie Jane Ogden
Officers: Lynda Jane Amner, Secretary; Natalie Jane Ogden [1985] Director/Skincare Manufacturer

Alice in Perfume Limited
Incorporated: 13 March 2014
Net Worth: £1,290 *Total Assets:* £13,039
Registered Office: Red Sky House, Fairclough Hall, Halls Green, Weston, Herts, SG4 7DP
Major Shareholder: Marie Still
Officers: Marie Still [1958] Director

Alkaiser Perfumes Ltd
Incorporated: 8 September 2018
Registered Office: Aramex House, Old Bath Road, Colnbrook, Slough, Berks, SL3 0NS
Shareholders: Yamen Muneer Albakour; Safaa Mohamed Ali Mohamed Ali Mohamed
Officers: Yamen Muneer Albakour [1979] Director/Manager [Syrian]

All Good Skincare Limited
Incorporated: 23 July 2018
Registered Office: 10 The Triangle, Nottingham, NG2 1AE
Major Shareholder: Luke Thomas Baldwin
Officers: Luke Thomas Baldwin [1990] Director

The Ally Dog Company Limited
Incorporated: 28 November 2018
Registered Office: 71-75 Shelton Street, London, WC2H 9JQ
Major Shareholder: William Illingworth-Dennis
Officers: William Illingworth-Dennis, Secretary; William Illingworth-Dennis [1994] Director

Almond & Avocado Ltd
Incorporated: 27 April 2010
Net Worth Deficit: £9,575 *Total Assets:* £4,083
Registered Office: First Floor, 85 Great Portland Street, London, W1W 7LT
Major Shareholder: Annette Yvonne Clark Headley
Officers: Annette Yvonne Clark Headley [1977] Director/Consultant

Ray Alteraifi Limited
Incorporated: 14 July 2015
Net Worth Deficit: £5,688 *Total Assets:* £1,004
Registered Office: Victoria House, Stanbridge Park, Staplefield Lane, Staplefield, W Sussex, RH17 6AS
Major Shareholder: Rihab Alteraifi Abdelkarim
Officers: Dr Rihab Alteraifi Abdelkarim [1970] Director

AM Fragrances Limited
Incorporated: 29 November 2018
Registered Office: 451 Moseley Road, Birmingham, B12 9BX
Major Shareholder: Mohammed Ali Sayed
Officers: Mohammed Ali Sayed [1996] Director

Amaranthine Beauty Ltd
Incorporated: 16 January 2017
Net Worth Deficit: £1,251 *Total Assets:* £1,099
Registered Office: 101 Rose Street, South Lane, Edinburgh, EH2 3JG
Major Shareholder: Sarah Rueger
Officers: Sarah Rueger [1974] Director/Clinical Support Worker [Irish]

Anuvaayum Ltd
Incorporated: 15 January 2018
Registered Office: 17 Falconers Road, Luton, Beds, LU2 9ET
Major Shareholder: Karunakaran Subramaniam
Officers: Karunakaran Subramaniam [1978] Director/Consultant

Anyki Ltd
Incorporated: 22 January 2019
Registered Office: 20-22 Wenlock Road, London, N1 7GU
Shareholders: Anya Kruger; Kim Brown
Officers: Kim Brown [1963] Director/Project Consultant; Anya Kruger [1978] Director/Consultant [South African]

Anyone Limited
Incorporated: 25 February 2019
Registered Office: 87 Hewell Road, Barnt Green, Birmingham, B45 8NL
Major Shareholder: Brian Harry Fox
Officers: Brian Harry Fox [1959] Director

Aqua Natural Limited
Incorporated: 19 December 1988
Net Worth Deficit: £261,403 *Total Assets:* £25,703
Registered Office: Unit 50 Leyland Trading Estate, Irthlingborough Road, Wellingborough, Northants, NN8 1RT
Major Shareholder: Hafiz Anver Khandwala
Officers: Rosemeen Hafiz Khandwala, Secretary; Hafiz Anver Khandwala [1954] Director; Noor Hafiz Khandwala [1987] Director/Marketing Manager; Rosemeen Hafiz Khandwala [1958] Director; Tayab Hafiz Khandwala [1980] Director

Arbar Ltd
Incorporated: 28 January 2019
Registered Office: 114 St Mary's Road, London, SE15 2DU
Major Shareholder: Rosemary MacGregor
Officers: Rosemary MacGregor [1989] Director

Arcania Apothecary Ltd
Incorporated: 12 September 2000 *Employees:* 28
Net Worth: £890,583 *Total Assets:* £2,481,689
Registered Office: Second Floor, The Fragrance House, Haydon, Wells, Somerset, BA5 3FF
Major Shareholder: Richard Geoffrey Howard
Officers: Nigel Bond, Secretary; Richard Geoffrey Howard [1963] Director/Cosmetic Designer

Archem (N.I.) Ltd
Incorporated: 9 July 2003
Net Worth: £57,931 *Total Assets:* £133,839
Registered Office: 158 High Street, Holywood, Co Down, BT18 9HT
Shareholders: Brian Alexander Hunniford; Lynne Diane Dorothy Joan Hunniford
Officers: Brian Alexander Hunniford, Secretary; Brian Alexander Hunniford [1952] Director; Lynne Diane Dorothy Joan Hunniford [1953] Director

Arco England Limited
Incorporated: 8 April 2008 *Employees:* 33
Net Worth: £1,044,079 *Total Assets:* £2,549,470
Registered Office: Crusader Park, Roman Way, Warminster, Wilts, BA12 8SP
Shareholders: Roger John Biles; Philippa Jane Biles
Officers: Roger John Biles, Secretary; Philippa Jane Biles [1967] Director/Designer; Roger John Biles [1966] Director/Designer

Argos International Fragrances Ltd
Incorporated: 12 November 2018
Registered Office: 71-75 Shelton Street, Covent Garden, London, WC2H 9JQ
Major Shareholder: Christian Petrovich
Officers: Christian Petrovich, Secretary; Christian Petrovich [1978] Director/Fragrance Manufacturer [American]

Arizona Botaniq Limited
Incorporated: 19 October 2016
Net Worth Deficit: £7,703 *Total Assets:* £200
Registered Office: 43 Gaitside Drive, Aberdeen, AB10 7BH
Major Shareholder: Arizona Arizona Brodie
Officers: Arizona Brodie [1992] Director

Ark Perfumeries Limited
Incorporated: 12 February 2018
Registered Office: Kemp House, 160 City Road, London, EC1V 2NX
Shareholders: Manulla Kanchwala; Alham Kanchwala
Officers: Alham Kanchwala, Secretary; Manulla Kanchwala, Secretary; Alham Kanchwala [1995] Director/Businessman [Indian]; Manulla Kanchwala [1971] Director/Businessman [Indian]

Aroma Amour Ltd
Incorporated: 27 December 2017
Registered Office: Unit 19 The Mall, Hyde, Cheshire, SK14 2QT
Major Shareholder: Karena Dawn Dawson
Officers: Karena Dawn Dawson, Secretary; Karena Dawn Dawson [1980] Director/Sales & Marketing

Aroma Body Treats Limited
Incorporated: 6 December 2017
Registered Office: 45 The Grove, Sidcup, Kent, DA14 5NG
Shareholders: Marili Datema; Daniela Maria Luengo
Officers: Marili Datema [1988] Director [German]; Daniela Maria Luengo [1969] Director

Aroma Cosmetics Laboratory Limited
Incorporated: 28 April 2014
Registered Office: 30 Manstone Lane, Sidmouth, Devon, EX10 9TU
Major Shareholder: Seng Koon Lim
Officers: Seng Koon Lim [1959] Director [Singaporean]; Andrew Stuart Young [1980] Director

Aroma Design Ltd
Incorporated: 21 June 2018
Registered Office: Badgemore House, Badgemore, Henley on Thames, Oxon, RG9 4NR
Major Shareholder: Frank Paul Julian Carter
Officers: Frank Paul Julian Carter [1947] Director

Aroma Trading Limited
Incorporated: 18 March 1992 *Employees:* 9
Net Worth: £6,168,710 *Total Assets:* £6,605,720
Registered Office: c/o APS Accountancy Limited, 4 Cromwell Court, New Street, Aylesbury, Bucks, HP20 2PB
Shareholders: John Francis Black; Sharon Margaret Black
Officers: John Francis Black, Secretary/Director [Irish]; John Francis Black [1959] Director [Irish]; Sharon Margaret Black [1965] Director

Aromabar (Scotland) Ltd
Incorporated: 5 December 2017
Registered Office: Unit 9-11 Robertson Street, Barrhead, E Renfrewshire, G78 1QW
Shareholders: Alan Grant; Catherine Grant
Officers: Alan Grant [1963] Director; Catherine Grant [1964] Director

Aromaherb Limited
Incorporated: 24 January 1996
Registered Office: Lambert Chapman, 3 Warners Mill, Silks Way, Braintree, Essex, CM7 3GB
Major Shareholder: Clive Lionel Bendon
Officers: Clive Lionel Bendon [1955] Director/Analytical Perfumer

Aromatherapy Infusions Ltd
Incorporated: 13 November 2015
Net Worth Deficit: £3,571 *Total Assets:* £1,721
Registered Office: 83 Ducie Street, Manchester, M1 2JQ
Major Shareholder: Ginina Houghton
Officers: Ginina Houghton [1972] Director/Manager

Aromatic Answers Ltd
Incorporated: 18 January 2018
Registered Office: Units 4 & 5 Brightwell Barns, Waldringfield Road, Brightwell, Ipswich, Suffolk, IP10 0BJ
Major Shareholder: Donna Walker
Officers: Donna Walker [1973] Director

Aromatic Scents Ltd
Incorporated: 20 April 2017
Registered Office: 18 Hall Street, Bury, Lancs, BL8 1RY
Shareholder: Barbara Allen
Officers: Barbara Allen, Secretary; Paul Mainwaring [1958] Director

Arriva Fragrances Limited
Incorporated: 3 August 1987 *Employees:* 2
Net Worth: £42,621 *Total Assets:* £80,790
Registered Office: 1 Holtspur Lane, Wooburn Green, High Wycombe, Bucks, HP10 0AA
Shareholders: Stanley Peter Koziol; Gillian Koziol
Officers: Gillian Koziol, Secretary; Gillian Koziol [1955] Director/Housewife; Stanley Peter Koziol [1954] Director/Perfumer

Arrivatech Limited
Incorporated: 1 December 2016
Registered Office: Unit 1 Holtspur Lane, Wooburn Green, High Wycombe, Bucks, HP10 0AA
Major Shareholder: Stanley Peter Koziol
Officers: Stanley Peter Koziol [1954] Creative & Technical Director

Art de Parfum Ltd.
Incorporated: 1 May 2015 *Employees:* 1
Net Worth Deficit: £61,749 *Total Assets:* £26,687
Registered Office: 86-90 Paul Street, London, EC2A 4NE
Major Shareholder: Ruta Degutyte
Officers: Ruta Degutyte [1974] Director/Founder [Lithuanian]

Artemis Oils Ltd
Incorporated: 21 June 2018
Registered Office: Badgemore House, Badgemore, Henley on Thames, Oxon, RG9 4NR
Major Shareholder: Frank Paul Julian Carter
Officers: Frank Paul Julian Carter [1947] Director

Artisane Aromatherapy Limited
Incorporated: 15 May 2018
Registered Office: 38 Victoria Street, Harwich, Essex, CO12 3AR
Officers: Susan Elizabeth Burgess [1959] Director/Manufacturer

AS Manufacturing Ltd
Incorporated: 29 October 2018
Registered Office: 157 School Road, Hall Green, Birmingham, B28 8JF
Major Shareholder: Asim Mehmood
Officers: Asim Mehmood [1990] Managing Director

Askett & English Ltd
Incorporated: 9 February 2011
Net Worth: £50 *Total Assets:* £50
Registered Office: Mercury House, 19-21 Chapel Street, Marlow, Bucks, SL7 3HN
Major Shareholder: Matthew David Jeffs
Officers: Matthew David Jeffs [1962] Director

Aspire Eden Ltd
Incorporated: 15 September 2014
Registered Office: 107e Vassall Road, London, SW9 6NJ
Major Shareholder: Dola Alika Akinola
Officers: Dola Alika Akinola [1981] Director/Project Accountant

Astarra Ltd
Incorporated: 13 August 2018
Registered Office: 21 Beech Road, Darlington, Co Durham, DL1 3HQ
Major Shareholder: Deborah Jackson
Officers: Deborah Jackson [1959] Director

Astroscent Ltd
Incorporated: 20 February 2019
Registered Office: Little Barn, Castle Rocks Barns, Wiveliscombe, Taunton, Somerset, TA4 2TL
Major Shareholder: Velma Claire Lyrae
Officers: Velma Claire Lyrae [1960] Director/Perfumer

Aswad P.S.S Ltd
Incorporated: 28 December 2016
Net Worth: £3,594 *Total Assets:* £5,630
Registered Office: 729 Ixworth Place, London, SW3 3QF
Major Shareholder: Omar Al-Ayoubi
Officers: Omar Al-Ayoubi [1991] Director/Entrepreneur

Athena Cosmetics Limited
Incorporated: 8 October 2013
Registered Office: c/o 7Side Secretarial Limited, 14-18 City Road, Cardiff, CF24 3DL
Officers: Dr Michael Curt Brinkenhoff [1948] Director [American]

Atlas Group Limited
Incorporated: 23 August 1988
Registered Office: Swallowfield House, Station Road, Wellington, Somerset, TA21 8NL
Officers: Jane Fletcher [1967] Director/Sales & Marketing; Matthew Gazzard [1971] Group Financial Director; Timothy James Perman [1962] Director

Atmosy Ltd
Incorporated: 27 December 2018
Registered Office: 3 Norton Close, Smethwick, W Midlands, B66 3JA
Shareholders: Abdulaziz Omar Noor; Safiya Issa
Officers: Safiya Issa [1988] Director/Engineer [Dutch]; Abdulaziz Omar Noor [1992] Director/Optometrist

Atypical Cosmetics Ltd
Incorporated: 25 January 2019
Registered Office: 311 Byres Road, Glasgow, G12 8UQ
Major Shareholder: Marwa Sayed Ahmed Ebrahim Hashem Ebrahim
Officers: Marwa Sayed Ahmed Ebrahim Hashem Ebrahim [1995] Director/Chief Executive [Bahraini]

Aube Laboratories Ltd
Incorporated: 8 February 2018
Registered Office: 27 Old Gloucester Street, London, WC1N 3AX
Parent: Swit Pharma SP Z O.O
Officers: Waldemar Siwak [1969] Director [Polish]

Auli London Ltd
Incorporated: 15 September 2016
Net Worth Deficit: £45,197 *Total Assets:* £8,526
Registered Office: 78 York Street, London, W1H 1DP
Major Shareholder: Joshua Christian
Officers: Joshua Christian [1981] Director; Aakanksha Sharma [1987] Director [Indian]

Aura Organics Limited
Incorporated: 1 December 2015
Net Worth: £2,923 *Total Assets:* £2,923
Registered Office: Studio 92, Hackney Downs Studios, 17 Amhurst Terrace, London, E8 2BT
Major Shareholder: Danielle Alexandra Andrean
Officers: Danielle Andrean [1987] Director; Elizabeth Ann Andrean [1956] Director

Authenticus Ltd
Incorporated: 10 May 2018
Registered Office: 23 Stage House, 23-27 London Road, East Grinstead, W Sussex, RH19 1AL
Officers: Stanley Williams [1960] Managing Director

Ava Corporations Ltd
Incorporated: 7 July 2017
Registered Office: 14 Abbey Street, Armagh, BT61 7DX
Major Shareholder: Collin Grayson
Officers: Collin Grayson [1970] Director/Businessman

Avenge Skincare Limited
Incorporated: 28 February 2018
Registered Office: 71 Lima Court, Bath Road, Reading, Berks, RG1 6NF
Major Shareholder: Nikita Jain
Officers: Nikita Jain [1994] Director/Sales and Marketing Specialist

Aventual Ltd
Incorporated: 9 January 2015
Net Worth Deficit: £47,705 *Total Assets:* £120,318
Registered Office: 38 Ermine Road, London, SE13 7JS
Shareholder: Lillian Amoah
Officers: Lillian Amoah [1962] Director

Awake Organics Ltd
Incorporated: 22 September 2017
Registered Office: 30 Harborough Road, Northampton, NN2 7AZ
Officers: James Alexander Kimbell [1974] Director; Melissa Kimbell [1979] Director

Axwood Limited
Incorporated: 29 January 2018
Registered Office: Kemp House, 160 City Road, London, EC1V 2NX
Major Shareholder: Alexandre Seewald-Butzerin
Officers: Alexandre Seewald-Butzerin, Secretary; Alexandre Seewald-Butzerin [1979] Director/Manager [French]

Ayuroma Limited
Incorporated: 13 September 2017
Registered Office: P O Box 72048, 28 Brondesbury Villas, London, NW6 9TY
Shareholders: Raghav Malik; Ripul Agarwal
Officers: Ripul Agarwal [1988] Director/Entrepreneur [Indian]; Raghav Malik [1991] Director/Product Manager [Indian]

Ayurveda Pura Ltd
Incorporated: 24 October 2003
Net Worth Deficit: £700,336 *Total Assets:* £480,253
Registered Office: Saffron House, 61b Elmstead Lane, Chislehurst, Kent, BR7 5EQ
Major Shareholder: Vasudev Raju Ravindra Apte
Officers: Dr Deepa Apte, Secretary/Medical Doctor; Dr Deepa Apte [1973] Director/Medical Doctor; Vasudev Raju Ravindra Apte [1973] Director/Solicitor; Vikas Jain [1977] Director/Engineer [Indian]

Ayurveda Wellness Ltd
Incorporated: 3 November 2017
Registered Office: Office 9 & 10, Anna House, Dunmurry Office Park, 37a Upper Dunmurry Lane, Dunmurry, Belfast, BT17 0AA
Major Shareholder: Upendra Shenoy Umesh Vijayam
Officers: Veena Gopalakini [1978] Director/Supervisor; Upendra Shenoy Umesh Vijayam [1971] Director/Self Employed

B Luxury Scents Ltd
Incorporated: 9 January 2019
Registered Office: 22 Everest Close, Great Sutton, Ellesmere Port, Cheshire, CH66 2RH
Major Shareholder: Luke Daniel Rochell
Officers: Luke Daniel Rochell [1989] Director/Security Guard

B. Silki Naturally Ltd
Incorporated: 18 October 2017
Registered Office: 62d Clifford Road, Barnet, Herts, EN5 5NY
Major Shareholder: Nancy Tanscia Smith
Officers: Nancy Tanscia Smith [1973] Director

B.S. Eurochem Limited
Incorporated: 31 December 2003
Net Worth: £348 *Total Assets:* £65,019
Registered Office: 40 Carrington Avenue, Borehamwood, Herts, WD6 2HA
Officers: Susan Lynne Rossi, Secretary; Jennifer Mary Bissmire [1950] Director/Administrator; Susan Lynne Rossi [1960] Director/Administrator; Simon Paul Salvage [1963] Director/Administrator

Bahoma Limited
Incorporated: 10 March 2006 *Employees:* 17
Net Worth: £266,330 *Total Assets:* £625,243
Registered Office: 2-4 Packhorse Road, Gerrards Cross, Bucks, SL9 7QE
Major Shareholder: James Bruce
Officers: Margaret Strug [1968] Sales Director [Polish]

Balance By Nora Limited
Incorporated: 29 October 2013
Previous: Balanced By Nora Limited
Net Worth Deficit: £1,056 *Total Assets:* £7,332
Registered Office: 7 St Petersgate, Stockport, Cheshire, SK1 1EB
Major Shareholder: Obiechina Nkemena
Officers: Maryam Nkemena, Secretary; Obiechina Nkemena [1972] Director/Cosmetics Distributor

Balm House Limited
Incorporated: 8 January 2018
Registered Office: Office 7, 35-37 Ludgate Hill, London, EC4M 7JN
Officers: Charlotte Priestley [1993] Director; Anthony David Sneath [1987] Director

Balmpots Limited
Incorporated: 21 November 2016
Net Worth: £92 *Total Assets:* £92
Registered Office: 7 Islay Avenue, Rutherglen, Glasgow, G73 5NH
Officers: Christian Andre Tischhauser [1962] Director/Support Worker [American]

Bamboobar Online Ltd
Incorporated: 10 January 2019
Registered Office: 36 Fifth Avenue, Havant, Hants, PO9 2PL
Major Shareholder: Daniel James Holloway
Officers: Daniel James Holloway [1987] Director/Marketing

Banyan Skincare Ltd
Incorporated: 2 August 2018
Registered Office: Frog Hall, Rectory Lane, Breadsall, Derby, DE21 5LL
Shareholders: Megan Heather Barstow; Judy Lynn Sturgis
Officers: Megan Heather Barstow [1981] Marketing Accounts Director [American]; Judy Lynn Sturgis [1960] Director, Therapist, Psychotherapist [American]

Barony Universal Products PLC
Incorporated: 19 November 1999 *Employees:* 202
Net Worth Deficit: £2,676,000 *Total Assets:* £35,509,000
Registered Office: 5 Riverside Way, Riverside Business Park, Irvine, N Ayrshire, KA11 5DJ
Officers: Eliot Swan, Secretary; Andrei Borshchev [1971] Director [Russian]; Steven David Groden [1970] Director/Sales and Marketing; Victor Lobashkov [1974] Director [Russian]; Alexandre Matytsine [1958] Director [Russian]; Sergei Popov [1969] Director [Russian]; Eliot Swan [1966] Finance Director

Bath Candy Ltd
Incorporated: 4 December 2017
Registered Office: 21a Devon Close, Nuneaton, Warwicks, CV10 8ES
Major Shareholder: Baljot Kaur
Officers: Baljot Kaur [1998] Director

Bathroom Cosmetics Ltd
Incorporated: 30 January 2018
Registered Office: 18 Church Street, Ashton under Lyne, Lancs, OL6 6XE
Major Shareholder: Serina Claire Wagstaffe
Officers: Serina Claire Wagstaffe [1980] Director

Baum of London Limited
Incorporated: 25 July 2017
Registered Office: H5 Ash Tree Court, Nottingham Business Park, Nottingham, NG8 6PY
Shareholders: Marc Bauwens; Baum of London
Officers: Marc Bauwens, Secretary; Marc Bauwens [1954] Director/Retired [Belgian]

Baylis & Harding Public Limited Company
Incorporated: 19 September 1978 *Employees:* 77
Net Worth: £13,352,501 *Total Assets:* £21,126,496
Registered Office: Nash Road, Park Farm, Redditch, Worcs, B98 7AS
Shareholders: Adrian David Slater; Tania Angelina Slater
Officers: Daniel Stephen Wall, Secretary; Christopher Charles Fallon [1962] Sales Director; Adrian David Slater [1974] Director/Executive; Tania Angelina Slater [1970] Director

BCM Limited
Incorporated: 20 August 1992
Net Worth: £61,600,000 *Total Assets:* £90,600,000
Registered Office: 1 Thane Road West, Nottingham, NG2 3AA
Parent: Fareva UK Limited
Officers: Andrew John Mortimer [1959] Director/Country Manager UK; Christophe Petras [1969] Director/Vice President Global Operations [French]; Richard David Whall [1962] Managing Director

Bear Head Grooming Products Limited
Incorporated: 14 September 2017
Registered Office: 7 Kilbean Drive, Falkirk, FK1 5PH
Major Shareholder: Grant Taylor
Officers: Grant Taylor [1992] Director

Beard Armour Limited
Incorporated: 20 June 2017
Registered Office: 18 Burnawn Place, Galston, E Ayrshire, KA4 8JY
Shareholders: Gordon Alexander Larmour; Helen Gaythorpe Larmour
Officers: Helen Gaythorpe Larmour, Secretary; Gordon Alexander Larmour [1966] Director/Civil Servant

Beard Nature Limited
Incorporated: 13 February 2017
Net Worth: £519 *Total Assets:* £519
Registered Office: 82a Delce Road, Rochester, Kent, ME1 2DH
Officers: Edgars Miezitis [1987] Director [Latvian]

Beard Oil Company Limited
Incorporated: 10 April 2015
Net Worth: £6,132 *Total Assets:* £21,930
Registered Office: 43 Ardaveen Drive, Newry, Co Down, BT35 8UH
Major Shareholder: James Richard Harte
Officers: James Richard Harte [1987] Director [Irish]

Bearface Industries Limited
Incorporated: 19 February 2015
Net Worth: £93 *Total Assets:* £15,496
Registered Office: Brewery House, High Street, Twyford, Winchester, Hants, SO21 1RG
Shareholders: Emma Louise Findley; Matthew Wood; James Sebastian Wood
Officers: Emma Louise Findley [1984] Director/Designer; James Sebastian Wood [1978] Director/Fitness Instructor; Matthew Wood [1976] Creative Director

The Beautiful Mind Series Limited
Incorporated: 22 July 2009
Net Worth: £1,610 *Total Assets:* £1,329,002
Registered Office: 5-6 Underhill Street, London, NW1 7HS
Officers: Paul Douglas White, Secretary; Paul Douglas White [1959] Director/Designer

Beauty 4 Me Ltd
Incorporated: 4 November 2013
Registered Office: 119 Hoarwithy Road, Hereford, HR2 6HD
Shareholders: Elaine Edwards; Elaine Edwards
Officers: Elaine Edwards [1964] Director/Business Consultant

The Beauty Alliance International Limited
Incorporated: 21 September 2018
Registered Office: Unit 3 Heads of The Valley Industrial Estate, Rhymney, Tredegar, Blaenau Gwent, NP22 5RL
Major Shareholder: Mitchell Laurence Field
Officers: Mitchell Laurence Field [1952] Director

Beauty Core Limited
Incorporated: 20 July 2017
Registered Office: c/o Livingstones Accountants Limited, 309 Harrow Road, Wembley, Middlesex, HA9 6BD
Officers: Jelena Miladinovic-Delic [1972] Director

Beauty Essentials (Scotland) Limited
Incorporated: 28 June 2013
Registered Office: 3 Newmains Avenue, Inchinnan, Renfrew, PA4 9RR
Officers: Brian Aitken [1954] Director/Accountant; Stephen James MacDonough [1962] Director

Beauty Exchange Limited
Incorporated: 28 June 2013
Registered Office: 3 Newmains Avenue, Inchinnan, Renfrew, PA4 9RR
Officers: Brian Aitken [1954] Director/Accountant; Stephen James MacDonough [1962] Director

Beauty Handmade Limited
Incorporated: 19 May 2017
Net Worth: £354 *Total Assets:* £1,844
Registered Office: 352 Fulham Road, London, SW10 9UH
Major Shareholder: Zagorka Colovic
Officers: Zagorka Colovic [1973] Director

Bedeaux Ltd
Incorporated: 27 September 2017
Registered Office: Kingfisher House, Hurstwood Lane, Haywards Heath, W Sussex, RH17 7QX
Major Shareholder: Amanda Beadle
Officers: Amanda Beadle [1964] Director/Accountant

Beever Retail Limited
Incorporated: 24 September 2003 *Employees:* 1
Net Worth Deficit: £7,492 *Total Assets:* £28,492
Registered Office: 3 Park Square, Leeds, LS1 2NE
Major Shareholder: Stephen Colin Beever
Officers: Diana Beever, Secretary; Stephen Colin Beever [1964] Managing Director

Bell & Loxton Innovations Ltd
Incorporated: 10 January 2018
Registered Office: Upton Barton, South Milton, Kingsbridge, Devon, TQ7 3JF
Shareholders: Jon Bell; Peter Elliott Luebcke
Officers: Jon Bell [1969] Director/Farmer

Benefit & Riley Healthcare Ltd
Incorporated: 15 September 2017
Registered Office: 1 Torrent Complex, 9 Hillview Avenue, Dungannon, Co Tyrone, BT70 3DL
Parent: Riley & Sons Ltd
Officers: Charlotte Riley [1974] Director/Businesswoman

Berachah Consulting Limited
Incorporated: 16 December 2013
Registered Office: Apartment 12148, Chynoweth House, Trevissome Park, Truro, Cornwall, TR4 8UN
Officers: Gloria Petrina Youri, Secretary; Gloria Petrina Youri [1966] Director/Human Resources [Ghanaian]

Berry Inc Ltd
Incorporated: 30 July 2018
Registered Office: Kemp House, 160 City Road, London, EC1V 2NX
Major Shareholder: Evbi O'Sullivan
Officers: Evbi O'Sullivan, Secretary; Evbi O'Sullivan [1972] Director/Consultant

Bespoke Natural Health Ltd
Incorporated: 6 December 2018
Registered Office: 54 Mansfield Road, London, NW3 2HT
Shareholders: Daniel Swaby; Joseph Warden Garfinkel
Officers: Joseph Warden Garfinkel [1984] Director; Daniel Swaby [1978] Director

Bex London Ltd
Incorporated: 1 February 2011
Net Worth Deficit: £46,516 *Total Assets:* £9,376
Registered Office: 11 Dallington Road, Hove, E Sussex, BN3 5HS
Major Shareholder: Rebecca Louise Goswell
Officers: Maria Graham, Secretary; Rebecca Louise Goswell [1966] Creative Director

Bigben Healthcare Limited
Incorporated: 12 August 2015
Registered Office: Foerster Chambers, Fernhills House, Todd Street, Bury, Lancs, BL9 5BJ
Officers: Jimmy Taylor [1960] Director/Businessman

Bill & Artisans Ltd
Incorporated: 20 November 2017
Registered Office: Unit 232, 405 Kings Road, London, SW10 0BB
Major Shareholder: Palo William Balle
Officers: Palo William Balle [1988] Director/Designer

Biologico Cosmetics Limited
Incorporated: 14 February 2018
Registered Office: 3rd Floor, Citypoint, 65 Haymarket Terrace, Edinburgh, EH12 5HD
Major Shareholder: Craig McKay
Officers: Craig McKay [1983] Director

Bixie Group Ltd
Incorporated: 9 May 2017
Registered Office: 12 Hadleigh Close, Shenley, Radlett, Herts, WD7 9LT
Major Shareholder: Abike Abu
Officers: Abike Abu [1983] Director

BL Cosmetics Limited
Incorporated: 5 May 2000 *Employees:* 2
Net Worth Deficit: £41,009 *Total Assets:* £17,223
Registered Office: Condy Mathias, 6 Houndiscombe Road, Plymouth, PL4 6HH
Shareholders: Paul Lewis Ricketts; William Paul Ricketts; Lesley Ricketts
Officers: William Paul Ricketts, Secretary/Director; Lesley Ricketts [1958] Director; William Paul Ricketts [1953] Director

Black Cat Manufacturing Ltd
Incorporated: 24 February 2015
Net Worth: £943 *Total Assets:* £12,627
Registered Office: 212 Upholland Road, Billinge, Wigan, Lancs, WN5 7DJ
Major Shareholder: Philip Anthony Fouracre
Officers: Philip Anthony Fouracre [1972] Director/Cosmetic Chemist

Black Gem Cosmetics Ltd
Incorporated: 7 April 2016
Net Worth: £260 *Total Assets:* £710
Registered Office: 27b Mason Street, London, SE17 1HF
Officers: Felicity Nyekpunwo Amure [1975] Director

Blackbird and Rain Limited
Incorporated: 25 January 2018
Registered Office: 37 Chandos Road, Stroud, Glos, GL5 3QT
Shareholders: Evaleen Brinton; Valentin Damian
Officers: Evaleen Brinton [1989] Director/Entrepreneur; Valentin Damian [1987] Director/Software Engineer [Romanian]

Blank Factory Limited
Incorporated: 14 May 2018
Registered Office: Flat 7, 19 Royal Road, Ramsgate, Kent, CT11 9LE
Shareholders: Alexander Peter Verier; Frederick Augustus Fenton Sharpe
Officers: Frederick Augustus Fenton Sharpe [1996] Director; Alexander Peter Verier [1993] Director

Blazergold Limited
Incorporated: 24 March 1999
Net Worth: £1,806,500 *Total Assets:* £1,806,500
Registered Office: St Stephen's House, Laburnum Avenue, Robin Hoods Bay, Whitby, N Yorks, YO22 4RR
Officers: Seamus Foley, Secretary; Maurice Anthony Foley [1957] Director/Marketing Executive [Irish]; Seamus Foley [1947] Director; Timothy Bernard Foley [1950] Director/Marketing Consultant

Bleu D'Argan Skincare Limited
Incorporated: 6 August 2018
Registered Office: 71-75 Shelton Street, London, WC2H 9JQ
Major Shareholder: Chloe Pressoir de Valcy
Officers: Chloe Pressoir de Valcy [1968] Director/Formulation Scientist [Swedish]

Bloom Aromatics Limited
Incorporated: 22 March 2018
Registered Office: 24 Church Road, Crystal Palace, London, SE19 2ET
Major Shareholder: Tahir Masood Begg
Officers: Tahir Masood Begg [1954] Director/Chartered Certified Accountant

Bloom Remedies Ltd
Incorporated: 23 February 2018
Registered Office: 32 Pendarves Road, Penzance, Cornwall, TR18 2AJ
Shareholders: Stephen Richard Hall; Marie Elizabeth Hall
Officers: Marie Elizabeth Hall [1974] Director; Stephen Richard Hall [1970] Director

Bloomtown Ltd
Incorporated: 8 March 2018
Registered Office: Bloomtown Ltd, Unit 3 Empire Way, Tregoniggie Industrial Estate, Falmouth, Cornwall, TR11 4RX
Shareholders: Medwin John Culmer; Preyanka Jayanti Clark Prakash
Officers: Preyanka Jayanti Clark Prakash [1982] Director [American]; Medwin John Culmer [1977] Managing Director

Bluhans Ltd
Incorporated: 10 December 2018
Registered Office: 102a Redhill Drive, Bournemouth, BH10 6AW
Major Shareholder: Jaume Barfull Giralt
Officers: Jaume Barfull Giralt [1986] Director/Watchmaker [Spanish]

BLVNCO Limited
Incorporated: 25 May 2017
Registered Office: BLVNCO, 1 Blenhiem Court, Welwyn Garden City, Herts, AL7 1AD
Officers: Mohsin Khan [1982] Director; Sam Naqvi [1989] Director

Body & Face St. Cyrus Limited
Incorporated: 22 June 1993 *Employees:* 8
Net Worth Deficit: £69,208 *Total Assets:* £74,285
Registered Office: 252 Union Street, Aberdeen, AB10 1TN
Shareholders: William Milne Ritchie Carr; Angela Rosemary Carr
Officers: Angela Rosemary Carr [1947] Director; William Milne Ritchie Carr [1943] Director

Body Candy Ltd.
Incorporated: 15 February 2018
Registered Office: Kemp House, 160 City Road, London, EC1V 2NX
Officers: Michal Gasior [1982] Director [Polish]

Body Reform Limited
Incorporated: 28 June 2006
Net Worth: £10,001 *Total Assets:* £10,001
Registered Office: 96a Cardiff Road, Llandaff, Cardiff, CF5 2DT
Major Shareholder: Klaus Georg Ueber
Officers: Klaus Georg Ueber, Secretary; Klaus Georg Ueber [1947] Director

Body Station Limited
Incorporated: 6 November 2018
Registered Office: 71-75 Shelton Street, London, WC2H 9JQ
Major Shareholder: Thomas Hadleigh
Officers: Thomas Hadleigh [1974] Director

Body Thyme Limited
Incorporated: 18 September 2017
Registered Office: 2 Ryeburn Close, Kessingland, Lowestoft, Suffolk, NR33 7UH
Major Shareholder: Michelle Wendy Steers
Officers: Gordon John Cullingworth, Secretary; Michelle Wendy Steers [1974] Director

Bonita Lou Ltd
Incorporated: 3 November 2014
Registered Office: 81 Blyth Road, Hayes, Middlesex, UB3 1DB
Major Shareholder: Robert Day
Officers: Robert Day [1957] Director/Laboratory Technician

Boselli Europe Ltd
Incorporated: 1 February 2018
Registered Office: International House, 142 Cromwell Road, London, SW7 4EF
Officers: Tommaso Boselli [1966] Director

Andre Boyard Perfumes Limited
Incorporated: 25 September 2002
Net Worth Deficit: £124,150 *Total Assets:* £49,878
Registered Office: Equity House, 128-136 High Street, Edgware, Middlesex, HA8 7TT
Shareholders: Constantine Leo Borissoff; Ameet Chandubhai Rughani; Constantine Leo Borissoff; Ameet Chandubhai Rughani
Officers: Constantine Leo Borissoff [1958] Director/Executive; Ameet Chandubhai Rughani [1963] Director

Braw Beard Oils Ltd
Incorporated: 14 August 2013 *Employees:* 1
Net Worth: £4,107 *Total Assets:* £33,188
Registered Office: 48 Court Street, Haddington, E Lothian, EH41 3NP
Major Shareholder: John Jackson
Officers: John Jackson [1984] Director/Graphic Designer

Brigantia Personal Care Ltd
Incorporated: 22 September 2017
Registered Office: Unit 5 Whitley Street, Bingley, W Yorks, BD16 4JH
Major Shareholder: Mark Barton
Officers: Mark Barton [1986] Director

Belinda Brown Limited
Incorporated: 25 November 2009
Net Worth Deficit: £225,268 *Total Assets:* £75,958
Registered Office: 32 Maypole Road, Ashurst Wood, W Sussex, RH19 3QY
Major Shareholder: Tari-Ere Belinda Osoru Brown
Officers: Ian McNair Brown, Secretary; Tari-Ere Belinda Osoru Brown [1965] Director

Buachi Limited
Incorporated: 23 June 2014
Net Worth Deficit: £9,038 *Total Assets:* £8,073
Registered Office: 4 Hill Rise, Ruislip, Middlesex, HA4 7JL
Major Shareholder: Donald Nyampong Boakye
Officers: Karen Larbi, Secretary; Donald Nyampong Boakye [1967] Director/Pharmacist

Bubble-Bubble Ltd
Incorporated: 4 February 2019
Registered Office: Suite 18, Equity Chambers, 249 High Street North, Poole, Dorset, BH15 1DX
Major Shareholder: Aleksandra Ewa Krakowska
Officers: Aleksandra Ewa Krakowska [1995] Director [Polish]

Buddy Direct Ltd
Incorporated: 13 December 2016
Registered Office: PKW Accountancy, 1 Church Square, Leighton Buzzard, Beds, LU7 1AE
Major Shareholder: Richard Jonothon Walkling
Officers: Richard Jonothon Walkling, Secretary; Richard Jonothon Walkling [1968] Director

Luissa Burton Limited
Incorporated: 4 December 2018
Registered Office: The Hawthorns, Brockhill Lane, Norton, Worcester, WR5 2PP
Major Shareholder: Luissa Burton
Officers: Luissa Burton [1990] Director/Entrepreneur

Busy Bees Cosmetics Limited
Incorporated: 7 February 2018
Registered Office: 75 Head Lane, Great Cornard, Sudbury, Suffolk, CO10 0JS
Shareholder: Julie Anne Thorn
Officers: Julie Anne Thorn [1969] Director/Business Owner; Kevin Barry Thorn [1965] Director/Business Owner

Butterbur and Sage Limited
Incorporated: 2 November 1983
Net Worth: £115,966 *Total Assets:* £519,549
Registered Office: Victoria House, 18 Dalston Gardens, Stanmore, Middlesex, HA7 1BU
Major Shareholder: Jagat Ram Sandhu
Officers: Jagat Ram Sandhu [1955] Director

By Kathryn Ltd
Incorporated: 7 June 2011
Previous: Katie Forman Limited
Net Worth Deficit: £5,139 *Total Assets:* £18,061
Registered Office: 103-105 Brighton Road, Coulsdon, Surrey, CR5 2NG
Major Shareholder: Katie Forman
Officers: Claire Mackin, Secretary; Katie Foreman [1968] Director

Cactus Skincare Limited
Incorporated: 30 July 2018
Registered Office: Flat 8, Colmore House, Frazer Nash Close, Isleworth, Middlesex, TW7 5FR
Shareholders: Callum John Taylor; Amanda Ruth Merrifield
Officers: Amanda Ruth Merrifield [1994] Director [American]; Callum John Taylor [1993] Director/Financial Adviser

Caldey Island Estate Company Limited
Incorporated: 24 February 1971 *Employees:* 25
Net Worth: £171,342 *Total Assets:* £334,766
Registered Office: Caldey Abbey, Caldey Island, Tenby, Pembrokeshire, SA70 7UH
Parent: Caldey Abbey Trustees
Officers: Rev Gerardus Arnoldus Van Santvoort, Secretary; Michael Anthony Cestaro [1959] Director/Religious Brother; Ben Geoffrey Childs [1964] Director/Estate Manager; Reverend Alan Thomas Michael Gage [1948] Director/Priest; Aloysius Nicolass Keet [1948] Director/Religious Brother [Dutch]; Rev Desmond Mahony [1937] Director/Priest [Irish]; Jan Leon Rossey [1957] Director/Priest [Belgian]; Rev Kevin Gordon Simpson [1954] Director/Accounts and Administration Manager; Rev Gerardus Arnoldus Van Santvoort [1956] Director/Priest

Caley's of Exeter Ltd
Incorporated: 10 May 2018
Registered Office: Flat 1, 78 Longbrook Street, Exeter, Devon, EX4 6AP
Major Shareholder: Judy Caley
Officers: Judy Caley [1988] Director/Manufacturer

Calibria Ltd
Incorporated: 13 June 2007
Registered Office: 456 Rochester Road, Burham, Rochester, Kent, ME1 3RH
Major Shareholder: Latoya Makayla Alleyne
Officers: Latoya Alleyne, Secretary; Latoya Makayla Alleyne [1981] Director/Entrepreneur

Calmen Lifestyle Company Ltd
Incorporated: 23 January 2019
Registered Office: Cassidys Chartered Accountants, South Stour Offices, Mersham, Kent, TN25 7HS
Shareholders: Kevin Godlington; Stephen Manderson
Officers: Kevin Godlington [1975] Director; Stephen Manderson [1983] Director

Camblabs Ltd
Incorporated: 19 April 2018
Registered Office: Unit 5 Drakes Courtyard, 291 Kilburn High Road, London, NW6 7JR
Parent: Top Meadow Ltd
Officers: Kim Sec Tran [1987] Director

Cambridge Genefit Technologies Ltd
Incorporated: 27 June 2017
Registered Office: Crown House, 27 Old Gloucester Street, London, WC1N 3AX
Major Shareholder: Xue Gong
Officers: Xue Gong [1989] Director [Chinese]

Canco Candles Limited
Incorporated: 2 May 2018
Registered Office: 4 Kenswick Manor, Kenswick, Lower Broadheath, Worcester, WR2 6QB
Major Shareholder: Sarah Kate Burton
Officers: Sarah Kate Burton [1987] Director

Carapoll Chemicals Ltd
Incorporated: 2 February 2018
Registered Office: 19 The Hawthorns, Kirkby in Ashfield, Notts, NG17 8NL
Officers: Andrew Harpham Dennis Harpham [1966] Company Secretary/Director

Care By Jords Ltd
Incorporated: 19 June 2018
Registered Office: Rear Ground Floor, Unit 226-234 Barr Street, Hockley, Birmingham, B19 3AG
Shareholders: Jordan Ward Hamilton; Yvonne Williams-Hamilton
Officers: Jordan Hamilton, Secretary; Jordan Ward Hamilton [1993] Managing Director; Yvonne Williams-Hamilton [1964] Research & Development Director

Carefree Toiletries Limited
Incorporated: 5 October 2017
Registered Office: 19 Regal Drive, Walsall Enterprise Park, Walsall, W Midlands, WS2 9HQ
Officers: Sunil Sohpal, Secretary; Sunil Sohpal [1989] Director/Manager

Carrie Wilson Limited
Incorporated: 17 April 2013
Net Worth Deficit: £5,994 *Total Assets:* £131
Registered Office: 20-22 Wenlock Road, London, N1 7GU
Major Shareholder: Christopher Rushworth
Officers: Christopher Rushworth [1974] Director

Carzel Limited
Incorporated: 21 March 2017
Registered Office: 12 Courtleas, Cobham, Surrey, KT11 2PW
Major Shareholder: Akis Akis Tzortzis
Officers: Akis Zafirios Tzortzis [1965] Director

Castlefields Cosmetics Ltd.
Incorporated: 11 December 2017
Registered Office: HPC, High Bradley Lane, Keighley, W Yorks, BD20 9EX
Major Shareholder: Philip Neil Ramshaw
Officers: Philip Neil Ramshaw [1963] Director/Plastic Moulding Manufacturer; Stephen John Richardson [1961] Director/General Manager

CC Business Limited
Incorporated: 2 January 2019
Registered Office: 71-75 Shelton Street, Covent Garden, London, WC2H 9JQ
Major Shareholder: Cyril Francis Chresta
Officers: Cyril Chresta, Secretary; Cyril Francis Chresta [1932] Director

Chapel House Skincare Limited
Incorporated: 11 February 2019
Registered Office: Chapel House, Lower Road, Loosley Row, Princes Risborough, Bucks, HP27 0PE
Major Shareholder: Amanda Elizabeth Thomas
Officers: Amanda Elizabeth Thomas [1965] Director/Service Delivery Manager

Charles Jordi Limited
Incorporated: 7 October 1997
Net Worth Deficit: £12,361 *Total Assets:* £56,947
Registered Office: Frodsham Business Centre, Bridge Lane, Frodsham, Cheshire, WA6 7FZ
Parent: Charles Jordi (International) Limited
Officers: June Emma Hutchinson, Secretary; Lynda June Hutchinson [1957] Managing Director

Charmpits Ltd
Incorporated: 26 July 2018
Registered Office: Milland, Lower Park Road, Braunton, Devon, EX33 2LQ
Shareholders: Nicola Anne Relph; David Charles John Relph
Officers: David Charles John Relph [1971] Director; Dr Nicola Anne Relph [1974] Director

Chaud Solutions Limited
Incorporated: 9 March 2018
Registered Office: 11 Spindle Grove, Darlington, Co Durham, DL1 1LY
Officers: John Edo Aba [1981] Director/Analyst

Cheshire Fragrances Limited
Incorporated: 14 April 2016
Net Worth Deficit: £21,692 *Total Assets:* £1,931
Registered Office: 85 Conway Road, Sale, Cheshire, M33 2TE
Major Shareholder: Nasir Ali
Officers: Kashif Ijaz Ahmad [1973] Director/Doctor; Nasir Ali [1976] Director/Doctor

Chirps London Ltd
Incorporated: 28 August 2018
Registered Office: 71 Pulborough Road, London, SW18 5UL
Shareholders: Saeed Muayad Al-Rubeyi; Katy Rutherford-Mills
Officers: Saeed Muayad Al-Rubeyi [1986] Director; Katy Rutherford-Mills [1985] Director/Designer

Chuckling Goat Limited
Incorporated: 3 April 2014 *Employees:* 20
Net Worth: £682,116 *Total Assets:* £1,173,789
Registered Office: Glynmelyn, Brynhoffnant, Llandysul, Ceredigion, SA44 6DS
Parent: Glynmelyn Investments Limited
Officers: Richard Mansel Jones [1962] Director; Shann Erin Jones [1966] Director [American]

Cinsce Ltd
Incorporated: 3 November 2015
Net Worth Deficit: £924 *Total Assets:* £1
Registered Office: 71-75 Shelton Street, Covent Garden, London, WC2H 9JQ
Major Shareholder: Mia Amor Fields
Officers: Mia Fields [1975] Director [Barbadian]

Claes Heavenly Therapies and Aromas Ltd
Incorporated: 28 March 2017
Net Worth: £5,837 *Total Assets:* £5,837
Registered Office: 6 The Olde Watermill, Dickensian Shopping Village, Faldo Road, Barton-le-Clay, Bedford, MK45 4RF
Officers: Denise Frances Louise Lewis [1959] Director/Clinical Aromatherapist

Clarins & Felix Healthcare Ltd
Incorporated: 22 September 2017
Registered Office: Lot 28, 17-21 Hunter's Mill, Downpatrick, Co Down, BT30 6BL
Parent: Felix Medical Group Ltd
Officers: Dr Karren Brady [1976] Director/Businessman

Clay Club Skincare Limited
Incorporated: 13 July 2018
Registered Office: 19 Rodney Road, Cheltenham, Glos, GL50 1HX
Major Shareholder: Rachel Michelle Green
Officers: Rachel Michelle Green [1971] Director/Founder

Claycoco Limited
Incorporated: 20 February 2018
Registered Office: 31 Cardigan Road, Bournemouth, BH9 1BD
Major Shareholder: Samuel James Fahey
Officers: Samuel James Fahey [1989] Director/Telephonist

Clover Chemicals Limited
Incorporated: 1 March 1990 *Employees:* 80
Net Worth: £3,770,953 *Total Assets:* £4,944,551
Registered Office: Clover House, Macclesfield Road, Whaley Bridge, High Peak, Derbys, SK23 7DQ
Parent: Christeyns UK Ltd
Officers: Julie Susan Roberts, Secretary; Desmond Charles Eustace [1956] Managing Director; Nicholas James Garthwaite [1957] Director; Julie Susan Roberts [1969] Director; James Mark Tobias [1967] Director; Jozef Maria Jaak Wittouck [1962] Director [Belgian]

Cocoa Lime Limited
Incorporated: 2 February 2018
Registered Office: 44 Cornflower Grove, Ketley, Telford, Salop, TF1 5ZH
Major Shareholder: Helen Baines
Officers: Helen Baines, Secretary; Helen Baines [1968] Director/Senior Manager

Cocoa Twist Limited
Incorporated: 7 May 2013
Registered Office: 1 Surrey Mount, Forest Hill, London, SE23 3PF
Officers: Julia Williams [1976] Director

Cocobubble Ltd
Incorporated: 5 April 2017
Net Worth Deficit: £10,414 *Total Assets:* £24
Registered Office: 26 Smithies Avenue, Sully, Penarth, Vale of Glamorgan, CF64 5SS
Major Shareholder: Lauren Jones
Officers: Lauren Jones [1990] Director/Accountant

Combe International Limited
Incorporated: 13 March 1974 *Employees:* 10
Net Worth: £3,571,132 *Total Assets:* £8,769,294
Registered Office: Cedar Court, Guildford Road, Leatherhead, Surrey, KT22 9RX
Officers: Adrian McCulloch, Secretary; Keech Combe-Shetty [1977] Director/Co-Chief Executive Officer [American]; Akshay Anand Shetty [1977] Director/SVP Global Operations Co-Head Asia & Latin America [Indian]; Clare Want [1966] Managing Director

Concept: Skin Limited
Incorporated: 28 March 2012
Net Worth Deficit: £6,094 *Total Assets:* £497
Registered Office: 31 Tower Way, Canterbury, Kent, CT1 2DP
Major Shareholder: Chioma Esther Copeman
Officers: Nnena Ezi Ukpai, Secretary; Chioma Esther Copeman [1979] Director/Pharmaceutical Chemist; James Edward Copeman [1985] Director/Development Manager

A. & E. Connock (Perfumery & Cosmetics) Limited
Incorporated: 24 June 1975 *Employees:* 15
Net Worth: £703,401 *Total Assets:* £1,537,840
Registered Office: 146 New London Road, Chelmsford, Essex, CM2 0AW
Officers: Catherine Jane Connock, Secretary; Elizabeth Connock [1948] Technical Director; Rosemary Diana Connock [1981] Sales Director; Tim Connock [1974] Managing Director

Continental Fragrances Limited
Incorporated: 26 October 1966 *Employees:* 3
Net Worth: £189,305 *Total Assets:* £210,816
Registered Office: 43-45 Molesworth Street, Wadebridge, Cornwall, PL27 7DR
Officers: Odile Marie Francoise Faull, Secretary; Odile Marie Francoise Faull [1949] Director/Interpreter [French]

Contour and More London Limited
Incorporated: 23 January 2017
Net Worth: £4,080 *Total Assets:* £12,749
Registered Office: P O Box 314, St Neots, Cambs, PE19 9FX
Shareholders: Callum Morgan; Jasmine Golding
Officers: Jasmine Golding [1996] Director/Cosmetics Designer; Callum Morgan [1991] Director/Export Sales

Convoy Fragrances Ltd
Incorporated: 2 October 2018
Registered Office: 1st Floor, 85 Great Portland Street, London, W1W 7LT
Major Shareholder: Charnjit Singh Aujla
Officers: Charnjit Singh Aujla [1981] Director

Cool Gell Limited
Incorporated: 29 April 1999
Net Worth: £104,283 *Total Assets:* £134,916
Registered Office: The Maltings, Burton Row, Leeds, LS11 5NX
Officers: Martin Stead, Secretary; Robert Anthony Deegan [1946] Director; Joseph Orbell [1998] Director/Accounts Manager; Martin Stead [1980] Company Secretary/Director; Chloe Stead Deegan [1994] Director; Hannah Stead Deegan [1998] Director; Nathan Lee Telford [1993] Director

Corincraft Limited
Incorporated: 8 April 1999 *Employees:* 2
Net Worth Deficit: £59,307 *Total Assets:* £40,536
Registered Office: Unit 6 Bates Green Farm, Tye Hill Road, Arlington, Polegate, E Sussex, BN26 6SH
Major Shareholder: Robin Christopher Thomas Taylor
Officers: Suzanne Shepherd Taylor, Secretary; Robin Christopher Thomas Taylor [1961] Director

Coriungo Limited
Incorporated: 15 September 2017
Registered Office: 1 Golden Court, Richmond, Surrey, TW9 1EU
Officers: Pieter-Jan Beyls [1987] Director [Belgian]

Cosmetic Hooligans Ltd
Incorporated: 29 June 2017
Registered Office: 153 Caledonia Road, Wolverhampton, W Midlands, WV2 1JA
Officers: Patrycja Kalkowska [1995] Director/Cosmetic Production [Polish]

Cosmetics a la Carte Limited
Incorporated: 7 May 1973 *Employees:* 11
Net Worth: £125,213 *Total Assets:* £368,897
Registered Office: 102 Avro House, Havelock Terrace, London, SW8 4AS
Shareholders: Robert Cecil Gifford Dodds; Hermione Lynne Cecilia Sanders
Officers: Hermione Lynne Cecilia Sanders, Secretary; Robert Cecil Gifford Dodds [1957] Director; Hermione Lynne Cecilia Sanders [1950] Director/Chemist

Cosmos Cosmetics Limited
Incorporated: 30 November 2018
Registered Office: 71-75 Shelton Street, Covent Garden, London, WC2H 9JQ
Shareholders: Alptekin Aydin; Funda Hocaoglu
Officers: Funda Hocaoglu, Secretary; Alptekin Aydin [1973] Director; Funda Hocaoglu [1973] Director [Turkish]

Costradis Limited
Incorporated: 18 August 2015
Net Worth Deficit: £13,775 *Total Assets:* £5,135
Registered Office: 39 Huntly Street, Aberdeen, AB10 1TJ
Shareholders: Henry Darroch Juszczak; David William Lawton Birkmyre
Officers: David William Lawton Birkmyre [1952] Director/Financial Adviser; Henry Darroch Juszczak [1972] Director

Coty Manufacturing UK Limited
Incorporated: 23 January 1947 *Employees:* 306
Net Worth: £24,224,000 *Total Assets:* £107,977,000
Registered Office: Eureka Park, Ashford, Kent, TN25 4AQ
Parent: Coty Inc
Officers: Emma Walters, Secretary; Alberto Meloni [1976] Director [Italian]; Vengadan Swaminathan [1977] Director; Emma Morag Dorothy Walters [1974] Director/Financial Controller

CPL Aromas (Holdings) Limited
Incorporated: 13 September 1999
Net Worth: £53,550,000 *Total Assets:* £81,190,000
Registered Office: CPL Aromas, Quarry Road, Brixworth, Northampton, NN6 9UB
Officers: Philip Jonathan Gardner, Secretary; Bruce Forbes [1956] IT Director; Philip Jonathan Gardner [1963] Finance Director; Peter Jonathan Jacobs [1955] Director; Anthony Ewart Lloyd [1973] Director; Christopher Pickthall [1968] Director; Francis Pickthall [1967] Director; Nicholas Pickthall [1976] Director; Terence Pickthall [1939] Director

CPL Aromas Limited
Incorporated: 16 November 1971 *Employees:* 535
Net Worth: £66,265,000 *Total Assets:* £93,899,000
Registered Office: CPL Aromas Limited, Quarry Road, Brixworth, Northampton, NN6 9UB
Parent: CPL Aromas Holdings Limited
Officers: Philip Jonathan Gardner, Secretary; Bruce Forbes [1956] IT Director; Philip Jonathan Gardner [1963] Finance Director; Peter Jonathan Jacobs [1955] Director; Anthony Ewart Lloyd [1973] Director; Christopher Pickthall [1968] Director; Francis Pickthall [1967] Director; Nicholas Pickthall [1976] Director; Terence Pickthall [1939] Director/Chairman

Creative Perfumers London Ltd
Incorporated: 30 September 2013
Net Worth: £283 *Total Assets:* £30,943
Registered Office: 21 Arlington Street, London, SW1A 1RN
Major Shareholder: Anastasia Meta de Brauwere Brozler
Officers: Anastasia de Brauwere Brozler [1966] Director [Austrian]

Credence Hair Venture Limited
Incorporated: 6 November 2018
Registered Office: 1a Torphichen Street, Edinburgh, EH3 8HX
Shareholders: Philip John Anderton; Claire Katherine Mary Anderton
Officers: Philip John Anderton [1965] Director

Credo Felix Ltd
Incorporated: 6 December 2018
Registered Office: H5 Ash Tree Court, Nottingham Business Park, Nottingham, NG8 6PY
Officers: Chachar Salman [1989] Director/Marketing [Pakistani]

Creightons PLC
Incorporated: 29 September 1975 *Employees:* 365
Net Worth: £9,605,000 *Total Assets:* £16,646,000
Registered Office: 1210 Lincoln Road, Werrington, Peterborough, Cambs, PE4 6ND
Shareholder: William Oliver McIlroy
Officers: Nicholas Desmond John O'Shea, Secretary; Mary Teresa Carney [1953] Director/Tax Consultant; Philippa Clark [1969] Sales & Marketing Director; Paul Forster [1958] Director/Chartered Accountant; William Torrance Glencross [1946] Director/Marketing Consultant; Bernard James Mary Johnson [1945] Director/Management Consultant; William Oliver McIlroy [1945] Director/Company Investor; Nicholas Desmond John O'Shea [1954] Director/Chartered Management Accountant; Martin Stevens [1961] Technical Director

CS Holistic Therapy Products Limited
Incorporated: 18 September 2017
Registered Office: 2 Victoria Court, Victoria Road, Romford, Essex, RM1 2NU
Major Shareholder: Catarina Scaramuzza
Officers: Catarina Scaramuzza [1963] Director/Holistic Therapy Products

Culpeper Limited
Incorporated: 21 January 2016
Net Worth Deficit: £19,598 *Total Assets:* £100
Registered Office: Flat 2, Studley Court, 166 Woodside Green, London, SE25 5EW
Major Shareholder: Martin James Edgerton Gill
Officers: Jacqueline Ann Webber, Secretary; Martin James Edgerton Gill [1939] Director

Custom Skin Lab Limited
Incorporated: 28 June 2018
Registered Office: Kemp House, 160 City Road, London, EC1V 2NX
Major Shareholder: Lauranne Vleeming
Officers: Lauranne Vleeming [1989] Director/Business Development [Dutch]

Cutelovelee Limited
Incorporated: 25 April 2018
Registered Office: 339 High Street, West Bromwich, W Midlands, B70 9QG
Major Shareholder: Leanna Natasha Campbell
Officers: Leanna Natasha Campbell [1990] Director

Cybele UK Ltd
Incorporated: 19 July 2016
Registered Office: 71-75 Shelton Street, Covent Garden, London, WC2H 9JQ
Major Shareholder: Kathryn Walters
Officers: Kathryn Walters, Secretary; Kathryn Walters [1976] Director [Australian]

Cyclax Limited
Incorporated: 22 March 1994
Net Worth: £2 *Total Assets:* £2
Registered Office: Unit 3 Heads of The Valleys Industrial Estate, Rhymney, Tredegar, Gwent, NP22 5RL
Officers: Mitchell Lawrence Field, Secretary/Director; Mitchell Lawrence Field [1952] Director; Dilip Raichand Shah [1953] Director

D'lusso Collection Ltd
Incorporated: 31 May 2018
Registered Office: 145 Great Ancoats Street, Manchester, M4 6DH
Major Shareholder: Emmanuel Iretomi Temofeh
Officers: Emmanuel Iretomi Temofeh [1977] Managing Director [Nigerian]

Dach Cosmeceutics Limited
Incorporated: 20 September 2017
Registered Office: 118 Richmond Road, Southampton, SO15 8FS
Officers: Dr Chidinma Udegbunam Ibie [1984] Director/Pharmaceutical Scientist [Nigerian]

Dareen London Ltd.
Incorporated: 10 July 2015
Registered Office: 5 Welby Close, Maidenhead, Berks, SL6 3PY
Shareholders: Walid Boujarwa; Athari Jehail
Officers: Walid Boujarwa [1967] Director [Kuwaiti]

Daughters of Circe Ltd
Incorporated: 22 October 2018
Registered Office: 81 Upper Tollington Park, London, N4 4LP
Major Shareholder: Sarah Louise Montague
Officers: Sarah Louise Montague [1983] Director/Teacher

DBI Innovations Group Limited
Incorporated: 12 May 2017
Registered Office: 24 Elliot Road, Hendon, London, NW4 3DL
Major Shareholder: Robert Hatefi Mofrad
Officers: Robert Hatefi Mofrad [1976] Director [French]

De La Baie Arctic Skincare Ltd
Incorporated: 26 July 2011
Net Worth Deficit: £24,771 *Total Assets:* £18,054
Registered Office: 12 Madeley Road, Church Crookham, Fleet, Hants, GU52 6AR
Major Shareholder: Rev Miriam Alexandra Good
Officers: Rev Miriam Alexandra Good, Secretary; Rev Miriam Alexandra Good [1946] Director/Retired

J Deboy & Co Limited
Incorporated: 14 July 2015 *Employees:* 1
Net Worth Deficit: £4,036 *Total Assets:* £100
Registered Office: 19-20 Bourne Court, Southend Road, Woodford Green, Essex, IG8 8HD
Shareholders: Debra Ann Wood; Joy Beverley Wood
Officers: Debra Ann Wood [1968] Director/Childcare Provider; Joy Beverley Wood [1963] Director/Legal Secretary

Department Health & Beauty Ltd
Incorporated: 11 March 2018
Registered Office: Flat 32, Zenith House, 69 Lawrence Road, London, N15 4EY
Major Shareholder: Ebi Peniella Osuobeni
Officers: Ebi Peniella Osuobeni [1992] Director [British/Nigerian]

Dermafood Limited
Incorporated: 21 November 2011
Net Worth Deficit: £5,568 *Total Assets:* £191
Registered Office: 53 Bothwell Street, Glasgow, G2 6TS
Major Shareholder: Teodora Georgieva Caldwell
Officers: Teodora Georgieva Caldwell [1969] Director

Dermamaitre Ltd.
Incorporated: 10 October 2012
Registered Office: Curzon House, Cavendish Place, Brighton, BN1 2HS
Shareholders: Gabriella Bethany Tamsin Harman; Michelle Lorraine Angela Harman
Officers: Gabriella Bethany Tamsin Harman [1991] Director/Company Management & Product Development

Dermapharm Skincare Limited
Incorporated: 29 September 2003
Registered Office: The Roothings, 45 Foley Road, Claygate, Surrey, KT10 0LU
Major Shareholder: Timothy James Lovett
Officers: Timothy James Lovett, Secretary/Director; Jennifer Margaret Lovett [1949] Director/Retired Teacher; Timothy James Lovett [1948] Director

Dermaplaning Pro Official Ltd
Incorporated: 6 September 2018
Registered Office: 264 St Helens Road, Bolton, Lancs, BL3 3RS
Major Shareholder: Jamila Jangaria
Officers: Jamila Jangaria [1979] Director/Beautician

Designer Fragrances Limited
Incorporated: 21 May 2001
Net Worth: £915,180 *Total Assets:* £1,230,000
Registered Office: 202c Burcott Road, Bristol, BS11 8AP
Major Shareholder: Carol Ann Coleman
Officers: Carol Ann Coleman, Secretary; Carol Ann Coleman [1948] Director; Thomas Martin Coleman [1986] Director

Designer IP (2) Ltd
Incorporated: 16 August 2013
Registered Office: 78 The Green, Twickenham, Middlesex, TW2 5AG
Major Shareholder: Grant Dean Miller
Officers: Grant Dean Miller [1974] Director

Designer Shaik Limited
Incorporated: 21 June 2000
Net Worth: £1,000 *Total Assets:* £1,000
Registered Office: 12 Haviland Road, Ferndown Industrial Estate, Wimborne, Dorset, BH21 7RG
Major Shareholder: Mohammed Al Asfoor
Officers: Deborah Al Asfoor, Secretary; Mohammed Al Asfoor [1957] Designer Director [Bahraini]

Dilecta Cosmetics Limited
Incorporated: 15 March 2013
Registered Office: Primrose Bank, Catterlen, Penrith, Cumbria, CA11 0BQ
Officers: Steven Smith [1977] Director/Laboratory Manager

Divine Earth Ltd
Incorporated: 28 March 2018
Registered Office: 14 Knox Green, Binfield, Bracknell, Berks, RG42 4NZ
Major Shareholder: Elizabeth Low
Officers: Elizabeth Low [1981] Director [Australian]

The Divine Hag Ltd
Incorporated: 20 January 2017
Net Worth Deficit: £6,487 *Total Assets:* £2,187
Registered Office: 117 Saltmarket, Glasgow, G1 5LF
Major Shareholder: Margaret Morrison-MacLeod
Officers: Margaret Morrison-MacLeod [1961] Director/Manufacturer

Dolphin Eco Ltd
Incorporated: 24 January 2019
Registered Office: 2 Ness Way, Fortrose, Ross-shire, IV10 8SS
Major Shareholder: Gavin Innes Ross
Officers: Gavin Innes Ross [1961] Director/Engineer

Double Take Limited
Incorporated: 21 May 2015 *Employees:* 4
Net Worth Deficit: £1,000,989 *Total Assets:* £243,557
Registered Office: Grenville Court, Britwell Road, Burnham, Bucks, SL1 8DF
Parent: Mash Holdings Limited
Officers: Matilda Elvira Ashley [1996] Director [Swedish]

Jenni Douglas Limited
Incorporated: 30 August 2017
Registered Office: 40 Boreham Holt, Elstree, Borehamwood, Herts, WD6 3QJ
Officers: Jennifer Douglas, Secretary; Jennifer Douglas [1981] Director

Dr Jackson Ltd
Incorporated: 9 September 2008 *Employees:* 15
Net Worth: £16,566 *Total Assets:* £228,257
Registered Office: Albion Dockside Estate, Hanover Place, Bristol, BS1 6UT
Officers: Mauro Barazarte Durant [1965] Director; Shaari Ergas [1952] Director [American]; Peter William Gordon [1963] Director/Chef; Oliver Hicks [1971] Director

Dr. Organic Limited
Incorporated: 28 June 2007 *Employees:* 46
Net Worth: £17,220,000 *Total Assets:* £26,357,000
Registered Office: Dr Organic Limited, Valley Way, Swansea Enterprise Park, Swansea, SA6 8QP
Parent: NBTY (2015) Limited
Officers: Nicholas John Heywood Collins [1962] Director/Chief Strategy & Product Supply Officer International; Stephen Kelsey Ford [1968] Finance Director; Matthew James Richard Harvey [1980] Director/Chartered Accountant; Michael Henryk Lightowlers [1972] Managing Director; Stephen Ronald Price [1964] Group Export Director

Dreamweave Products Ltd
Incorporated: 24 January 2012
Net Worth: £577,620 *Total Assets:* £832,350
Registered Office: 11 Dalton Court, Commercial Road, Darwen, Lancs, BB3 0DG
Shareholders: Steven Mather; Elaine Mather
Officers: Elaine Mather [1965] Director/Cosmetics Manufacturer; Steven Mather [1965] Director/Cosmetics Manufacturer

Owen Drew Luxury Candles Limited
Incorporated: 12 September 2016
Net Worth: £505 *Total Assets:* £8,014
Registered Office: Unit 5, 254 Brook Street, Birkenhead, Merseyside, CH41 3PH
Major Shareholder: Peter Drew George Cockton
Officers: Peter Drew George Cockton [1986] Director

Drom International UK Limited
Incorporated: 9 October 1995 *Employees:* 3
Net Worth Deficit: £2,562,730 *Total Assets:* £237,067
Registered Office: Northline Business Consultants Ltd, 3-4 Wharfside, The Boatyard, Worsley, Manchester, M28 2WN
Officers: Dr Andreas Storp [1969] Director/General Manager [German]; Dr Ferdinand Storp [1966] Director [German]

Drops of Humanity Ltd
Incorporated: 22 October 2015
Net Worth Deficit: £7,424 *Total Assets:* £895
Registered Office: Acre House, 11-15 William Road, London, NW1 3ER
Major Shareholder: Kathia May Yin Sya
Officers: Kathia May Yin Sya [1981] Director [Malaysian]

Eabir Ltd
Incorporated: 5 November 2018
Registered Office: 16 Arlington Road, Stretford, Manchester, M32 9HJ
Major Shareholder: Ambreen Abdul
Officers: Ambreen Abdul [1989] Director [French]

Liz Earle Beauty Co. Limited
Incorporated: 20 June 1995 *Employees:* 923
Net Worth: £27,686,640 *Total Assets:* £38,463,136
Registered Office: The Green House, Nicholson Road, Ryde, Isle of Wight, PO33 1BD
Parent: Alliance Boots Holdings Limited
Officers: Andrew Richard Thompson, Secretary; Rosemary Frances Counsell [1963] Director/Chief Financial Officer - Global Brands; Anne Louise Murphy [1967] Director; David Waller [1980] Director

Earth Aroma Limited
Incorporated: 27 March 2018
Registered Office: 82 Dennis Way, Liss, Hants, GU33 7HL
Shareholder: Dona Anushika Madhuwanthi Rupasinghe
Officers: Dona Anushika Madhuwanthi Rupasinghe [1974] Director [Sri Lankan]

Earth Mother Soul Sister Limited
Incorporated: 20 March 2006 *Employees:* 2
Net Worth Deficit: £18,683 *Total Assets:* £13,186
Registered Office: 66 Bridge Street, Ramsbottom, Bury, Lancs, BL0 9AG
Shareholders: Joanna Helen Kelly-Morris; Rachel Elizabeth Kelly
Officers: Joanna Helen Kelly-Morris, Secretary; Rachel Elizabeth Kelly [1972] Director; Joanna Helen Kelly-Morris [1975] Director

Earthwhile Ltd
Incorporated: 2 July 2018
Registered Office: The Beacon, Westgate Road, Newcastle upon Tyne, NE4 9PQ
Major Shareholder: Xenia Steinhardt
Officers: Xenia Steinhardt [1992] Director [German]

East China Sourcing Ltd
Incorporated: 8 October 2018
Registered Office: Kemp House, 160 City Road, London, EC1V 2NX
Major Shareholder: Terence Lamb
Officers: Terence Lamb [1958] Director/Buyer

Eastwing Grooming Co. Limited
Incorporated: 24 April 2017
Net Worth Deficit: £6,487 *Total Assets:* £5,025
Registered Office: 38 Connaught Avenue, Shoreham-by-Sea, W Sussex, BN43 5WJ
Shareholders: Gary James Easton; James Paul Wingate
Officers: Gary James Easton [1984] Director/Business Manager; James Paul Wingate [1979] Director/Mortgage Advisor

Ebex International Limited
Incorporated: 7 September 1998
Net Worth Deficit: £5,326 *Total Assets:* £22,904
Registered Office: 22 Park Road, Tiverton, Devon, EX16 6BA
Officers: Stephen Paul Nicholson, Secretary; Archibald Dincan Ogilvie McIntyre [1940] Director

Eco Earth Limited
Incorporated: 8 February 2018
Registered Office: Eco-Earth, Chapel Street, Wellesbourne, Warwicks, CV35 9QU
Major Shareholder: Thomas Karl Rogers
Officers: Thomas Karl Rogers [1992] Director

Eco Labyrinth Limited
Incorporated: 18 May 2017
Registered Office: 16 Harold Close, Totton, Southampton, SO40 8UB
Officers: Monika Ewa Piasecka [1975] Director/General Manager [Polish]

Ecocrushuk Ltd
Incorporated: 29 October 2018
Registered Office: Flat 4, 44 Langdon Park Road, London, N6 5QG
Major Shareholder: Verity Elizabeth Crush
Officers: Verity Elizabeth Crush [1980] CRM Director

Ecopel Corporation Limited
Incorporated: 30 March 2016 *Employees:* 4
Net Worth Deficit: £25,873 *Total Assets:* £4,736
Registered Office: Northside House, Mount Pleasant, Barnet, Herts, EN4 9EE
Shareholders: Roy Henry Presswell; June Linda Presswell
Officers: Joanne Sarah Hurst [1972] Director; James Stephen Presswell [1978] Director; June Linda Presswell [1950] Director; Roy Henry Presswell [1948] Director

Ed N' Grace Ltd
Incorporated: 11 February 2019
Registered Office: 84-86 Bravington Road, London, W9 3AL
Major Shareholder: Edman Relox Ocampo
Officers: Edman Relox Ocampo [1981] Director/Healthcare

Eden Classics Limited
Incorporated: 25 May 2006 *Employees:* 4
Net Worth: £87,562 *Total Assets:* £93,934
Registered Office: Unit 7 Bermer Place, Imperial Way, Watford, Herts, WD24 4AY
Shareholders: Dinesh Chhabildas; Jayshree Dinesh Shah
Officers: Mahendra Kanabar, Secretary; Dinesh Chhabildas Shah [1958] Director; Jayshree Dinesh Shah [1963] Director

Eden in Valley Soapworks Limited
Incorporated: 1 November 2018
Registered Office: 904 Christian Street, London, E1 1AW
Officers: Aggie Him Yau Yu [1991] Director/Financial Advisor

Eden's Legends Limited
Incorporated: 14 December 2017
Registered Office: Bank Gallery, 13 High Street, Kenilworth, Warwicks, CV8 1LY
Officers: Donniece Greene-Smith [1966] Director [American]; Matthew Nathaniel Smith [1969] Director

EEM Botanicals Limited
Incorporated: 5 January 2018
Registered Office: Kemp House, City Road, London, EC1V 2NX
Major Shareholder: Ese Ejiro Mudanohwo
Officers: Ese Ejiro Mudanohwo [1979] Director

Eifelcorp Consumer Care Ltd
Incorporated: 3 February 2016
Registered Office: 161 St Andrews Road, Northampton, NN2 6HL
Officers: Williams Aspinall [1972] Director/Businessman; Trang Huyen Thi Le [1987] Director/Businesswoman [Vietnamese]

Ekstaze London Limited
Incorporated: 4 January 2019
Registered Office: 71-75 Shelton Street, Covent Garden, London, WC2H 9JQ
Major Shareholder: Kiran Kumar Arya
Officers: Kiran Kumar Arya [1977] Director [Indian]

Elan Skincare Ltd
Incorporated: 18 September 2017
Registered Office: 73 Dairsie Road, London, SE9 1XN
Major Shareholder: Joanna Wiktoria Silva
Officers: Rafael Dos Santos Silva, Secretary; Joanna Wiktoria Silva [1978] Director

Elegant Boss Ltd
Incorporated: 6 July 2018
Registered Office: 98 Ponsonby House, Bishops Way, Bethnal Green, London, E2 9HS
Major Shareholder: Phillip Johnson
Officers: Phillip Johnson [1966] Director/Security Controller [German]

Elemental Beauty Limited
Incorporated: 10 July 2007 Employees: 2
Net Worth Deficit: £576 Total Assets: £13,635
Registered Office: 4th Floor, Park Gate, 161-163 Preston Road, Brighton, BN1 6AF
Shareholders: Simon Clifford Pacey; Nicola Farrington
Officers: Simon Clifford Pacey, Secretary/Computer Engineer; Nicola Farrington [1975] Director/Cosmetic Production; Simon Clifford Pacey [1964] Director/Computer Engineer

Elemis Limited
Incorporated: 22 July 1988 Employees: 505
Net Worth: £41,931,088 Total Assets: £61,136,348
Registered Office: Unit D, Poplar Way East, Cabot Park, Avonmouth, Bristol, BS11 0DD
Parent: Nemo (UK) Holdco, Ltd
Officers: Daniel Michael Chambers, Secretary; Michael Stephan Haringman, Secretary; Oriele Anne Dunbar [1965] Director/Chief Marketing Officer [Canadian]; Noella Gabriel [1956] Managing Director [Irish]; Michael Stephan Haringman [1944] Director/Solicitor; Sean Harrington [1966] Director; Christopher Vieth [1965] Director [American]

Elequra Limited
Incorporated: 21 October 2011
Previous: Elethea Limited
Net Worth Deficit: £481,290 Total Assets: £111,570
Registered Office: Suite 316, 28 Old Brompton Road, London, SW7 3SS
Major Shareholder: Nausheen Qureshi
Officers: Nausheen Qureshi [1983] Director/Businesswoman

Eleuthere Ltd
Incorporated: 12 November 2015
Registered Office: Unit 3 Lake Farm House, Allington Lane, Fair Oak, Eastleigh, Hants, SO50 7DD
Major Shareholder: Julio Marcel Brugos Eleuterio
Officers: Julio Marcel Brugos Eleuterio [1976] Director [Spanish]

Elibec Limited
Incorporated: 8 June 2010 Employees: 1
Net Worth: £17,054 Total Assets: £38,447
Registered Office: Oldbury Cottage, Oldbury Road, Bridgnorth, Salop, WV16 5DY
Major Shareholder: Elizabeth Beckett
Officers: Elizabeth Beckett [1978] Director

Elie Consumer Care Ltd
Incorporated: 4 July 2017
Registered Office: 54 Elmwood Avenue, Belfast, BT9 6AZ
Major Shareholder: Mary Stephen
Officers: Trang Huyen Thi Le [1987] Director/Businesswoman [Vietnamese]; Mary Stephen [1972] Director/Businesswoman

Elinor Sophia Limited
Incorporated: 14 May 2018
Registered Office: Jamesons House, Compton Way, Witney, Oxon, OX28 3AB
Major Shareholder: Katherine Wyn-Davies
Officers: Katherine Wyn-Davies, Secretary; Katherine Wyn-Davies [1992] Director/Company CEO

Elinor-UK Ltd
Incorporated: 19 February 2018
Registered Office: 1st Floor, 2 Woodberry Grove, Finchley, London, N12 0DR
Major Shareholder: Vladislav Mihaylov Indzhov
Officers: Vladislav Mihaylov Indzhov, Secretary; Vladislav Mihaylov Indzhov [1986] Director [Bulgarian]

Elliott Nutrition Ltd
Incorporated: 24 July 2017
Registered Office: NI647055: Companies House, Default Address, 2nd Floor The Linenhall 32-38 Linenhall Street, Belfast, BT2 8BG
Major Shareholder: Laura Ashley
Officers: Prof Laura Ashley [1978] Director/Professor

Elmbronze Limited
Incorporated: 28 April 1994
Net Worth: £13,651 Total Assets: £23,031
Registered Office: Warrenpark Cottage, 6 Anthony Road, Largs, N Ayrshire, KA30 8EQ
Shareholder: David Stephen Eastabrook
Officers: David Stephen Eastabrook, Secretary/Herbologist; David Stephen Eastabrook [1952] Director/Herbologist; Winifred Eastabrook [1958] Director [Irish]

Elsan Limited
Incorporated: 10 May 1963 Employees: 20
Net Worth: £3,854,775 Total Assets: £4,644,513
Registered Office: Elsan House, 15 Brambleside, Bellbrook Park, Uckfield, E Sussex, TN22 1QF
Major Shareholder: Peter Timothy Warwick-Smith
Officers: Peter Timothy Warwick-Smith, Secretary; Stephen William Camp [1956] Works Director; Peter Timothy Warwick-Smith [1959] Director

EMC Botanica Limited
Incorporated: 20 September 2018
Registered Office: 37a Newington Green, London, N16 9PR
Major Shareholder: Emily McEwan Gibson
Officers: Emily McEwan Gibson [1985] Director/Make Up Artist

Emerald Kalama Chemical Limited
Incorporated: 13 March 2001 Employees: 86
Previous: Innospec Widnes Limited
Net Worth: £25,620,000 Total Assets: £34,191,000
Registered Office: Emerald Kalama Chemical Limited, Dans Road, Widnes, Cheshire, WA8 0RF
Officers: Wayne Thomas Byrne [1963] Director/EVP/CFO [American]; Paul Lawrence Hogan [1969] Director/Vice President, General Manager [Irish]; Graham Robert Smith [1962] Site Director

Emily Victoria Candles Limited
Incorporated: 18 December 2017
Registered Office: 32 Cringle Drive, Cheadle, Cheshire, SK8 1JJ
Major Shareholder: Emily Victoria Jeeves
Officers: Emily Victoria Jeeves [1994] Director

Es-Ssentially Yours Ltd
Incorporated: 12 October 2018
Registered Office: 5 Dublin Avenue, London, E8 4TP
Major Shareholder: Antoinette Stephanie Bourne
Officers: Antoinette Stephanie Bourne [1990] Director

Escentric Molecules Limited
Incorporated: 7 April 2009
Registered Office: 5-6 Underhill Street, London, NW1 7HS
Officers: David John Welsh, Secretary; Paul Douglas White [1959] Director/Designer

Esensi Skincare Ltd
Incorporated: 22 May 2017 *Employees:* 2
Net Worth Deficit: £2,806 *Total Assets:* £8,845
Registered Office: 149 Eastern Way, Ponteland, Northumberland, NE20 9RH
Shareholder: Edward Campbell
Officers: Edward Campbell, Secretary; Edward Campbell [1959] Director/Landlord; Elizabeth Anne Carden [1961] Director/Charity Worker

Essancy Limited
Incorporated: 14 September 2009
Net Worth Deficit: £17,477 *Total Assets:* £57,332
Registered Office: 1a Ludlow Avenue, Luton, Beds, LU1 3RW
Officers: Aroosa Neela Ali [1996] Managing Director

Essential Gent Ltd
Incorporated: 19 April 2016
Net Worth: £24 *Total Assets:* £24
Registered Office: 2nd Floor, Clyde Offices, 48 West George Street, Glasgow, G2 1BP
Major Shareholder: Antony Paul Ashraf
Officers: Antony Paul Ashraf [1979] Director/Financial Services Manager

Essential Spirit Limited
Incorporated: 29 February 2000 *Employees:* 2
Net Worth Deficit: £2,574 *Total Assets:* £9,652
Registered Office: 123 Irish Street, Dumfries, DG1 2PE
Major Shareholder: Marina Emma Lucy Vundum
Officers: Des Watts, Secretary; Marina Emma Lucy Vundum [1961] Director/Soap Maker

Essentially Yours Limited
Incorporated: 2 August 1999
Net Worth Deficit: £36,577 *Total Assets:* £103,849
Registered Office: 2nd Floor, Unicorn House, Station Close, Potters Bar, Herts, EN6 1TL
Major Shareholder: John Hamilton
Officers: John Hamilton [1957] Director

Ethical House Ltd
Incorporated: 3 December 2018
Registered Office: 34 Navigation Way, Victoria Dock, Hull, HU9 1SW
Major Shareholder: Faith Elizabeth Hanson
Officers: Faith Elizabeth Hanson [1991] Director and Company Secretary

Evans Vanodine International PLC
Incorporated: 10 April 1953 *Employees:* 151
Net Worth: £15,935,064 *Total Assets:* £20,189,306
Registered Office: Brierley Road, Walton Summit Centre, Bamber Bridge, Preston, Lancs, PR5 8AH
Shareholders: Peter David Evans; Anthony Ian Evans; Christopher John Evans
Officers: Christopher John Evans, Secretary; Anthony Ian Evans [1966] Systems Director; Christopher John Evans [1959] Operations Director; Derek Anthony Evans [1927] Director/Chairman; Peter David Evans [1955] Managing Director

Everlasting Youth Limited
Incorporated: 2 November 1995 *Employees:* 1
Net Worth Deficit: £95 *Total Assets:* £5
Registered Office: Lambert Chapman, 3 Warners Mill, Silks Way, Braintree, Essex, CM7 3GB
Major Shareholder: Clive Lionel Bendon
Officers: Clive Lionel Bendon [1955] Director/Analytical Perfumer

Evocativ Limited
Incorporated: 14 August 2017
Registered Office: 71-75 Shelton Street, Covent Garden, London, WC2H 9JQ
Shareholders: Thomas Bishop; Marta Blocka
Officers: Thomas Bishop, Secretary; Marta Bishop [1986] Director/Solicitor [Polish]; Thomas Bishop [1980] Director/Sales Executive

Evoiq International Ltd
Incorporated: 7 December 2018
Registered Office: c/o Talat Qazi Consulting, 58b Ilford Lane, Ilford, Essex, IG1 2JZ
Parent: Evoiq
Officers: Mona Mahmoud Saad Salama [1983] Director [Egyptian]

Excel (GS) Limited
Incorporated: 18 August 1999 *Employees:* 16
Net Worth: £361,943 *Total Assets:* £607,348
Registered Office: The Stables, Church Walk, Daventry, Northants, NN11 4BL
Shareholders: Paul Andrew Malone; John Anthony Malone
Officers: John Anthony Malone [1952] Director; Paul Andrew Malone [1974] Director

Experimental Perfume Club Ltd
Incorporated: 1 August 2016 *Employees:* 2
Net Worth: £45,308 *Total Assets:* £78,891
Registered Office: Studio 020, 1 Westgate Street, London, E8 3RL
Major Shareholder: Emmanuelle Moeglin
Officers: Emmanuelle Moeglin [1984] Director [French]

Eyegenius Ltd
Incorporated: 9 October 2013
Registered Office: 78 The Green, Twickenham, Middlesex, TW2 5AG
Major Shareholder: Grant Dean Miller
Officers: Grant Dean Miller [1974] Director

Pierre Fabre Limited
Incorporated: 12 August 1970 *Employees:* 74
Net Worth: £1,734,371 *Total Assets:* £7,420,965
Registered Office: Eversheds House, 70 Great Bridgewater Street, Manchester, M1 5ES
Officers: Xavier Pierre Marie Benoist [1966] Director/Pierre Fabre Dermo Cosmetique FC Manager [French]; Michael Frederic Danon [1969] Pierre Fabre SA General Director [French]; Frederic Marie Duchesne [1959] Pierre Fabre Medicament General Director [French]; Vincent Henri Francois Guiraud-Chaumeil [1964] Ethics Franchise & Europe Region Director [French]; Laura Adele McMullin [1973] Director/General Manager

Face Boutique Limited
Incorporated: 23 September 2004
Registered Office: Office 296, 56 Gloucester Road, London, SW7 4UB
Officers: Sarah Vorbach [1966] Director

Faces Cosmetics Limited
Incorporated: 18 August 2006
Net Worth: £1,061,000 *Total Assets:* £1,066,000
Registered Office: 27-28 Eastcastle Street, London, W1W 8DH
Officers: Marie Francoise Krin Chin Chung Kee Mew [1975] Director [Mauritian]; Amit Manocha [1978] Director [Indian]; Rajev Shukla [1969] Director [Indian]

Farasha-Cosmetics Ltd
Incorporated: 26 June 2018
Registered Office: 27 Old Gloucester Street, London, WC1N 3AX
Major Shareholder: Massimo Serra
Officers: Massimo Serra, Secretary; Massimo Serra [1965] Director/Self Employed [Italian]

Fashion Fragrances & Cosmetics UK Ltd
Incorporated: 14 October 2016 *Employees:* 15
Net Worth Deficit: £310,301 *Total Assets:* £959,217
Registered Office: 1st Floor, Sackville House, 143-149 Fenchurch Street, London, EC3M 6BN
Major Shareholder: Leslie Bayly Ledes
Officers: Leslie Bayly Ledes [1963] Director/President [American]

Felix Medical Group Ltd
Incorporated: 17 July 2017
Registered Office: NI646902: Companies House, Default Address, 2nd Floor The Linenhall 32-38 Linenhall Street, Belfast, BT2 8BG
Major Shareholder: Karren Brady
Officers: Dr Karren Brady [1976] Director/Businesswoman

Female Balance Shop Limited
Incorporated: 3 November 2014
Registered Office: 9 Wimpole Street, London, W1G 9SR
Major Shareholder: Tage Backstrom
Officers: Mikael Tage Valentin Backstrom [1963] Director [Swedish]

Ferndale Pharmaceuticals Limited
Incorporated: 2 April 2003 *Employees:* 24
Net Worth: £1,758,179 *Total Assets:* £2,920,641
Registered Office: Unit 740 Thorp Arch Estate, Street 2, Wetherby, W Yorks, LS23 7FX
Shareholders: Roger Mark Bloxham; Ferndale Pharma Group Inc
Officers: Roisin Wood, Secretary; Roger Mark Bloxham [1964] Managing Director; Doctor Michael John Burns [1955] Director & President; Sem Lloyd Davies [1965] International Director; James Thayer McMillan II [1946] Chairman & Director [American]

Field Fresh Skincare Ltd
Incorporated: 3 December 2014
Registered Office: 61 High Street, Cam, Dursley, Glos, GL11 5LD
Major Shareholder: Laura Jane Pardoe
Officers: Laura Jane Pardoe [1974] Director

Daniel Field Purity Project Ltd
Incorporated: 30 April 2009
Net Worth Deficit: £28,930 *Total Assets:* £55,624
Registered Office: Radnor House, Greenwood Close, Cardiff Gate Business Park, Pontprennau, Cardiff, CF23 8AA
Shareholders: Sara Shipman; Francesca Shipman
Officers: Francesca Shipman, Secretary; Jonathan David Shipman [1969] Director/Sales Agent; Marc Jason Shipman [1974] Director/Sales Agent

Fikkerts Limited
Incorporated: 9 April 1990 *Employees:* 29
Net Worth: £524,407 *Total Assets:* £905,822
Registered Office: The Design Studio, Royd Ings Avenue, Keighley, W Yorks, BD21 4BZ
Major Shareholder: Richard Nigel Fikkert
Officers: Julia Margaret Fikkert [1971] Sales & Marketing Director; Richard Nigel Fikkert [1965] Director

Fillcare Limited
Incorporated: 1 December 1981 *Employees:* 157
Net Worth: £10,460,000 *Total Assets:* £15,329,000
Registered Office: P O Box 66, Lanelay Road, Talbot Green, Pontyclun, Rhondda Cynon Taf, CF72 8YZ
Parent: Fareva UK Limited
Officers: Jean Pierre Fraisse [1959] Director [French]; Andrew John Mortimer [1959] Managing Director

Firmenich Holdings (UK) Limited
Incorporated: 1 October 1928
Net Worth: £3,062,000 *Total Assets:* £3,062,000
Registered Office: Hayes Road, Southall, Middlesex, UB2 5NN
Officers: Elodie Josiane Bouchard [1972] Senior Director Finance Europe [French]; Francois Paul Rohrbach [1964] Director [Swiss]

Firmenich UK Limited
Incorporated: 18 May 1990 *Employees:* 166
Net Worth: £25,586,000 *Total Assets:* £45,554,000
Registered Office: Hayes Road, Southall, Middlesex, UB2 5NN
Officers: Elodie Josiane Bouchard [1972] Senior Director Finance Europe [French]; Gary Charles Nelson [1961] Director; Paulo Sergio Menoita Nogueira [1966] Director [Brazilian/Portuguese]; Laetitia Christabel Pictet [1970] Director/Legal Counsel [Swiss]; Dominique Florence Zundel [1963] Director/VP Europe, Perfumery BHC [French]

Firmenich Wellingborough (UK) Limited
Incorporated: 18 June 1934
Registered Office: Hayes Road, Southall, Middlesex, UB2 5NN
Parent: Firmenich Holdings (UK) Limited
Officers: Elodie Josiane Bouchard [1972] Senior Director Finance Europe [French]; Francois Paul Rohrbach [1964] Director [Swiss]

First Natural Brands Ltd
Incorporated: 9 May 1984 *Employees:* 31
Net Worth: £1,546,100 *Total Assets:* £3,952,657
Registered Office: Millennium House, Unit 2 King Business Centre, Reeds Lane, Sayers Common, Hassocks, W Sussex, BN6 9LS
Parent: First Natural Limited
Officers: Robin Christopher Russell [1950] Director; Sanam Shah [1975] Director/Banker

First Natural Limited
Incorporated: 9 June 2006 *Employees:* 39
Net Worth: £868,732 *Total Assets:* £4,327,044
Registered Office: Millennium House, Unit 2 King Business Centre, Reeds Lane, Sayers Common, Hassocks, W Sussex, BN6 9LS
Shareholder: Robin Christopher Russell
Officers: Sanam Shah, Secretary; Robin Christopher Russell [1950] Director; Sanam Shah [1975] Director/Banker

The Fitzrovia Centre Ltd
Incorporated: 8 February 2016 *Employees:* 1
Net Worth Deficit: £21,633 *Total Assets:* £64,339
Registered Office: 71-75 Shelton Street, Covent Garden, London, WC2H 9JQ
Shareholders: Gemma Louise Clarke; Turpin Capital Limited
Officers: Gemma Clarke [1962] Director; Charles Edward Turpin [1973] Director/Financial Consultant

Fizzy Lizzy's Ltd
Incorporated: 2 January 2019
Registered Office: 20-22 Wenlock Road, London, N1 7GU
Major Shareholder: Elizabeth Joanna Taylor
Officers: Elizabeth Joanna Taylor [1986] Director/Veterinary Nurse

The Fizzy Thistle Ltd
Incorporated: 7 August 2018
Registered Office: 85 Inchmurrin Drive, Kilmarnock, E Ayrshire, KA3 2HY
Major Shareholder: Jason Gerald Harrison
Officers: Jason Generald Harrison [1984] Director/Regional Controller

Flo Ventures Ltd
Incorporated: 29 December 2009
Net Worth: £747 *Total Assets:* £747
Registered Office: 10 Round Mead, Stevenage, Herts, SG2 9PH
Shareholders: Wabuji Dore; Stephen Dore
Officers: Wabuji Dore, Secretary; Stephen Dore [1968] Director

Flowery Whiff Limited
Incorporated: 3 January 2018
Registered Office: 6 Victoria Street, Scarborough, N Yorks, YO12 7SS
Shareholders: Carolyn Popple; Alex Popple
Officers: Alex Popple [1996] Director of Marketing; Carolyn Popple [1963] Director of Manufacturing

Flynn Group of Companies Ltd
Incorporated: 17 July 2017
Registered Office: 18 Queen Street, Enniskillen, Co Fermanagh, BT74 7DB
Major Shareholder: Michael Bronson
Officers: Michael Bronson [1975] Director/Businessman

Foad Wax Limited
Incorporated: 20 June 2011
Net Worth: £360 *Total Assets:* £1,516
Registered Office: 27a Washington Road, Worcester Park, Surrey, KT4 8JG
Shareholders: Patrick Neil Foad; Leonie Rachel Foad
Officers: LeOne Rachel Foad [1986] Director; Patt Foad [1985] Director

Foltex Hair Technology Limited
Incorporated: 2 October 2018
Registered Office: Northside House, Mount Pleasant, Barnet, Herts, EN4 9EE
Shareholder: Roy Henry Presswell
Officers: Joanne Sarah Hurst [1972] Director; James Stephen Presswell [1978] Director; June Linda Presswell [1950] Director; Roy Henry Presswell [1948] Director

Forte Organics Ltd
Incorporated: 1 September 2017
Registered Office: 70 Jermyn Street, Mayfair, London, SW1Y 6NY
Major Shareholder: Irene Alisea Forte
Officers: Irene Alisea Forte [1988] Group Project Director at Rocco Forte

Fragrance and Glamour Ltd
Incorporated: 22 January 2018
Registered Office: 4 Glaisher Street, Liverpool, L5 1AB
Major Shareholder: Kleanthis Iordanidis
Officers: Kleanthis Iordanidis [1974] Director

Fragrance du Bois (UK) Limited
Incorporated: 5 December 2011
Net Worth Deficit: £20,425 *Total Assets:* £383
Registered Office: Towers Point, Wheelhouse Road, Rugeley, Staffs, WS15 1UN
Major Shareholder: Melanie Ann Copestake
Officers: David Michael Linell [1958] Director/Chartered Accountant

Fragrance Oils (International) Limited
Incorporated: 12 August 1974 *Employees:* 31
Net Worth: £23,283,736 *Total Assets:* £48,507,260
Registered Office: Eton Hill Industrial Estate, Eton Hill Road, Radcliffe, Manchester, M26 2FR
Officers: John Morgan, Secretary; Barbara Carter [1951] Director; Malcolm Charles Hogan [1956] Director/Buyer; John Morgan [1955] Director/Accountant; Mark Peter Ogden [1957] Director/Export Sales Manager; Martin Christopher Francis Potts [1959] Director; Jacqueline Radovic [1956] Personnel Director; Jeffrey Robert Slavin [1952] Director/Chartered Accountant; Barry Starr [1950] Laboratory Director; Richard Jeremy Thomas [1960] Sales Director

Fragrance Oils (Purchasing) Limited
Incorporated: 20 September 1967 *Employees:* 169
Net Worth: £9,934,622 *Total Assets:* £25,254,370
Registered Office: Eton Hill Industrial Estate, Eton Hill Road, Radcliffe, Manchester, M26 2FR
Officers: John Morgan, Secretary; Malcolm Charles Hogan [1956] Director; John Morgan [1955] Director/Accountant; Martin Christopher Francis Potts [1959] Director; Jeffrey Robert Slavin [1952] Director/Chartered Accountant

Fragrance Selection (UK) Limited
Incorporated: 27 June 2012
Net Worth: £7,931 *Total Assets:* £7,931
Registered Office: 63B Portland Road, Edgbaston, Birmingham, B16 9HS
Major Shareholder: Bhupendra Parmar
Officers: Bhupendra Parmar [1956] Director

Fragrances and Cosmetics Limited
Incorporated: 16 December 1999
Net Worth: £141,316 *Total Assets:* £1,109,992
Registered Office: Unit K, Penfold Trading Estate, Imperial Way, Watford, Herts, WD24 4YY
Major Shareholder: Gulam Abbas Megjhi
Officers: Ghulam Abbas Megjhi [1946] Director

Fragrances UK Limited
Incorporated: 29 November 2010 *Employees:* 37
Net Worth: £382,710 *Total Assets:* £712,273
Registered Office: Fragrances UK, Fen Lane, Metheringham, Lincoln, LN4 3AQ
Major Shareholder: Kabir Upkar Singh Sehmi
Officers: Zena Patricia Jones [1965] Director; Angela Marie Meekings [1976] Director

Fragrant Earth International Limited
Incorporated: 13 September 2007
Net Worth Deficit: £52,653 *Total Assets:* £548,683
Registered Office: Unit 21 Beckery Road, Glastonbury, Somerset, BA6 9NX
Shareholders: Shirley May Routley; Jan Brian Kusmirek
Officers: Ian John Cambray-Smith [1946] Director; Jan Brian Kusmirek [1946] Director; Shirley May Routley [1961] Director

Fragrant Spa Limited
Incorporated: 24 January 2018
Registered Office: Basement, 146 Ladbroke Grove, London, W10 5NE
Major Shareholder: Xiangrong Liu
Officers: Xiangrong Liu [1982] Director [Chinese]

Fragrantia Limited
Incorporated: 18 January 2019
Registered Office: Unit 24 Highcroft Industrial Estate, Enterprise Road, Horndean, Waterlooville, Hants, PO8 0BT
Major Shareholder: Haroon Abdul-Rauf
Officers: Haroon Abdul-Rauf [1975] Director

Freestyle Beauty Products Limited
Incorporated: 29 July 1999
Net Worth: £598 Total Assets: £598
Registered Office: Unit 7 Bermer Place, Imperial Way, Watford, Herts, WD24 4AY
Shareholder: Dinesh Chhabildas Shah
Officers: Mahendra Kanabar, Secretary; Dinesh Chhabildas Shah [1958] Director; Jayshree Dinesh Shah [1963] Director; Karan Shah [1988] Director

Freshly Whip'd Limited
Incorporated: 21 January 2019
Registered Office: 1 Heron Mead, Enfield, Middlesex, EN3 6FD
Major Shareholder: Nneoma Chibudibia Okeke
Officers: Dr Nneoma Chibudibia Okeke [1992] Director and Company Secretary

Freshorize Ltd
Incorporated: 26 March 2002 Employees: 11
Net Worth: £3,926,854 Total Assets: £4,209,926
Registered Office: University of East London, Royal Dock Business Centre, University Way, London, E16 2RD
Major Shareholder: Abdul Ebrahim Patel
Officers: Bilkis Master, Secretary; Abdul Ebrahim Patel, Secretary/Barrister; Abdul Ebrahim Patel [1963] Director

Frosts of London Limited
Incorporated: 6 July 2018
Registered Office: Kemp House, 160 City Road, London, EC1V 2NX
Shareholders: Andrew Philip Catlin; Katie Catlin
Officers: Andrew Catlin, Secretary; Andrew Philip Catlin [1961] Commercial Director; Katie Catlin [1989] Managing Director

Fumarette Ltd
Incorporated: 5 January 2012
Net Worth Deficit: £90,954 Total Assets: £37,706
Registered Office: Suite 29, 58 Acacia Road, London, NW8 6AG
Major Shareholder: Ingo Steyer
Officers: Ingo Steyer [1966] Director/Trader [German]

Fysifarm Limited
Incorporated: 16 January 2018
Registered Office: 27 Old Gloucester Street, London, WC1N 3AX
Major Shareholder: Nikolaos Chalvatzis
Officers: Panagiotis Laskaris [1966] Director [Greek]

G & G Skincare Ltd
Incorporated: 2 January 2019
Registered Office: Venthams Ltd, 51 Lincoln's Inn Fields, London, WC2A 3NA
Shareholders: Benjamin Gibbs; Mark Girven
Officers: Benjamin Gibbs [1980] Director/Sales; Mark Girven [1988] Director/Sales

G and B Beauty Products Ltd
Incorporated: 31 January 2003
Net Worth: £2 Total Assets: £2
Registered Office: 62 Wilson Street, London, EC2A 2BU
Major Shareholder: Tony Coveva
Officers: Tony Coveva, Secretary; Tony Coveva [1972] Director

Gagnon Essentials Limited
Incorporated: 20 March 2006
Net Worth: £17,475 Total Assets: £73,490
Registered Office: 4 Old Park Lane, London, W1K 1QW
Major Shareholder: Beth Gagnon
Officers: Simon Hosier, Secretary; Beth Gagnon [1951] Director [American]

Gallivant Perfumes Limited
Incorporated: 22 April 2016
Net Worth: £82,819 Total Assets: £110,328
Registered Office: Anchorage House, The Trampery Republic, 2 Clove Crescent, London, E14 2BE
Major Shareholder: Nicholas Steward
Officers: Cecile Marret [1973] Director [French]; Nicholas John Steward [1974] Director/Perfume Designer [Irish]

Garden Perfumers Ltd
Incorporated: 9 May 2018
Registered Office: 149 Dalling Road, London, W6 0ET
Major Shareholder: Linda Merrill Tipping
Officers: Linda Merrill Tipping [1958] Director [Canadian]

Garnier & Hemo Healthcare Ltd
Incorporated: 14 September 2017
Registered Office: 14 Whitehouse Road, Londonderry, BT48 0NE
Parent: Hemo Bioscience Ltd
Officers: Dr David Leppinen [1968] Director/Businessman

Gellure Ltd
Incorporated: 20 August 2012
Net Worth: £3,797 Total Assets: £3,797
Registered Office: 96a Cardiff Road, Llandaff, Cardiff, CF5 2DT
Officers: Klaus Ueber, Secretary; Catherine Hann [1974] Director; Klaus Georg Ueber [1947] Director

Gelspa Limited
Incorporated: 4 June 2018
Registered Office: Unit 27 Gelicity House, Castle Park Industrial Estate, Flint, CH6 5XA
Shareholders: Wayne Walton; Paul Morris
Officers: Paul Morris, Secretary; Paul Morris [1963] Director; Wayne Walton [1965] Director

Geltec Limited
Incorporated: 18 December 2014
Net Worth: £281,603 Total Assets: £293,570
Registered Office: Unit 16 Trojan Industrial Estate, Trojan Industrial Park, Paignton, Devon, TQ4 7EP
Major Shareholder: John Ellacott
Officers: John Ellacott, Secretary; John Ellacott [1956] Director/Company Manager

General Flavours & Fragrances Ltd
Incorporated: 14 April 1987
Net Worth Deficit: £5,200 Total Assets: £3,750
Registered Office: Stratton House, nr Micheldever, Winchester, Hants, SO21 3DP
Officers: David James Stride, Secretary; Belinda Mary Stride [1959] Director/Manager

M.S. George Limited
Incorporated: 20 March 1972 Employees: 19
Net Worth: £2,449,597 Total Assets: £3,202,793
Registered Office: Sterling House, 27 Hatchlands Road, Redhill, Surrey, RH1 6RW
Officers: Quentin Peter Davis, Secretary; Mark Simon Davis [1964] Director/Operations Manager; Quentin Peter Davis [1953] Director/Accountant

Get Lucky Inc Ltd
Incorporated: 21 October 2015
Net Worth: £6,700 *Total Assets:* £289,543
Registered Office: Studio 19, The Brewery Quarter, Unit H2, High Street, Cheltenham, Glos, GL50 3FF
Shareholders: Miles Maitland Spencer Dunkley; Steven Arthur Ross
Officers: Richard Mark Buckland [1977] Finance Director; Miles Spencer Maitland Dunkley [1967] Director; Steven Arthur Ross [1964] Director

Gillette U.K. Limited
Incorporated: 17 March 1931 *Employees:* 168
Net Worth: £29,559,000 *Total Assets:* £63,434,000
Registered Office: The Heights, Brooklands, Weybridge, Surrey, KT13 0XP
Parent: Gilette Industries Limited
Officers: Anthony Joseph Appleton, Secretary; Anthony Joseph Appleton [1962] Director/Solicitor; Alexander George Buckthorp [1973] Finance Director; Vijay Indroo Sitlani [1975] Finance Director [Singaporean]; Husnu Yilmaz [1971] Director/Plant Manager [Turkish]; Christopher John Young [1974] HR Director

Ginger & Vanilla Ltd
Incorporated: 18 January 2019
Registered Office: 4 Arundel Court, Newcastle upon Tyne, NE3 2UJ
Major Shareholder: Maria Dimichele
Officers: Maria Dimichele [1972] Director

Gio Natura Ltd
Incorporated: 8 May 2018
Registered Office: 153 Glenfield Road, Leicester, LE3 6DP
Major Shareholder: Joanna Tylko
Officers: Joanna Tylko [1972] Director/Cream Maker [Polish]

Glad Gent Ltd
Incorporated: 28 April 2017
Registered Office: 87 Fernleigh Road, London, N21 3AJ
Major Shareholder: Jonathan Wolfgang Draper
Officers: Jonathan Wolfgang Draper [1972] Director

Glamoessence Ltd
Incorporated: 9 June 2016
Registered Office: Kemp House, 152 City Road, London, EC1V 2NX
Officers: Abdulla Salih [1963] Director [Maldivian]; Abdulla Yasir [1973] Director [Maldivian]

Glamour Natural Cosmetics Ltd
Incorporated: 17 February 2017
Net Worth Deficit: £8,969 *Total Assets:* £6
Registered Office: Unit 15 Cavendish Centre, Winnall Close, Winchester, Hants, SO23 0LB
Shareholder: Tamas V.David
Officers: Krisztin V.David [1969] Director [Hungarian]; Tamas V.David [1965] Director [Hungarian]

Glory Skin Ltd
Incorporated: 12 February 2018
Registered Office: 37b Bredgar Road, London, N19 5BW
Major Shareholder: Eunice Asante
Officers: Eunice Asante [1986] Director

Good By Nature Ltd
Incorporated: 8 November 2018
Registered Office: Flat 9, Tiggap House, 20 Cable Walk, London, SE10 0TP
Shareholders: Tara Louise O'Malley; Julian Ruiz
Officers: Tara Louise O'Malley [1993] Director/Editor

Good Mela Ltd
Incorporated: 3 April 2018
Registered Office: 1 Richmond Close, Rushden, Northants, NN10 0NT
Shareholders: Andrea Haughton; Ruth Haughton
Officers: Ruth Haughton [1995] Director

Good Skin Care Company Limited
Incorporated: 5 February 2014
Registered Office: Enterprise House, 38 Tyndall Court, Commerce Road, Lynchwood, Peterborough, Cambs, PE2 6LR
Officers: Christopher Mark Taylor, Secretary; Alan Leslie Taylor [1952] Director; Christopher Mark Taylor [1963] Director; Raymond Neil Taylor [1957] Director; Evelyn May Taylor [1932] Director

John Gosnell & Company, Limited
Incorporated: 4 August 1933 *Employees:* 27
Net Worth: £2,620,999 *Total Assets:* £2,833,054
Registered Office: Unit F, Malling Brooks, Brooks Road, Lewes, E Sussex, BN7 2QG
Major Shareholder: David Alan Warner
Officers: David Alan Warner, Secretary; Matthew Peter Fry [1977] Director [Irish]; Nicola Lesley Tickner [1969] Director; Christopher Robert Warner [1972] Director; David Alan Warner [1942] Director

Gotvox Limited
Incorporated: 26 September 2014 *Employees:* 3
Net Worth: £27,717 *Total Assets:* £43,273
Registered Office: 6 Northlands Road, Southampton, SO15 2LF
Shareholders: Stephen James Cross; Melanie Rose Cross
Officers: Melanie Rose Cross, Secretary; Stephen James Cross [1980] Director

Grace & Hartland Ltd
Incorporated: 23 November 2018
Registered Office: 9 Puttingthorpe Drive, Weston-Super-Mare, Somerset, BS22 8LE
Officers: Ray Anthony Brearley [1954] Director/IT Consultant; Nicola Grace Clifton [1984] Director/Nurse; Sheila Mary Clifton [1954] Director/Accounts Manager; Amy Louise Trevaskus [1979] Director/Creative Writer

Gracetree Ltd
Incorporated: 1 March 2010 *Employees:* 2
Net Worth: £16,614 *Total Assets:* £84,566
Registered Office: 4 Old Park Lane, Mayfair, London, W1K 1QW
Major Shareholder: Antonia Burrell
Officers: Antonia Burrell [1972] Managing Director

Greatest of All Time Soapworks Ltd
Incorporated: 23 August 2017
Registered Office: Booley House, Booley, Stanton upon Hine Heath, Shrewsbury, Salop, SY4 4LY
Shareholders: Adam Jarvis; Sarah Jarvis
Officers: Adam Jarvis [1981] Director; Sarah Jarvis [1987] Director

Green Jiva Ltd
Incorporated: 26 November 2015
Previous: Lilitu Ltd
Registered Office: 99 Heol Senni, Foxglove Meadows, Bettws, Newport, NP20 7GB
Shareholders: Jessica Grace Element; Andrew Christopher Hunter
Officers: Jessica Grace Element [1981] Director/R&D Software Technician; Andrew Christopher Hunter [1975] Director/R&D Software Technician

Green Ladies N.I Ltd
Incorporated: 19 September 2018
Registered Office: 48 Crawfordstown Road, Downpatrick, Co Down, BT30 8QA
Major Shareholder: Tracy Megoran
Officers: Tracy Megoran [1982] Director/Entrepreneur

Green Mass Limited
Incorporated: 14 January 2019
Registered Office: Flat 32, Adventures Court, 12 Newport Avenue, London, E14 2DN
Major Shareholder: Chunxiang Yang
Officers: Chunxiang Yang [1980] Director/Businessman [Chinese]

Groomers Limited
Incorporated: 18 April 2000 *Employees:* 36
Net Worth: £500,978 *Total Assets:* £1,879,278
Registered Office: 137 Seventh Street, Greenham Business Park, Greenham, Thatcham, Newbury, Berks, RG19 6HW
Major Shareholder: Graham Searle
Officers: Deborah Jane Searle [1958] Director; Graham Searle [1951] Managing Director

H H Formulations Ltd
Incorporated: 11 April 2018
Registered Office: 121 Hide Tower, Regency Street, London, SW1P 4AB
Major Shareholder: Rupinder Singh Mangat
Officers: Rupinder Singh Mangat [1968] Director/Therapist

Hair Systems Europe Limited
Incorporated: 23 December 1998 *Employees:* 8
Net Worth Deficit: £469,693 *Total Assets:* £487,853
Registered Office: 141-143 Camford Way, Sundon Park, Luton, Beds, LU3 3AN
Major Shareholder: Marjorie Minehan Covey
Officers: Marjorie Minehan Covey, Secretary; William Edward Covey Jr [1962] Director/President Hair Systems Inc [American]; Sharon Griffith [1965] Director/Secretary [American]

Hairs & Graces Cosmetics Ltd
Incorporated: 1 November 2018
Registered Office: 142 Cromwell Road, Kensington, London, SW7 4EF
Major Shareholder: Natalie Jones
Officers: Natalie Jones [1981] Director

Hamiltons of Canterbury Limited
Incorporated: 24 May 2017
Registered Office: 49 The Drive, Hove, E Sussex, BN3 3JE
Major Shareholder: Max Richard Leslie Burton
Officers: Max Richard Leslie Burton, Secretary; Max Richard Leslie Burton [1950] Director

Hampshire Cosmetics Limited
Incorporated: 26 April 2015
Registered Office: Brambles House, Waterberry Drive, Waterlooville, Hants, PO7 7UW
Parent: Solab Group Limited
Officers: Mark Polding [1963] Operations Director

Hanan Pacha Ltd
Incorporated: 3 January 2019
Registered Office: 20-22 Wenlock Road, London, N1 7GU
Major Shareholder: Paloma Castro Romero
Officers: Paloma Castro Romero [1977] Director [Spanish]

Hands Organic Ltd
Incorporated: 22 February 2019
Registered Office: Unit 34 The Maltings Business Centre, The Maltings, Stanstead Abbotts, Herts, SG12 8HG
Major Shareholder: Katherine Victoria Frederick
Officers: Katherine Frederick, Secretary; Katherine Victoria Frederick [1981] Director/Aromatherapist

Happy Melon Skin Care Limited
Incorporated: 23 March 2018
Registered Office: 16 Fenney Street, Salford, M7 2ZL
Major Shareholder: Kirsten Kiernan
Officers: Kirsten Kiernan [1991] Director

Happy Products Limited
Incorporated: 5 January 2015
Net Worth Deficit: £1,768 *Total Assets:* £13,962
Registered Office: Elizabeth House, 8 Queen Elizabeth Close, Shefford, Beds, SG17 5LE
Officers: Matthew Bibb [1970] Director; Suzanne Bibb [1966] Director

Haromatic Ltd
Incorporated: 22 August 2018
Registered Office: 3 Bray Lane, Telford, Salop, TF3 5HH
Shareholders: Richard Molli Boulock; Sonia Molli Boulock
Officers: Sonia Molli Boulock, Secretary; Richard Molli Boulock [1981] Director/Teacher [Cameroonian]

Hart Enterprise Limited
Incorporated: 27 February 2018
Registered Office: 18 Fern Close, Kirkby, Merseyside, L32 1BH
Major Shareholder: Dean Anthony Hart
Officers: Dean Anthony Hart [1986] Director

Haych Cosmetics Limited
Incorporated: 2 December 2016
Net Worth Deficit: £8,585 *Total Assets:* £45,429
Registered Office: Unit 5 Meadowcroft Mill, Bury Road, Bamford, Rochdale, Lancs, OL11 4AU
Major Shareholder: Joy Elizabeth Howieson
Officers: Kenneth Howieson, Secretary; Joy Elizabeth Howieson [1990] Director

HBNatura Ltd
Incorporated: 24 June 2016
Registered Office: 71-75 Shelton Street, London, WC2H 9JQ
Major Shareholder: Herve Sczerbyna
Officers: Herve Sczerbyna [1955] Director/Engineer [French]

HE FE Ltd
Incorporated: 18 January 2016
Net Worth Deficit: £9,376 *Total Assets:* £586
Registered Office: P O Box 2784, 27 Old Gloucester Street, London, WC1N 3XX
Major Shareholder: Adrian Pozniak
Officers: Adrian Pozniak [1986] Director

Heaven Scent Incense Limited
Incorporated: 9 October 1997 *Employees:* 36
Net Worth: £2,186,209 *Total Assets:* £2,646,548
Registered Office: 33 Duke Street, Trowbridge, Wilts, BA14 8EA
Shareholders: Daniel John Pettitt; Mark Thomas Pettitt
Officers: Daniel John Pettitt, Secretary/Director; Daniel John Pettitt [1965] Director; Mark Thomas Pettitt [1964] Director

Heavenly Fragrance (UK) Limited
Incorporated: 12 August 2010
Registered Office: Dalton House, 60 Windsor Avenue, London, SW19 2RR
Major Shareholder: Titty Pappachen Thomas
Officers: Titty Pappachen Thomas [1974] Director/Engineer [Indian]

Heidi J Naturals Limited
Incorporated: 28 April 2018
Registered Office: 43 Whitecross Road, Weston-Super-Mare, Somerset, BS23 1EN
Major Shareholder: Craig Conway
Officers: Craig Conway [1980] Director

Hemo Bioscience Ltd
Incorporated: 6 July 2017
Registered Office: 6 St Colman's Park, Newry, Co Down, BT34 2BX
Major Shareholder: David Leppinen
Officers: Dr David Leppinen [1968] Director/Businessman

The Hemp Garden Ltd
Incorporated: 8 January 2018
Registered Office: 22 Heol Y Felin, Pontyberem, Llanelli, Carmarthenshire, SA15 5EH
Major Shareholder: Robert Turner
Officers: Robert Turner [1983] Director

Herbfarmacy Ltd
Incorporated: 29 November 2012 *Employees:* 9
Net Worth Deficit: £52,929 *Total Assets:* £153,836
Registered Office: The Field, Eardisley, Hereford, HR3 6NB
Shareholders: Gordon Paul Richards; Carol Elizabeth Richards
Officers: Carol Elizabeth Richards [1952] Director; Gordon Paul Richards [1948] Director

Herc Ltd.
Incorporated: 4 February 2006
Net Worth Deficit: £20,790 *Total Assets:* £97,450
Registered Office: Lewis House, Great Chesterford Court, Great Chesterford, Essex, CB10 1PF
Major Shareholder: Arun Dev Kumar
Officers: Narinder Kumar, Secretary; Dr Ajay Kumar [1981] Director/Doctor; Narinder Kumar [1961] Director/Manager

Herrmann + Herrmann Limited
Incorporated: 11 September 2012
Registered Office: 5-7 Broadway Drive, Halesworth, Suffolk, IP19 8QR
Shareholder: Nigel Kurt Herrmann
Officers: Nigel Kurt Herrmann [1951] Director; Susan Herrmann [1950] Director

Hi Energy Healing Limited
Incorporated: 16 November 2016
Net Worth Deficit: £5,827
Registered Office: 27a Maxwell Road, Northwood, Middlesex, HA6 2XY
Major Shareholder: Reena Cotsford-Dolden
Officers: Reena Cotsford-Dolden, Secretary; Reena Cotsford-Dolden [1962] Director

The Highland Soap Co. Limited
Incorporated: 17 July 2006 *Employees:* 23
Net Worth: £205,939 *Total Assets:* £294,882
Registered Office: The Highland Soap Co Ltd, Spean Bridge, Highland, PH34 4EP
Major Shareholder: Archibald Sven MacDonald
Officers: Angus Francis MacDonald [1962] Director; Archibald Sven MacDonald [1990] Director; Emma Parton [1973] Director

Hkka Limited
Incorporated: 31 July 2017
Registered Office: Flat 21, Stickle House, Creative Road, London, SE8 3FU
Major Shareholder: Adam Kanyog
Officers: Katalin Huse [1987] Director [Hungarian]; Adam Kanyog [1988] Director [Hungarian]

HMMT Holdings Ltd.
Incorporated: 20 November 2014
Previous: Resa Red Limited
Registered Office: 30-34 North Street, Hailsham, E Sussex, BN27 1DW
Shareholders: Milena Thacker; Heather Anne Mills
Officers: Heather Anne Mills [1968] Director/Entrepreneur

Hoc Parfum Ltd
Incorporated: 8 November 2017
Registered Office: 3rd Floor, Hathaway House, Popes Drive, London, N3 1QF
Major Shareholder: Maria Chumburidze
Officers: Ksenia Bejenar [1983] Director; Maria Chumburidze [1983] Director [French]

Hod Perfumes Limited
Incorporated: 31 January 2014
Net Worth Deficit: £12,536 *Total Assets:* £3,205
Registered Office: Flat 4, Aria House, 9 Haling Down Passage, South Croydon, Surrey, CR2 6FA
Major Shareholder: Dipty Hasmukh Patel
Officers: Dipty Hasmukh Patel [1976] Director/Perfumer

Hoff Beards Limited
Incorporated: 20 February 2018
Registered Office: 14 Tolworth Rise South, Tolworth, Surrey, KT5 9NN
Major Shareholder: Adam Reddyhoff
Officers: Adam Reddyhoff [1992] Director

Holistic Plant Technologies Ltd
Incorporated: 5 November 2015
Net Worth Deficit: £18,970 *Total Assets:* £35,000
Registered Office: Office 228, The Legacy Business Centre, 2a Ruckholt Road, London, E10 5NP
Major Shareholder: Tomasz Kwiecinski
Officers: Tomasz Kwiecinski [1985] Director/Coach [Polish]

Holistica Skin Ltd
Incorporated: 4 July 2017
Registered Office: 21 Bradford Street, Chester, CH4 7DE
Major Shareholder: Becky Laura May Symes
Officers: Becky Laura May Symes [1992] Director/Founder

Honesty Skincare Limited
Incorporated: 14 May 2015
Net Worth: £1,923 *Total Assets:* £2,373
Registered Office: 81 Castle Lodge Avenue, Rothwell, Leeds, LS26 0ZD
Major Shareholder: Cheryl Ruth Woodman
Officers: Cheryl Ruth Woodman [1987] Director

Honey Corn Limited
Incorporated: 28 September 2017
Registered Office: 71-75 Shelton Street, London, WC2H 9JQ
Major Shareholder: Ayesha Ibrahim
Officers: Mona Fofana [1954] Director; Ayesha Ibrahim [1976] Director

Hope and Rose Limited
Incorporated: 7 February 2017
Registered Office: 4 Watermans Close, Kingston upon Thames, Surrey, KT2 5AS
Officers: Susannah Rose-Innes [1978] Director/Solicitor

House of 18 Ltd
Incorporated: 9 August 2018
Registered Office: 24 Caractacus Green, Watford, Herts, WD18 6JU
Major Shareholder: Zala Markovic Ho
Officers: Zala Markovic Ho [1981] Director [Slovenian]

House of Sanders Limited
Incorporated: 19 February 2014
Registered Office: 28 Sandpiper Close, Colchester, Essex, CO4 3GE
Major Shareholder: Mark Sanders
Officers: Tracey Sanders, Secretary; Mark Sanders [1978] Director

House of Unique Parfum Limited
Incorporated: 6 March 2018
Registered Office: Lynwood House, 373-375 Station Road, Harrow, Middlesex, HA1 2AW
Major Shareholder: Linda Crane
Officers: Linda Crane [1950] Director

Hunk Grooming Ltd
Incorporated: 16 November 2018
Registered Office: Kemp House, 160 City Road, London, EC1V 2NX
Major Shareholder: Alexander David Jarman
Officers: Alexander Jarman, Secretary; Alexander David Jarman [1987] Director

Hypha Cosmetics Ltd
Incorporated: 19 August 2015
Net Worth: £300 *Total Assets:* £400
Registered Office: 491 Davidson Road, Croydon, Surrey, CR0 6DT
Officers: Vivienne Okafor [1991] Director

Hypothesis One Ltd
Incorporated: 13 May 2015
Registered Office: 23 Morrison Avenue, London, N17 6TU
Major Shareholder: Jan Bolton
Officers: Stephen Wilkins, Secretary; Jan Bolton [1978] Director; Stephen Wilkins [1978] Director/Secretary

I Love Myself Ltd
Incorporated: 29 May 2018
Registered Office: 1 Danes Way, Oxshott, Leatherhead, Surrey, KT22 0LU
Major Shareholder: Kathryn Caroline Bennett Rea
Officers: Kathryn Caroline Bennett Rea [1979] Director

Iam By Nature Ltd.
Incorporated: 30 August 2002
Net Worth Deficit: £567,927 *Total Assets:* £210,488
Registered Office: Vox Studios, Unit W112, 1-45 Durham Street, London, SE11 5JH
Shareholder: Mai Abdulatif Aljadawi
Officers: Mai Abdulatif Aljadawi [1976] Director [Saudi Arabian]

IAP Cosmetics International Ltd
Incorporated: 12 January 2018
Registered Office: Ground Floor, 14 High Street, Stoke on Trent, Staffs, ST6 5TG
Major Shareholder: Kirsten Ankersoe
Officers: Kirsten Ankersoe [1950] Director [Danish]

Icaro Sana Limited
Incorporated: 9 July 2018
Registered Office: 12 Fairfield Way, Stevenage, Herts, SG1 6BF
Major Shareholder: Michelle Imelda Martin
Officers: Michelle Imelda Martin [1968] Director [Irish]

Icebox Brands EU Limited
Incorporated: 29 January 2019
Registered Office: Third Floor, 207 Regent Street, London, W1B 3HH
Major Shareholder: Sean Omara
Officers: Sean Omara, Secretary; Sean Omara [1977] Director [American]

Icilda's Ltd
Incorporated: 22 October 2018
Registered Office: 71-75 Shelton Street, London, WC2H 9JQ
Major Shareholder: Diane Hutchinson
Officers: Diane Hutchinson, Secretary; Diane Hutchinson [1972] Director

Ikaa Cosmetics Limited
Incorporated: 27 December 2017
Registered Office: 71-75 Shelton Street, Covent Garden, London, WC2H 9JQ
Major Shareholder: Ravi Kumar Nagarajan
Officers: Ravi Kumar Nagarajan, Secretary; Vivek Kumar [1985] Director [Indian]; Ravi Kumar Nagarajan [1968] Director [Indian]

Image Hub Limited
Incorporated: 2 June 2014 *Employees:* 1
Net Worth Deficit: £24,600 *Total Assets:* £15,937
Registered Office: Old Town Hall, Fore Street, Wellington, Somerset, TA21 8LS
Major Shareholder: Alfred Handley
Officers: Alfred Handley [1962] Director/Marketing Consultant; Juliet Anne Handley [1965] Director/Development Officer

In Line Health and Beauty Limited
Incorporated: 8 July 1997 *Employees:* 24
Net Worth: £1,227,043 *Total Assets:* £2,264,920
Registered Office: BCL House, 2 Pavilion Business Park, Royds Hall Road, Leeds, LS12 6AJ
Shareholders: Christian Miles Cain; Adele Cain
Officers: Adele Cain, Secretary; Christian Miles Cain [1962] Director/Chemist

Inari Skincare Ltd
Incorporated: 19 August 2014
Net Worth Deficit: £9,030 *Total Assets:* £26,594
Registered Office: 50 Skylark Way, Shinfield, Reading, Berks, RG2 9AJ
Major Shareholder: Christopher Willem Smit
Officers: Christopher Willem Smit [1973] Director

Incoplex Limited
Incorporated: 8 June 2016
Net Worth Deficit: £489 *Total Assets:* £1,498
Registered Office: Kemp House, 152 City Road, London, EC1V 2NX
Major Shareholder: Abubakara Ademola Gborigi
Officers: Abubakara Ademola Gborigi [1992] Director/Student

Indult Paris Ltd
Incorporated: 3 September 2014
Net Worth Deficit: £4,169 *Total Assets:* £64,351
Registered Office: 113 Tivoli Court, Rotherhithe Street, London, SE16 5UD
Major Shareholder: Kim Christopher Charles
Officers: Keston Robinson-Price, Secretary; Kim Christopher Charles [1955] Director; Keston Robinson-Price [1977] Director/Chartered Accountant

Infinity Global Corporation & Investment - IGCI Ltd
Incorporated: 11 December 2018
Registered Office: c/o Talat Qazi Consulting, 58b Ilford Lane, Ilford, Essex, IG1 2JZ
Shareholders: Saleh Abdullah Al Damegh; Mohamed Ahmed Mohamed Ahmed Alrefaey
Officers: Saleh Abdullah Al Damegh [1961] Director [Saudi Arabian]; Saleh Mohammad Al Harkan [1960] Director [Saudi Arabian]

Ink of Coco Skincare Ltd
Incorporated: 22 January 2019
Registered Office: 20b Bridge Street, Killamarsh, Sheffield, S21 1AH
Major Shareholder: Shane Paul Craig
Officers: Shane Paul Craig [1984] Director

Inovair Limited
Incorporated: 4 September 2002
Net Worth Deficit: £167,903 *Total Assets:* £45,422
Registered Office: Companies House, Default Address, Cardiff, CF14 8LH
Major Shareholder: Hubert Willem Maat
Officers: Hubert Willem Maat [1965] Director [Dutch]

Insensed Ltd
Incorporated: 31 December 2018
Registered Office: 8 Cwmdraw Court, Pontllanfraith, Blackwood, Monmouthshire, NP12 2GH
Major Shareholder: Sasha King
Officers: Sasha King [1972] Director/Manufacturer

Inspired Diffusing Ltd
Incorporated: 31 December 2018
Registered Office: 33 Vale Road, Northfleet, Kent, DA11 8DD
Major Shareholder: Katie Spaticchia
Officers: Katie Spaticchia [1993] Director/Owner

Inspired Health & Beauty Products Limited
Incorporated: 4 November 2014
Net Worth: £145,502 *Total Assets:* £145,502
Registered Office: Old Bank House, 1-3 High Street, Arundel, W Sussex, BN18 9AD
Shareholder: Christopher Andrew Jones
Officers: Janet Jones, Secretary; Christopher Andrew Jones [1957] Director/Businessman; Daniel Christopher Jones [1985] Director/Designer; Janet Elizabeth Jones [1955] Director/Secretary

International Toiletries & Cosmetics Limited
Incorporated: 14 December 1998 *Employees:* 11
Net Worth: £703,968 *Total Assets:* £1,768,367
Registered Office: 36 Cambridge Road, Hastings, E Sussex, TN34 1DU
Officers: George Payne, Secretary/Cosmetics Consultant; Brian Ernest Murdoch [1951] Director/Cosmetics Consultant; Mrs Linda Margaret Murdoch [1950] Director; George Payne [1958] Director/Cosmetics Consultant; Shelagh Margaret Payne [1958] Director

Intradicted Ltd
Incorporated: 23 July 2018
Registered Office: 214a Kettering Road, Northampton, NN1 4BN
Major Shareholder: Louise Bunn
Officers: Vilma Alvarez [1964] Director [Filipino]

IQ-Area Ltd
Incorporated: 10 February 2015
Net Worth: £114,756 *Total Assets:* £120,256
Registered Office: 71-75 Shelton Street, Covent Garden, London, WC2H 9JQ
Major Shareholder: Eugeniusz Siedlecki
Officers: Eugeniusz Siedlecki [1982] Director/IT Developer [Polish]

Sarah Ireland Perfumes Ltd
Incorporated: 4 April 2018
Registered Office: Crown House, 27 Old Gloucester Street, London, WC1N 3AX
Major Shareholder: Sarah Louise Ireland
Officers: Sarah Louise Ireland [1981] Director/Perfumer

Irregular Cosmetics Company Ltd
Incorporated: 7 December 2018
Registered Office: 32 Meadow View, Newtownabbey, Co Antrim, BT37 0US
Officers: George Philip Holtom [1965] Director; Leslie John Morrow [1965] Director; Rachel Lesley Morrow [1994] Director; Angie Frances Morton [1963] Director

Ishga Ltd
Incorporated: 11 December 2015
Registered Office: 47 Westview Terrace, Stornoway, Isle of Lewis, HS1 2HP
Officers: Martin MacLeod [1975] Director; Malcolm Robert MacRae [1970] Director; Hans Hermann Rissmann [1974] Director; Leon Keith Trayling [1974] Director; Robert Julio Vagnoni [1957] Director [Australian]

Islestarr Holdings Limited
Incorporated: 20 July 2011 *Employees:* 772
Net Worth: £9,401,657 *Total Assets:* £61,629,924
Registered Office: 50 Brook Green, Hammersmith, London, W6 7BJ
Major Shareholder: Charlotte Emma Bow Tilbury
Officers: Michael Mark Lynton [1960] Director/Chairman, Snap Inc [American]; Michael Jonathan Moritz [1954] Director/Investor [American]; Lady Demetra Aikaterini Pinsent [1974] Director/Chief Executive Officer; Charlotte Emma Bow Tilbury [1973] Director/Make Up Artist; Thomas Harry Walker [1961] Director/Investor [American]; George Edward Guilford Waud [1967] Director/Film Producer

Itaconix (U.K.) Limited
Incorporated: 27 October 2005 *Employees:* 27
Previous: Revolymer (U.K.) Limited
Net Worth Deficit: £20,604,000 *Total Assets:* £3,310,000
Registered Office: Fieldfisher, Riverbank House, 2 Swan Lane, London, EC4R 3TT
Parent: Revolymer PLC
Officers: Michael John Norris, Secretary; Laura Elizabeth Denner [1983] Director [American]; John Roger Shaw [1959] Director [American]

Its All About The Skin Limited
Incorporated: 17 September 2015
Net Worth Deficit: £56,876 *Total Assets:* £9,305
Registered Office: c/o Laconica Ltd, 25 Meades Lane, Chesham, Bucks, HP5 1ND
Major Shareholder: Steven Alistair Standring
Officers: Steven Alistair Standring [1959] Director

J2NR Ltd
Incorporated: 21 November 2016
Registered Office: 11 Spindle Grove, Darlington, Co Durham, DL1 1LY
Officers: John Edo Aba [1981] Director/Advisor

Agnes Jackson Limited
Incorporated: 11 August 2017
Registered Office: 5 Scoter Close, Woodford Green, Essex, IG8 7DH
Major Shareholder: Agnes Marfo-Jackson
Officers: Agnes Marfo-Jackson [1966] Director/Aromatherapist

Jaemae Ltd
Incorporated: 3 August 2017
Registered Office: 10 Rowley Way, Northampton, NN2 8XD
Major Shareholder: Manuel Thompson-Oloko
Officers: Manuel Thompson-Oloko, Secretary; Manuel Thompson-Oloko [1984] Director

Jamal London Ltd
Incorporated: 31 August 2012
Net Worth Deficit: £12,977 *Total Assets:* £43,049
Registered Office: 13 Baggrave Street, Leicester, LE5 3QU
Major Shareholder: Mohammed Sadik Jamal
Officers: Mohammed Sadik Jamal [1976] Director/Perfumer

Nicholas James (UK) Limited
Incorporated: 12 February 1982 *Employees:* 22
Net Worth: £142,687 *Total Assets:* £884,281
Registered Office: Tower House, Westfield Industrial Estate, Kirk Lane, Yeadon, Leeds, LS19 7LX
Officers: Alan David Ingram [1973] Logistics Director; Peter Eric Liversidge [1980] Director/Chemist; Paul Mottram [1948] Director; Susan Mottram [1947] Director; Paul Richard Schofield [1974] Sales Director

Jardins D'Eden Ltd
Incorporated: 27 December 2018
Registered Office: 2nd Floor, Hanover House, 30 Charlotte Street, Manchester, M1 4EX
Major Shareholder: Zeina Nazer
Officers: Zeina Nazer, Secretary; Zeina Nazer [1975] Director

Jarvis Cosmetic Developments Ltd.
Incorporated: 13 April 1978 *Employees:* 44
Previous: Peter Jarvis Cosmetic Developments Limited
Net Worth: £1,448,164 *Total Assets:* £2,257,317
Registered Office: 7-9 Hadleigh Business Park, Pond Hall Road, Hadleigh, Suffolk, IP7 5PW
Major Shareholder: Quentin Jarvis
Officers: Quentin Jarvis, Secretary/Director; Daphne Joy Jarvis [1934] Director; Peter Arthur Watson Jarvis [1931] Director/Chemist; Quentin Jarvis [1961] Director

Jean Christian Perfumes Limited
Incorporated: 12 September 1997
Net Worth: £143,800 *Total Assets:* £289,970
Registered Office: 202c Burcott Road, Avonmouth, Bristol, BS11 8AP
Major Shareholder: Carol Ann Coleman
Officers: Carol Ann Coleman, Secretary; Carol Ann Coleman [1948] Managing Director; Thomas Martin Coleman [1986] Director

JLP Cosmetics Ltd
Incorporated: 29 June 2016 *Employees:* 5
Net Worth: £44,453 *Total Assets:* £140,019
Registered Office: 58 Church Street, Louth, Lincs, LN11 9BY
Major Shareholder: Jasper Elliot Dicker
Officers: Jasper Elliot Dicker [1994] Director

Jogb Limited
Incorporated: 11 January 2016
Registered Office: 23 Derby Road, Cheam, Sutton, Surrey, SM1 2BL
Shareholder: James Raymond Stanton
Officers: Jo Glanville-Blackburn [1964] Director/Journalist; James Raymond Stanton [1963] Art Director

Jorum of Scotland Limited
Incorporated: 29 November 2018
Registered Office: 3-8 Rodney Street, Edinburgh, EH7 4EN
Major Shareholder: Euan David McCall
Officers: Euan David McCall [1989] Director/Perfumer, Entrepreneur

Jove London Ltd
Incorporated: 12 April 2016
Net Worth: £16,732 *Total Assets:* £19,128
Registered Office: Suite 188, 8 Shepherd Market, London, W1J 7JY
Major Shareholder: Tatiana Pankova
Officers: Tatiana Pankova [1985] Director [Russian]

JST Exports (UK) Ltd
Incorporated: 4 October 2018
Registered Office: Kemp House, 160 City Road, London, EC1V 2NX
Officers: Sunita Kapoor, Secretary; Sunita Kapoor [1963] Director/Beauty Therapist [Australian]

Jubilee Capital (UK) Ltd
Incorporated: 3 April 2017
Net Worth: £100 *Total Assets:* £100
Registered Office: 70 Devonshire Drive, Mickleover, Derby, DE3 9HD
Officers: Geoff Bye [1965] Director/Engineer/Chemist; John Lindsay Coote [1949] Director/International Financier [Australian]

Julie's Natural Health Ltd
Incorporated: 10 July 2017
Registered Office: 3F River House Business Centre, Castle Lane, Coleraine, Co Londonderry, BT51 3DR
Major Shareholder: Thomas Jones
Officers: Prof Thomas Jones [1966] Director

Juni Cosmetics Limited
Incorporated: 23 March 2018
Registered Office: Lovewell Blake LLP, The Gables, Old Market Street, Thetford, Norfolk, IP24 2EN
Shareholders: Madeleine White; Suzanne White; Kevin White
Officers: Kevin White [1964] Director; Madeleine White [1997] Director/Make Up Artist; Suzanne White [1962] Director

Just Skincare Limited
Incorporated: 9 January 2017
Registered Office: Cameron Rait Boxfield, 15 Knowle Road, Budleigh Salterton, Devon, EX9 6AR
Major Shareholder: Cameron Alexander Rait
Officers: Cameron Alexander Rait [1997] Director

JWO Beauty Limited
Incorporated: 9 December 2015 *Employees:* 1
Net Worth Deficit: £153,974 *Total Assets:* £67,061
Registered Office: 5a Bear Lane, London, SE1 0UH
Major Shareholder: Josephine Alice Wood
Officers: Josephine Alice Wood [1955] Director/Founder

K.K. Toiletries Limited
Incorporated: 16 June 1997 *Employees:* 19
Net Worth: £807,084 *Total Assets:* £954,436
Registered Office: One Bell Lane, Lewes, E Sussex, BN7 1JU
Parent: Area 16 Holdings Limited
Officers: Kenneth Derek Brownless [1967] Director/Manager; Timothy William Coates [1961] Director; Sharon Elizabeth Hindle [1971] Director

Kadiricosmetics Ltd
Incorporated: 2 August 2018
Registered Office: 53 Iverson Approach, Leeds, LS16 6NT
Major Shareholder: Amina Kadiri
Officers: Amina Kadiri [1999] Director/Student

Kaira Luchi Ltd
Incorporated: 15 December 2011
Registered Office: 16 Stelfox House, Penton Rise, London, WC1X 9EA
Major Shareholder: Kaosochi Ezigboh
Officers: Kaosochi Ezigboh [1988] Director

Kairn Holding Limited
Incorporated: 28 August 2018
Registered Office: 24 Junction Road, Bath, BA2 3NH
Shareholders: Derek Nairn Hood; Douglas Killick
Officers: Derek Nairn Hood [1965] Director/Master Bookbinder; Douglas Killick [1979] Director/Marketing Consultant

Kao (UK) Limited
Incorporated: 27 June 2002 *Employees:* 93
Net Worth: £19,323,000 *Total Assets:* £42,610,000
Registered Office: 21 Holborn Viaduct, London, EC1A 2DY
Officers: Edward Barham, Secretary; Edward Barham [1983] Director/Solicitor; Bjorn Erich [1970] Finance Director [Dutch]; Deborah Rix [1962] Director/General Manager; Joseph Bernard Workman [1962] Director [American]

Karaama Fragrances Ltd
Incorporated: 16 May 2017
Net Worth Deficit: £28,744 *Total Assets:* £145,319
Registered Office: Omega Accountants, 54 Lower Addiscombe Road, Croydon, Surrey, CR0 6AA
Major Shareholder: Runu Miah
Officers: Runu Miah [1973] Director

Karamat Collection Ltd
Incorporated: 28 September 2018
Registered Office: 71-75 Shelton Street, London, WC2H 9JQ
Officers: Zakaria Ahajiou [1988] Director [Belgian]

Karma Cosmetics Co Ltd
Incorporated: 7 January 2019
Registered Office: c/o Hillside, 55 Rectory Grove, Leigh on Sea, Essex, SS9 2HA
Major Shareholder: Jane Sharon Richards
Officers: Jane Sharon Richards [1987] Director

KD Trading (UK) Limited
Incorporated: 18 June 2014
Net Worth: £585,594 *Total Assets:* £670,729
Registered Office: 9 Stoughton Road, Oadby, Leicester, LE2 4DS
Shareholders: Kunal Dattani; Keval Dattani; Savan Dattani
Officers: Keval Dattani [1984] Director; Kunal Dattani [1988] Director; Savan Dattani [1993] Director

Kehal Ltd
Incorporated: 2 November 2018
Registered Office: Premier Business Centre, 47-49 Park Royal Road, London, NW10 7LQ
Major Shareholder: Abdulazeez Althefeeri
Officers: Abdulazeez Althefeeri [1979] Director [Kuwaiti]

Kensa Chemicals Limited
Incorporated: 11 December 1987
Registered Office: Unit 6a Redbrook Business Park, Wilthorpe Road, Barnsley, S Yorks, S75 1JF
Major Shareholder: Iain William McCallum
Officers: Iain William McCallum [1957] Managing Director

Khali Min Limited
Incorporated: 17 January 2019
Registered Office: 32 Cubitt Street, London, WC1X 0LR
Shareholders: Anna Vanessa Karlo; Jehan Marei
Officers: Anna Vanessa Karlo [1980] Director/Founder [American]; Jehan Marei [1977] Director/Founder [Egyptian]

Khushi Skincare Limited
Incorporated: 21 November 2017
Registered Office: 6 Sycamore Court, Leeds, LS8 2NY
Major Shareholder: Surinder Kaur Rall
Officers: Surinder Kaur Rall [1985] Director/Manager

Kingdom Scotland Limited
Incorporated: 26 February 2016
Net Worth: £2,070 *Total Assets:* £17,190
Registered Office: 15 Young Street, Edinburgh, EH2 4HU
Officers: Imogen Russon-Taylor [1970] Director

Kingsmill Cosmetic Preparations Limited
Incorporated: 27 June 1978
Net Worth: £100 *Total Assets:* £364
Registered Office: 7-9 Hadleigh Business Park, Pond Hall Road, Hadleigh, Suffolk, IP7 5PW
Parent: Jarvis Cosmetic Developments Ltd
Officers: Quentin Jarvis, Secretary/Director; Daphne Joy Jarvis [1934] Director/Secretary; Peter Arthur Watson Jarvis [1931] Director; Quentin Jarvis [1961] Director

Kinski Limited
Incorporated: 2 August 2011
Net Worth: £637 *Total Assets:* £165,901
Registered Office: 5-6 Underhill Street, London, NW1 7HS
Major Shareholder: Paul Douglas White
Officers: Paul Douglas White [1959] Director/Designer

The Top UK Perfume and Toilet Preparations Manufacturers

Kisens Ltd
Incorporated: 11 November 2016
Net Worth Deficit: £788 *Total Assets:* £1,701
Registered Office: 71-75 Shelton Street, Covent Garden, London, WC2H 9JQ
Shareholders: Kyriaki Drosou; Iraklis Tsekouras
Officers: Kyriaki Drosou [1984] Director/Musician [Greek]; Iraklis Tsekouras [1984] Director/Lead Software Developer [Greek]

Kisu Skincare Ltd
Incorporated: 15 October 2018
Registered Office: 98 St Denis Road, Birmingham, B29 4LU
Major Shareholder: Rachel Angharad Davies
Officers: Dr Rachel Angharad Davies [1973] Director/Medical Doctor

Ko. Essentials Ltd.
Incorporated: 26 February 2018
Registered Office: 161 Tinshill Lane, Leeds, LS16 6EE
Major Shareholder: Megan Landreth-Smith
Officers: Christine Gilland Robinson [1984] Director/Entrepreneur; Joseph Landreth-Smith [1990] Director/Entrepreneur; Megan Landreth-Smith [1991] Director/Entrepreneur; Naomi Joy Partridge [1984] Director/Entrepreneur; Thomas Michael Partridge [1981] Director/Entrepreneur

Thomas Kosmala Parfums Ltd
Incorporated: 17 April 2014
Net Worth Deficit: £15,363 *Total Assets:* £39,284
Registered Office: Suites 2 & 3, Marine Trade Centre, Lockside, Brighton Marina Village, Brighton, BN2 5HA
Shareholders: Andrew Roger Moss; Tomasz Kosmala
Officers: Tomasz Kosmala [1981] Director/Perfumer [Polish]

Koze Limited
Incorporated: 25 April 2018
Registered Office: 45 Lye Avenue, Birmingham, B32 3UE
Major Shareholder: Aime Moses Baransananiye
Officers: Aime Moses Baransananiye [1966] Director/General Manager [Burundian]

KPSS (UK) Limited
Incorporated: 27 February 1958 *Employees:* 98
Net Worth: £439,000 *Total Assets:* £14,330,000
Registered Office: 130 Shaftesbury Avenue, London, W1D 5EU
Parent: Kao Germany GmbH
Officers: Edward Barham, Secretary; Edward Barham [1983] Director/Solicitor; Bjorn Erich [1970] Finance Director [Dutch]; Mark Giannandrea [1972] Director/General Manager

Kropp & Hem Ltd
Incorporated: 21 May 2018
Registered Office: 44 Alexandra Park, Nottingham, NG3 4JD
Major Shareholder: Rebecca Louise Burgin
Officers: Rebecca Louise Burgin [1995] Director

Kylah K Skincare Ltd
Incorporated: 14 August 2017
Registered Office: 15 Old School Lane, Bristol, BS13 7SY
Major Shareholder: Chantel Latoya Broomfield
Officers: Chantel Latoya Broomfield [1991] Director

Kyoka Pro Ltd
Incorporated: 10 September 2018
Registered Office: 264 St Helens Road, Bolton, Lancs, BL3 3PZ
Major Shareholder: Jamila Jangaria
Officers: Jamila Jangaria [1979] Director/Beautician

L & A Natural Limited
Incorporated: 15 October 2018
Registered Office: 5 St Marys Road, Faversham, Kent, ME13 8EH
Shareholders: Asya Yaneva; Louisa Tidy
Officers: Asya Yaneva, Secretary; Louisa Tidy [1980] Director; Asya Yaneva [1981] Director

The L A Partnership Limited
Incorporated: 4 May 1995 *Employees:* 1
Net Worth Deficit: £4,782 *Total Assets:* £48
Registered Office: Unit 1 Cambridge House, Camboro Business Park, Oakington Road, Girton, Cambridge, CB3 0QH
Major Shareholder: Lala Akhter
Officers: Rahila Abid, Secretary; Dr Lalarukh Akhter [1957] Director

L'Ocean Limited
Incorporated: 27 February 2008
Net Worth Deficit: £55,712 *Total Assets:* £5,005
Registered Office: c/o Ozkan Accountants Ltd, Suite 12, 2nd Floor, Vantage Point, New England Road, Brighton, BN1 4GW
Major Shareholder: Poppy Emma Mosbacher
Officers: Janet Elizabeth Mosbacher, Secretary; Janet Elizabeth Mosbacher [1963] Director

L.A Life Limited
Incorporated: 3 April 2002
Registered Office: Unit 1 Cambridge House, Camboro Business Park, Oakington Road, Girton, Cambridge, CB3 0QH
Major Shareholder: Lala Akhter
Officers: Rahila Abid, Secretary; Dr Lalarukh Akhter [1957] Managing Director

L.E.C.(L'pool) Limited
Incorporated: 27 April 1976 *Employees:* 59
Net Worth: £3,913,771 *Total Assets:* £5,224,663
Registered Office: Lec House, Alfred Street, off Picton Road, Liverpool, L15 4LH
Major Shareholder: Laurence John Clare
Officers: Lily May Blackhurst, Secretary; Lily May Blackhurst [1946] Director/Company Secretary; Laurence John Clare [1937] Director; Stephen Charles Daly [1943] Director; Deborah Diane Dwyer [1972] Director/Administration Manager; Mark Paul Johnson [1979] Director/Production Manager

La Maison Hedonique Limited
Incorporated: 7 February 2017 *Employees:* 1
Net Worth Deficit: £17,703 *Total Assets:* £9,167
Registered Office: 27 Old Gloucester Street, London, WC1N 3AX
Major Shareholder: Lucy Oldham
Officers: Lucy Oldham [1970] Director/Actor

La Mu London Limited
Incorporated: 9 January 2019
Registered Office: 71-75 Shelton Street, Covent Garden, London, WC2H 9JQ
Major Shareholder: Mariia Uvarova
Officers: Mariia Uvarova [1990] Director/Management [Russian]

La Parfumerie Anglaise Limited
Incorporated: 13 June 2016
Net Worth: £1,957 *Total Assets:* £2,421
Registered Office: 32 Paderborn Court, Bolton, Lancs, BL1 4TX
Officers: Lynn Cooper [1958] Director

La Riche Limited
Incorporated: 6 February 1981 *Employees:* 12
Net Worth: £581,526 *Total Assets:* £1,470,524
Registered Office: 10 Towerfield Close, Shoeburyness, Southend on Sea, Essex, SS3 9QP
Major Shareholder: Michael John Sambrook
Officers: Roy David Millington, Secretary; Roy David Millington [1973] Director; Celia Sambrook [1956] Director; Michael John Sambrook [1952] Director

La-Eva Limited
Incorporated: 17 September 2016
Net Worth Deficit: £68,921 *Total Assets:* £13,625
Registered Office: 12a Fleet Business Park, Sandy Lane, Church Crookham, Fleet, Hants, GU52 8BF
Officers: Dr Louisa Canham [1979] Director/Cosmetics Development; Tara Gail Donovan [1967] Director/Consultant

Laboratory Facilities Limited
Incorporated: 28 October 1943 *Employees:* 3
Net Worth: £531,615 *Total Assets:* £538,890
Registered Office: 79 Marine Gate Mansions, Promenade, Southport, Merseyside, PR9 0EF
Shareholder: Christopher Michael Holmes
Officers: Catherine Holmes [1947] Director; Christopher Michael Holmes [1945] Director; Patricia Ann Holmes [1943] Director/Secretary Typist

Ladd Cosmetics Ltd
Incorporated: 31 August 2017
Registered Office: 27 Old Gloucester Street, London, WC1N 3AX
Major Shareholder: Mark Barton
Officers: Mark Barton [1986] Director/Office Administrator

Lakeland Fragrances Limited
Incorporated: 11 December 1995
Net Worth: £8,526 *Total Assets:* £23,101
Registered Office: Oak Holme, Beemire Lane, Birthwaite Road, Windermere, Cumbria, LA23 1DW
Shareholders: Anthony Kingsley Young; Valerie Elizabeth Young
Officers: Anthony Kingsley Young, Secretary; Anthony Kingsley Young [1941] Director; Valerie Elizabeth Young [1950] Director

Lamer & Ava Healthcare Ltd
Incorporated: 14 September 2017
Registered Office: Unit 8d, Office 10, Kilroot Business Park, Carrickfergus, Co Antrim, BT38 7PR
Parent: Ava Corporations Ltd
Officers: Collin Grayson [1970] Director/Businessman

Lana-Rae Ltd Ltd
Incorporated: 23 June 2014
Previous: Lana-Rae Ltd
Registered Office: 3rd Floor, 207 Regent Street, London, W1B 3HH
Officers: Raechel Muhammad, Secretary; Raechel Muhammad [1989] Director/Student

Lathersmith Ltd
Incorporated: 31 January 2013
Net Worth: £929 *Total Assets:* £929
Registered Office: 129 Dairsie Road, London, SE9 1XL
Officers: Aiste Kekiene [1982] Director/Cosmetics [Lithuanian]

Thomas Laurie Naturals Limited
Incorporated: 20 June 2017
Net Worth Deficit: £5,451 *Total Assets:* £2,692
Registered Office: 23 Woodside Place, Bridgend, Linlithgow, W Lothian, EH49 6PF
Major Shareholder: Vicki Helen Macpherson
Officers: Vicki Helen Macpherson [1976] Director/Housewife

Legendes Products Ltd
Incorporated: 11 May 2004
Net Worth: £10,496 *Total Assets:* £20,397
Registered Office: 43 Townsend Way, Folksworth, Peterborough, Cambs, PE7 3TU
Major Shareholder: Kevin Eric Arnold
Officers: Dr Kevin Eric Arnold [1957] Director/Industrial Chemist

Lese & Lista Ltd
Incorporated: 19 November 2018
Registered Office: 2nd Floor, College House, 17 King Edwards Road, Ruislip, Middlesex, HA4 7AE
Major Shareholder: Randy Lindo Cornwall
Officers: Randy Cornwall, Secretary; Randy Lindo Cornwall [1977] Director/Entrepreneur

Nadeane Letisha Ltd
Incorporated: 17 November 2015 *Employees:* 1
Net Worth Deficit: £4,859 *Total Assets:* £263
Registered Office: White House, Wollaton Street, Nottingham, NG1 5GF
Major Shareholder: Nadeane McDonald
Officers: Nadeane McDonald [1987] Director

Leum Skin Care Ltd
Incorporated: 7 April 2014
Net Worth Deficit: £114 *Total Assets:* £35
Registered Office: 20-22 Wenlock Road, London, N1 7GU
Major Shareholder: Ieva Dos Santos Rita de Jesus
Officers: Ieva Dos Santos Rita de Jesus [1975] Director [Latvian]

Leviticus 19:27 Beard Company Limited
Incorporated: 4 January 2018
Registered Office: 16 Beatrice Street, Kempston, Bedford, MK42 8AE
Officers: Damien Kurt Scott Anderson, Secretary; Damien Kurt Scott Anderson [1981] Director

Lex Roris Ltd
Incorporated: 15 August 2018
Registered Office: Lex Roris LMT, P O Box 72396, London, SW18 9PW
Shareholders: Alexis Rosalia von Pfefer; Carlos Augusto Romero
Officers: Alexis Rosalia Von Pfefer [1988] Director

Libhairation Ltd
Incorporated: 21 January 2019
Registered Office: 20-22 Wenlock Road, London, N1 7GU
Major Shareholder: Kimberleen Duncan-Lajewski
Officers: Kimberleen Duncan-Lajewski [1985] Director/General Sales Advisor

Lick Labs Limited
Incorporated: 2 October 2018
Registered Office: 45 Mount Ambrose, Redruth, Cornwall, TR15 1NX
Shareholders: Ross Anthony Rosewarne; Levi Ripley
Officers: Levi Ripley [1987] Founder/Director; Ross Anthony Rosewarne [1986] Managing Director

Lily Her Limited
Incorporated: 19 May 2017
Registered Office: Fairview, Park Terrace, Nottingham, NG1 5DN
Major Shareholder: Lili He
Officers: Lili HE [1974] Managing Director

Christian Lincoln Enterprise Limited
Incorporated: 23 June 2015
Net Worth: £86,842 *Total Assets:* £87,042
Registered Office: 32 Schooner Way, Cardiff, CF10 4EQ
Major Shareholder: Adebimpe Titilope Lincoln
Officers: Doctor Adebimpe Titilope Lincoln [1979] Director/Academic

Linden and Lime Limited
Incorporated: 18 December 2018
Registered Office: Salisbury House, Station Road, Cambridge, CB1 2LA
Parent: L3 Point Limited
Officers: Paul Nigel Robert Bennett [1959] Director; Dr Mukund Unavane [1972] Director

Lip Sync Beauty Limited
Incorporated: 30 March 2016
Net Worth: £100 *Total Assets:* £100
Registered Office: Blue House Farm Office, Brentwood Road, West Horndon, Essex, CM13 3LX
Major Shareholder: Colin Meredith Barthelmy
Officers: Colin Meredith Barthelmy [1961] Director/Product Designer

Little Green Beehive Ltd
Incorporated: 23 April 2018
Registered Office: 7 Potts Close, Kenilworth, Warwicks, CV8 2SD
Shareholders: Josephine Cassell; Nikki Lee
Officers: Dr Josephine Cassell [1987] Director/Co-Founder; Dr Nikki Lee [1989] Director/Co-Founder [Canadian]

Little House of Wild Ltd
Incorporated: 2 January 2019
Registered Office: Winwick Hall, Winwick, Northampton, NN6 7PD
Officers: Bruce Green, Secretary; Bruce Green [1944] Director/Retired

Littlemore Candle Company Limited
Incorporated: 9 February 2018
Registered Office: 265 Cowley Road, Oxford, OX4 1XQ
Major Shareholder: Molly Stevenson
Officers: Molly Stevenson [1991] Director/Candle Maker/Barmaid

Liza.B. Glow Actives Ltd
Incorporated: 4 December 2018
Registered Office: Auldton Farm, Millburn Road, Ashgill, Larkhall, S Lanarks, ML9 3BH
Major Shareholder: Elizabeth Brown
Officers: Elizabeth Brown [1964] Director/Administrator

LJSP Ltd
Incorporated: 23 August 2016
Net Worth: £1,000 *Total Assets:* £1,000
Registered Office: First Floor, 85 Great Portland Street, London, W1W 7LT
Major Shareholder: Mark Boulos
Officers: Mark Boulos [1980] Director; Jonathan Sumner [1980] Director; Robert Bird Sumner [1982] Director

Lobal Ltd
Incorporated: 11 November 2013
Net Worth Deficit: £223,291 *Total Assets:* £66,354
Registered Office: c/o Wilkins Kennedy LLP, Anglo House, Bell Lane Office Village, Bell Lane, Amersham, Bucks, HP6 6FA
Major Shareholder: Sian Elizabeth Ellingworth-Hutley
Officers: Sian Elizabeth Ellingworth - Hutley [1971] Business Development Director

Lofty Gardens Ltd
Incorporated: 9 October 2018
Registered Office: 1st Floor, Block C, The Wharf, Manchester Road, Burnley, Lancs, BB11 1JG
Major Shareholder: Muhammad Mohsin Khan
Officers: Muhammad Mohsin Khan [1989] Director [Pakistani]

Lola's Apothecary Ltd
Incorporated: 11 November 2011
Net Worth Deficit: £44,520 *Total Assets:* £26,210
Registered Office: Colleton Manor, Colleton, Chulmleigh, Devon, EX18 7JS
Major Shareholder: Dominic Beavis Blake Phillips
Officers: Dominic Beavis Blake Phillips [1988] Director/Accountant; Grania Tiffany Phillips [1953] Director/Farmer; Simon Blake Phillips [1949] Director/Farmer

London Goddess Limited
Incorporated: 5 June 2017
Registered Office: 40 Boreham Holt, Elstree, Borehamwood, Herts, WD6 3QJ
Major Shareholder: Jennifer Douglas
Officers: Jennifer Douglas [1981] Director

Lovefro Ltd.
Incorporated: 7 October 2011
Net Worth: £100 *Total Assets:* £100
Registered Office: 9 Langlodge Road, Holbrook, Coventry, Warwicks, CV6 4EG
Major Shareholder: Jacqueline Annetta Derby
Officers: Jacqueline Annetta Laing [1970] Director

LTSC Ltd
Incorporated: 6 February 2018
Registered Office: 40 Albert Place, Cheltenham, Glos, GL52 2JX
Shareholders: Leigh Thompson; Steven Crumblehulme
Officers: Steven John Crumblehulme [1980] Director/Reflexologist; Leigh Thompson [1976] Director/Contractor

LU Aromatherapy Ltd
Incorporated: 20 February 2018
Registered Office: 2 Whinberry Drive, Kirkby, Merseyside, L32 9BA
Officers: Lucrecia Silvana Bianchi [1976] Director [Italian]; Eliseo Bustamante [1996] Director [Italian]

Lucayan Limited
Incorporated: 16 May 2017
Registered Office: 174 Rochfords Gardens, Slough, Berks, SL2 5XL
Officers: Meranda-Jade Peart [1992] Director

Lucidlure Ltd
Incorporated: 3 December 2015
Net Worth Deficit: £1,430 *Total Assets:* £1,160
Registered Office: Unit 1-2 Little Broom Street, Birmingham, B12 0EU
Officers: Sahdia Akhtar [1977] Director/Salesman

Lucidly Ltd
Incorporated: 30 December 2016
Registered Office: 33 Blairatholl Avenue, Glasgow, G11 7QJ
Major Shareholder: Reemah Shanab
Officers: Reemah Shanab [1992] Director

Lukas Products Limited
Incorporated: 10 January 2018
Registered Office: Rollsbridge House, Ide Lane, Exeter, Devon, EX2 9QU
Shareholder: Tobias Julian Blatchford-Tagg
Officers: Tobias Julian Blatchford-Tagg [1984] Director; Luke Stephen James Chitty [1987] Director/Barber; Stuart Paul Jolley [1986] Director; Harry William Jones [1991] Director

Lum Lifestyle Ltd.
Incorporated: 20 March 2018
Registered Office: 15 The Hamlet, Champion Hill, London, SE5 8AW
Officers: Anil Kumar Panda [1978] Director

Lumine Beauty Ltd
Incorporated: 13 September 2018
Registered Office: 50 Haines House, The Residence, 10 Charles Clowes Walk, London, SW11 7AH
Major Shareholder: Aie Chen
Officers: Aie Chen [1973] Director [Chinese]

Lush Ltd.
Incorporated: 17 June 1994 *Employees:* 282
Net Worth: £59,083,000 *Total Assets:* £133,899,000
Registered Office: 29 High Street, Poole, Dorset, BH15 1AB
Parent: Lush Cosmetics Limited
Officers: Karl Joseph Bygrave, Secretary; Rowena Jaqueline Bird [1959] Director/Retail Consultant; Karl Joseph Bygrave [1962] Director/Manager; Jack Constantine [1984] Director; Margaret Joan Constantine [1953] Director/Inventor; Mark Constantine [1952] Director; Hilary Anita Jones [1962] Director; Simon George Nicholls [1963] Director

Lush Manufacturing Limited
Incorporated: 5 March 1997 *Employees:* 1,271
Net Worth: £46,751,000 *Total Assets:* £53,155,000
Registered Office: 29 High Street, Poole, Dorset, BH15 1AB
Parent: Lush Limited
Officers: Karl Joseph Bygrave, Secretary; Margaret Joan Constantine [1953] Director/Inventor; David Jason Muller [1970] Director; Elizabeth Kate Smith [1976] Director/Manager

Luxurious Personal Care Ltd
Incorporated: 19 February 2019
Registered Office: 55 High Street, Hoddesdon, Herts, EN11 8TQ
Major Shareholder: James Shipton
Officers: James Shipton, Secretary; Bradley John Shipton [1995] Director; James Shipton [1993] Director

Luxury Personal Care Ltd
Incorporated: 15 February 2019
Registered Office: Kemp House, 160 City Road, London, EC1V 2NX
Major Shareholder: James Shipton
Officers: James Shipton, Secretary; Brad Shipton [1995] Director/Buyer; James Shipton [1993] Director/Buyer

M.88 Fragrances Ltd
Incorporated: 16 October 2017
Registered Office: Cirrus Building, Office 129, 6 International Avenue, A B Z Business Park, Dyce, Aberdeen, AB21 0BH
Major Shareholder: Daniel Labbe
Officers: Daniel Labbe [1988] Director [German]

M.C Skin Truth Ltd
Incorporated: 17 July 2015
Registered Office: 35 Ballards Lane, London, N3 1XW
Shareholders: Michelle Collins; Simon Paul Frost
Officers: Michelle Collins [1962] Director

MAC Professional Haircare Limited
Incorporated: 21 January 2008 *Employees:* 6
Net Worth: £355,550 *Total Assets:* £643,953
Registered Office: 34 Harbet Road, London, N18 3HT
Major Shareholder: Mehmet Ali Cetin
Officers: Mehmet Ali Cetin, Secretary; Esra Cetin [1986] Director; Ilhan Cetin [1984] Director

Macks Wax Ltd
Incorporated: 18 July 2018
Registered Office: Tresco, 3 Trevone Crescent, St Austell, Cornwall, PL25 5EB
Major Shareholder: Ruth Elizabeth McCoulough
Officers: Ruth Elizabeth McCoulough [1988] Director/Barmaid

Madalyn and Rose Ltd
Incorporated: 13 July 2015
Net Worth Deficit: £3,713 *Total Assets:* £599
Registered Office: 21 Dowanhill Road, London, SE6 1SU
Major Shareholder: Natalee Nelson
Officers: Natalee Nelson [1991] Director

Madre Skincare Limited
Incorporated: 13 April 2011
Net Worth Deficit: £1,270 *Total Assets:* £2,030
Registered Office: 98 Averil Road, Leicester, LE5 2DB
Major Shareholder: Ravinder Kandohla
Officers: Ravinder Kandohla [1976] Director

Magma London Ltd
Incorporated: 23 December 2014
Net Worth: £3,774 *Total Assets:* £26,567
Registered Office: 83 George Road, New Malden, Surrey, KT3 6BT
Officers: Kareem Rhouila [1980] Director/Perfumer

Magpie's Ocean Ltd
Incorporated: 19 September 2018
Registered Office: 34 Wain Street, Stoke on Trent, Staffs, ST6 4ES
Shareholders: Samantha Ophelia Chinnery; Eleanor Lunaria Hetherington
Officers: Samantha Ophelia Chinnery [1980] Director/Manufacturer; Eleanor Lunaria Hetherington [1992] Director/Manufacturer

Maison Ex Nihilo UK Limited
Incorporated: 21 August 2014 *Employees:* 6
Net Worth Deficit: £163,426 *Total Assets:* £294,310
Registered Office: 2nd Floor, Regis House, 45 King William Street, London, EC4R 9AN
Shareholder: Umiuchi Sas
Officers: Sylvie Loday [1977] Director/Business Owner [French]; Olivier Royere [1978] Director/Business Owner [Swedish]

Majestic Company London Limited
Incorporated: 4 July 2018
Registered Office: Ground Floor, Anchorage House, 2 Clove Crescent, East India Dock, London, E14 2BE
Major Shareholder: Hamza Mursaleen
Officers: Hamza Mursaleen [1993] Director/Manager

Make-Up Art Cosmetics (U.K.) Limited
Incorporated: 29 January 1993
Registered Office: One Fitzroy, 6 Mortimer Street, London, W1T 3JJ
Parent: The Estee Lauder Companies Inc.,
Officers: Edward Robert Hughes, Secretary; Sara Ellen Moss, Secretary/Lawyer [American]; Spencer Gary Smul, Secretary; Alison Claire Day [1971] Finance Director; Sara Ellen Moss [1946] Director/Lawyer [American]; Tracey Thomas Travis [1962] Director/Executive Vice President and CFO [American]

Making Scents Ltd
Incorporated: 21 August 2017
Registered Office: Thirtleby House, High Street, Eastrington, Goole, E Yorks, DN14 7PH
Officers: Joanne Winters [1973] Director

Mama Mio Distribution Limited
Incorporated: 28 July 2011
Registered Office: 5th Floor, Voyager House, Chicago Avenue, Manchester Airport, Manchester, M90 3DQ
Parent: Mama Mio Limited
Officers: James Patrick Pochin, Secretary; John Andrew Gallemore [1969] Director; Paul Jonathan Gedman [1981] Director/Retailer

Man Mask Ltd
Incorporated: 12 December 2018
Registered Office: 1 Park Farm Court, Clapham, Bedford, MK41 6EF
Shareholders: Benjamin Gibbs; Mark Girven
Officers: Benjamin Gibbs [1980] Director/Sales; Mark Girven [1988] Director/Sales

Man Mountain Beard Care Ltd
Incorporated: 4 July 2017
Registered Office: 39 Ferry View, Thorngumbald, Hull, HU12 9GB
Major Shareholder: Vincent Patrick Glen McAllister
Officers: Vincent Patrick Glen McAllister [1983] Director

The Manhattan Group Ltd.
Incorporated: 19 June 2017
Registered Office: The White House, 5 Staines Green, Hertford, SG14 2LN
Major Shareholder: Zarina Zarina Morris
Officers: Zarina Zarina Morris [1989] Director

Victoria March Skincare Ltd
Incorporated: 2 October 2018
Registered Office: 129 Corporation Road, Workington, Cumbria, CA14 2PW
Major Shareholder: Victoria McTiernan
Officers: Victoria McTiernan [1979] Director/Civil Servant

Maribella London Limited
Incorporated: 31 October 2017
Registered Office: 11 Gateway, Walworth Road, London, SE17 3HQ
Major Shareholder: Godman Usman
Officers: Godman Usman [1986] Director/Banker

Marine Beauty Care Limited
Incorporated: 2 April 2001
Net Worth Deficit: £46,205 *Total Assets:* £14,255
Registered Office: 155 The Ryde, Old Hatfield, Herts, AL9 5DP
Major Shareholder: Kerstin Birgit Holman-Schmidt
Officers: Kerstin Birgit Holman-Schmidt [1953] Director [German]

Marinical Limited
Incorporated: 9 January 2018
Registered Office: 4 Haxton House, Bothwell, S Lanarks, G71 8DR
Major Shareholder: Donna Marie Tierney
Officers: Donna Marie Tierney [1982] Director/Chief Executive

Marsh Organics Limited
Incorporated: 18 July 2017
Registered Office: Mill House, Mill Lane, Irby-in-the-Marsh, Skegness, Lincs, PE24 5BB
Major Shareholder: Marianne Jennifer Cowdery
Officers: Marianne Jennifer Cowdery [1966] Director

Mary Jean Limited
Incorporated: 25 November 2008
Net Worth Deficit: £7,579 *Total Assets:* £832
Registered Office: Whincroft Braehead, Orton, Fochabers, Moray, IV32 7QH
Shareholders: Leslie Thomas Quinn; Elizabeth Quinn
Officers: Elizabeth Quinn [1954] Director; Leslie Thomas Quinn [1972] Director

Maskalin Ltd
Incorporated: 15 August 2017
Registered Office: Maskalin, Riverpark Road, Manchester, M40 2XP
Major Shareholder: Stephen Neale
Officers: Stephen Neale [1992] Director

Maskologist Ltd
Incorporated: 5 June 2018
Registered Office: Kemp House, 160 City Road, London, EC1V 2NX
Major Shareholder: Sam Nouri
Officers: Sam Nouri, Secretary; Sam Nouri [1993] Director [Iranian]

Mast - Art Group Limited
Incorporated: 13 December 2018
Registered Office: 17 Green Lanes, London, N16 9BS
Shareholder: Umran Aysan
Officers: Umran Aysan [1976] Director [Turkish]

Mata Labs Cosmetics Ltd
Incorporated: 4 July 2018
Registered Office: 17 Mead Plat, Stonebridge, London, NW10 0PD
Major Shareholder: Mata Marielle Mumvadi
Officers: Mata Marielle Mumvadi [1998] Director/Artist

Mavala (U.K.) Limited
Incorporated: 19 June 1970 *Employees:* 22
Net Worth: £582,874 *Total Assets:* £2,004,162
Registered Office: 5th Floor, 6 St Andrew Street, London, EC4A 3AE
Major Shareholder: Hans August Maute
Officers: Jonathan Hodge [1970] Managing Director; Hans August Maute [1938] Director [Swiss]

Christina May Limited
Incorporated: 29 September 2000 *Employees:* 31
Net Worth: £364,412 *Total Assets:* £964,391
Registered Office: Rotherdale, Fir Toll Road, Mayfield, E Sussex, TN20 6NB
Parent: Stompee Holdings Limited
Officers: Christina Juliet Butts, Secretary; Christina Juliet Butts [1949] Director/Company Secretary; Courtenay Arthur Robert Butts [1951] Director; Oliver Courtenay Richard Butts [1985] Director

Mayen Velvaere Limited
Incorporated: 25 March 2016
Previous: Mayen Botanicals TIB Limited
Net Worth: £1 *Total Assets:* £1
Registered Office: 4th Floor, 18 St Cross Street, London, EC1N 8UN
Major Shareholder: Stephanie Efefiong Effiom
Officers: Stephanie Efefiong Effiom [1992] Managing Director

Mayfair Perfumes Limited
Incorporated: 15 January 1999
Net Worth: £314,688 *Total Assets:* £326,083
Registered Office: Amertrans Park, Bushey Mill Lane, Watford, Herts, WD24 7JG
Parent: Shaneel Enterprises Ltd
Officers: Hitesh Bhogilal Mehta, Secretary; Dilesh Bhogilal Mehta [1960] Director; Hitesh Bhogilal Mehta [1956] Director/Secretary

Mayla Skincare Ltd
Incorporated: 10 December 2018
Registered Office: 14 Bishop Ramsey Close, Ruislip, Middlesex, HA4 8GY
Major Shareholder: Karen Elsbeth Helpap
Officers: Karen Elsbeth Helpap [1967] Director [German]

Mbikudi Ltd
Incorporated: 29 March 2016
Net Worth: £6,515 *Total Assets:* £9,015
Registered Office: 272 Bath Street, Glasgow, G2 4JR
Officers: Hermine Makangu, Secretary; Natalie Cita [1980] Director/Administrator; Sara Ntumba Kalukenda [1991] Director/Manager [Congolese]; Hermine Makangu [1989] Director

Robert McBride Ltd
Incorporated: 9 March 1927 *Employees:* 1,114
Net Worth: £4,536,000 *Total Assets:* £170,578,000
Registered Office: Middleton Way, Middleton, Manchester, M24 4DP
Shareholders: McBride PLC; McBride Holdings Limited
Officers: Carol Williams, Secretary; David Thomas Rattigan [1969] Director/Accountant; Christopher Ian Charles Smith [1964] Director/Accountant; Rik Jean Pierre Dora Albert de Vos [1960] Director [Belgian]

McCallum Manufacturing Limited
Incorporated: 10 December 1987 *Employees:* 10
Net Worth: £452,066 *Total Assets:* £636,003
Registered Office: 6a Redbrook Business Park, Wilthorpe Road, Barnsley, S Yorks, S75 1JF
Major Shareholder: Iain William McCallum
Officers: Iain William McCallum [1957] Director/Chemist

Meadow Farm Friends Ltd
Incorporated: 14 July 2014
Registered Office: Meadow Cottage, 23 Church Road, Sparkford, Somerset, BA22 7JN
Major Shareholder: Verity Kate Bracher
Officers: Verity Kate Bracher [1975] Director

Mechmark Ltd
Incorporated: 14 April 2015
Net Worth: £18,525 *Total Assets:* £23,833
Registered Office: 70 Aberford Drive, Houghton-le-Spring, Co Durham, DH4 4ZH
Shareholders: Peter Spencer; Julie Spencer
Officers: Peter Spencer [1962] Director

Meek and Mild Essentials Ltd
Incorporated: 21 February 2019
Registered Office: Kemp House, 160 City Road, London, EC1V 2NX
Major Shareholder: Samara Allan
Officers: Samara Allan, Secretary; Samara Allan [1990] Director

Meiyume (UK) Limited
Incorporated: 15 June 1950 *Employees:* 646
Previous: LF Beauty (UK) Limited
Net Worth: £28,370,000 *Total Assets:* £75,902,000
Registered Office: Aintree Avenue, White Horse Business Park, Trowbridge, Wilts, BA14 0XB
Parent: Lornamead Group Limited
Officers: Stephanie Little [1964] Director/VP HR; Gerard Jan Raymond [1957] Director [Australian]; Robert Adrian Sharpe [1956] Director; Paul Victor Taylor [1960] Director; Cheang Chin Wooi [1967] Director [Malaysian]

Mibelle Ltd
Incorporated: 4 November 2005 *Employees:* 194
Net Worth: £10,323,000 *Total Assets:* £24,631,000
Registered Office: Units 3-5 City Link Industrial Park, Phoenix Way, Tyersal, Bradford, W Yorks, BD4 8JP
Parent: Mibelle AG
Officers: Amanda Frances Louise Caldwell, Secretary; Amanda Frances Louise Caldwell [1971] Director/Chartered Accountant; Gary Brian Clarke [1968] Commercial Director; Massimiliano Costantini [1970] Commercial Director; Gregoire Filiatre [1976] Director/Chartered Accountant [French]; Walter Cornelio Huber [1957] Director [Swiss]; Dr Luigi Pedrocchi [1959] Director [Swiss]; Andrew Martin Sharp [1968] Operations Director

Doris Michaels Cosmetics Ltd
Incorporated: 18 November 2003 *Employees:* 1
Net Worth: £118,791 *Total Assets:* £148,860
Registered Office: 2 Exeter House, Beaufort Court, Sir Thomas Longley Road, Rochester, Kent, ME2 4FE
Major Shareholder: Doris Mary Edema Michaels
Officers: Doris Mary Edema Michaels, Secretary; Doris Mary Edema Michaels [1963] Director/Sales Executive

Lyn Michel Limited
Incorporated: 5 December 2014 *Employees:* 3
Net Worth: £3,515 *Total Assets:* £162,924
Registered Office: 46 Elsworthy Road, London, NW3 3BU
Shareholders: Christophe Francois Henri Michel; Carolyn Harris
Officers: Carolyn Harris [1968] Director/Perfumer; Christophe Francois Henri Michel [1972] Director [French]

Midha Limited
Incorporated: 1 August 2002
Net Worth: £11,184 *Total Assets:* £12,139
Registered Office: 461 Bradford Road, Pudsey, Leeds, LS28 8ED
Shareholders: Jatinder Midha; Baljit Singh
Officers: Baljit Arora Singh, Secretary; Jatinder Midha [1981] Director; Baljit Arora Singh [1958] Director

Midnight Apothecary Limited
Incorporated: 10 January 2017
Registered Office: Flat 8, 241-243 Hackney Road, London, E2 8NA
Major Shareholder: Simona Auteri
Officers: Simona Auteri [1985] Director [Italian]

Miller Harris Limited
Incorporated: 28 April 1992 *Employees:* 29
Net Worth Deficit: £9,158,432 *Total Assets:* £3,230,946
Registered Office: 116 Commercial Street, London, E1 6NF
Officers: David Belhassen [1970] Director/Investor [French]; Eytan Hanouna [1972] Director/Investor [French]; Tracey Huggett [1971] Director; Miles Stanley Clewley Johnson [1963] Director; Christophe Francois Henri Michel [1972] Director [French]; Sarah Rotheram [1973] Director; Ing-Nan Nancy Shen [1966] Director/Investor [American]

Millicent and Snob Limited
Incorporated: 15 May 2017
Registered Office: 8 Joyce Avenue, Enfield, London, N18 2TP
Major Shareholder: Philip Royer
Officers: Philip Royer [1963] Director

Milo and James Limited
Incorporated: 5 October 2017
Registered Office: 29 Mount Drive, Park Street, St Albans, Herts, AL2 2NP
Shareholders: Ross MacDonald; Anna Louise Howard-Macdonald
Officers: Anna Louise Howard-Macdonald [1979] Director/Financial Consultant; Ross MacDonald [1979] Director/IT Consultant

Mint Julip Ltd
Incorporated: 21 January 2019
Registered Office: XL Business Solutions, Catcraig Quarry, Craigie, Kilmarnock, E Ayrshire, KA1 5NB
Major Shareholder: Sheila Joyce Steele
Officers: Sheila Joyce Steele [1950] Director

Missy D Collection Limited
Incorporated: 27 February 2019
Registered Office: 297 Alwold Road, Birmingham, B29 5JH
Shareholders: Nichola Delita Donald; Shanay Talia Dixon
Officers: Nichola Delita Donald [1978] Director/Learning Support Assistant

Mitchell and Peach Limited
Incorporated: 18 June 2010 *Employees:* 1
Net Worth: £21,606 *Total Assets:* £320,669
Registered Office: Foxbury Farm, Stone Street, Sevenoaks, Kent, TN15 0LW
Major Shareholder: Jonathan Dominic Mitchell
Officers: Jonathan Dominic Mitchell [1975] Director/Magazine Editor

Mitchell London Limited
Incorporated: 11 April 2018
Registered Office: 30 Penrith Road, Cheltenham, Glos, GL51 3QB
Major Shareholder: Carrie Mitchell
Officers: Carrie Mitchell [1980] Director

MK Design & Art Direction Ltd
Incorporated: 2 May 2017
Net Worth Deficit: £3,931 *Total Assets:* £770
Registered Office: 90a Farleigh Road, London, N16 7TQ
Major Shareholder: Marina Kozlova
Officers: Marina Kozlova [1983] Director [German]

MLC Parfum & Oudh Ltd
Incorporated: 1 October 2018
Registered Office: 5 Loxley Garden, Burnley, Lancs, BB12 6PW
Major Shareholder: Chanel Leak
Officers: Malcolm Allan Leak [1970] Director/Ex Professional Basketball Player [American]

Mob Fragrances Ltd.
Incorporated: 4 January 2019
Registered Office: 9 Silesia Buildings, London, E8 3PX
Major Shareholder: Paul William John Martin
Officers: Paul William John Martin [1990] Director/Entrepreneur

The Model Handmade Limited
Incorporated: 12 June 2017 *Employees:* 2
Net Worth Deficit: £21,283 *Total Assets:* £1,778
Registered Office: 5 Technology Park, Colindeep Lane, Colindale, London, NW9 6BX
Shareholders: Harley Collins; Alexandra Collins
Officers: Harley Collins, Secretary; Alexandra Collins [1989] Director/Model/Actor/Author [Australian]; Harley Collins [1982] Director/Local Government Manager

Modernista London Limited
Incorporated: 14 January 2019
Registered Office: Yew Tree House, Lewes Road, Forest Row, E Sussex, RH18 5AA
Shareholders: Christine Masters; John Edward Masters
Officers: Christine Masters [1960] Director; John Edward Masters [1956] Director

Molecula Ltd
Incorporated: 5 December 2017
Registered Office: 20-22 Wenlock Road, London, N1 7GU
Major Shareholder: Martina Dragicevic
Officers: Danijel Palic, Secretary; Martina Dragicevic [1975] Director [Croatian]

Molton Brown Limited
Incorporated: 21 August 1989 *Employees:* 737
Net Worth: £33,251,000 *Total Assets:* £55,077,000
Registered Office: 130 Shaftesbury Avenue, London, W1D 5EU
Parent: Kao Corporation
Officers: Graham John Edgerton, Secretary; Eric Anthonius Brockhus [1964] Director/President Consumer Products [Dutch]; Graham John Edgerton [1961] Finance Director; Mark Johnson [1973] Director/President [American]; Yoshihiro Murakami [1963] Director/Chairman [Japanese]

Susan Molyneux Cosmetics Limited
Incorporated: 4 November 1988 *Employees:* 19
Net Worth: £814,855 *Total Assets:* £1,220,875
Registered Office: Windsor House, Bayshill Road, Cheltenham, Glos, GL50 3AT
Parent: Lavender Cosmetics Limited
Officers: Laurent Van Bekkum, Secretary/Director [Dutch]; Laurent Van Bekkum [1973] Director [Dutch]

Mono Naturoils Ltd
Incorporated: 29 March 2016
Net Worth Deficit: £3,240 *Total Assets:* £4,660
Registered Office: Cobweb Cottage, Weaverhead Close, Thaxted, Essex, CM6 2PP
Shareholders: Tracy Michelle Goodson; Kevin Joseph Goodson
Officers: Kevin Joseph Goodson [1974] Art Director; Tracy Goodson [1975] Creative Director [Canadian]

Monreale Limited
Incorporated: 19 September 2016
Registered Office: 393 Lordship Lane, London, N17 6AE
Major Shareholder: Thomas Tsavdaridis
Officers: Thomas Tsavdaridis [1971] Director [Greek]

Morgan's Pomade Company Limited
Incorporated: 2 March 1938 *Employees:* 20
Net Worth: £90,956 *Total Assets:* £1,031,126
Registered Office: Tyler Way, Swalecliffe, Whitstable, Kent, CT5 2RT
Parent: The Marie Antoinette Company Limited
Officers: Patricia Eleanor Martin [1936] Director; Deborah Frances Pearson [1956] Director

Moyy Limited
Incorporated: 3 October 2016
Registered Office: 91 Lichfield Grove, London, N3 2JL
Major Shareholder: Andrew James Smith
Officers: Andrew James Smith [1980] Director/Landlord

Mr Vanguard Limited
Incorporated: 15 May 2017
Net Worth Deficit: £7,603 *Total Assets:* £6,227
Registered Office: 15 Ingestre Place, London, W1F 0DU
Major Shareholder: Emmanuel Omoyele
Officers: Emmanuel Omoyele [1987] Director

Mrs Greens Hemp Remedies Ltd
Incorporated: 21 November 2018
Registered Office: Denant Farm, Dreenhill, Haverfordwest, Pembrokeshire, SA62 3TS
Major Shareholder: Mark John David George
Officers: Mark John David George [1983] Director

Muir Events Ltd
Incorporated: 20 June 2017
Registered Office: Kemp House, City Road, London, EC1V 2NX
Major Shareholder: Keith William David Bawden
Officers: Keith William David Bawden [1985] Director/Founder

Mulondon Limited
Incorporated: 7 August 2015
Net Worth: £9,787 *Total Assets:* £20,401
Registered Office: 64c Evelyn Street, London, SE8 5DD
Major Shareholder: Boris Zatezic
Officers: Boris Zatezic [1976] Director [Swedish]

MWK Cosmetics (UK) Ltd
Incorporated: 31 December 2018
Registered Office: 2/2, 37 Morar Drive, Paisley, Renfrewshire, PA2 9BG
Major Shareholder: Francis Nderitu Gatongi
Officers: Francis Nderitu Gatongi [1965] Managing Director

My Life But Greener Limited
Incorporated: 10 September 2013
Previous: Rose Plackett Limited
Registered Office: Keepers Retreat, Flecknoe, Rugby, Warwicks, CV23 8AT
Major Shareholder: Hannah Rose Plackett-Smith
Officers: Hannah Rose Plackett-Smith [1991] Director

Joy Myfanwy Limited
Incorporated: 6 March 2018
Registered Office: 117 Prices Court, Cotton Row, London, SW11 3YW
Major Shareholder: Joy Myfanwy Timmer
Officers: Joy Myfanwy Timmer [1997] Director/Student

Myroo Ltd
Incorporated: 12 May 2016
Net Worth: £11,510 *Total Assets:* £14,070
Registered Office: Myroo Skincare, 12 Grasmere Crescent, Harrogate, N Yorks, HG2 0ED
Shareholders: Philip Alexander Dunseath; Rachael Dunseath
Officers: Philip Alexander Dunseath [1971] Director; Rachael Dunseath [1975] Director/Skincare Industry Consultant

Nadarra Cosmetics Ltd
Incorporated: 21 November 2016 *Employees:* 1
Net Worth Deficit: £3,034 *Total Assets:* £2,483
Registered Office: 100 Church Street, Brighton, BN1 1UJ
Major Shareholder: Margaret Sinclair
Officers: Margaret Sinclair [1976] Director/Osteopath

Nars & Elliott Healthcare Ltd
Incorporated: 22 September 2017
Registered Office: Unit 41 Antrim Business Park, 25 Randalstown Road, Antrim, BT41 4LD
Parent: Elliott Nutrition Ltd
Officers: Prof Laura Ashley [1978] Director/Businesswoman

Naticuma Limited
Incorporated: 14 April 2015
Net Worth Deficit: £24,779 *Total Assets:* £21,090
Registered Office: Suite 86, 272 Kensington High Street, London, W8 6ND
Shareholders: Nilza Rosa Da Silva; Rosa Maria Rufino Dos Santos
Officers: Nilza Rosa Da Silva [1971] Director [Italian]; Rosa Maria Rufino Dos Santos [1972] Director [Italian]

Natural Aromatics Limited
Incorporated: 17 February 2016 *Employees:* 8
Net Worth Deficit: £363,786 *Total Assets:* £303,900
Registered Office: Millennium House, Unit 2 King Business Centre, Reeds Lane, Sayers Common, Hassocks, W Sussex, BN6 9LS
Parent: First Natural Limited
Officers: Sanam Shah, Secretary; Robin Christopher Russell [1950] Director; Sanam Shah [1975] Director

The Natural Deodorant Co Limited
Incorporated: 24 March 2015
Net Worth: £979 *Total Assets:* £28,566
Registered Office: Building 1, Unit 8 Lynderswood Lane, Lynderswood Farm, Braintree, Essex, CM77 8JT
Shareholders: Laurie Clare Hooper; Brett David Sanders
Officers: Laurie Clare Hooper [1984] Managing Director; Brett David Sanders [1985] Director

Natural Looks Trading Limited
Incorporated: 31 August 2000 *Employees:* 22
Net Worth Deficit: £225,208 *Total Assets:* £568,690
Registered Office: Unit 27 Mountbatten Road, Kennedy Way, Tiverton, Devon, EX16 6SW
Major Shareholder: Riyadh Ahmad Mohammed Alkury
Officers: Wendy Helen Alkury, Secretary; Riyadh Ahmad Mohammed Alkury [1955] Director [Jordanian]; Wendy Helen Alkury [1957] Director

Natural Products Factory Ltd
Incorporated: 22 September 2011 Employees: 8
Net Worth: £3,777 Total Assets: £151,404
Registered Office: Ashcombe Court, Woolsack Way, Godalming, Surrey, GU7 1LQ
Shareholders: Pauline Hili; David Peter Watts
Officers: David Abramson [1964] Director; Doctor Pauline Hili [1967] Director/Chemist [Australian]

Natural Science Aromas Ltd
Incorporated: 24 April 2014
Net Worth: £4,843 Total Assets: £32,471
Registered Office: Badgemore House, Badgemore, Henley on Thames, Oxon, RG9 4NR
Major Shareholder: Frank Paul Julian Carter
Officers: Frank Paul Julian Carter [1947] Director/Perfumer

Natural Sheaness Ltd
Incorporated: 30 March 2018
Registered Office: 122 Hurstbourne Gardens, Barking, Essex, IG11 9UT
Major Shareholder: Crystal Dale Browne
Officers: Crystal Dale Browne [1990] Director/Podiatrist

Natural Skincare London Limited
Incorporated: 25 March 2011
Net Worth Deficit: £50,600 Total Assets: £7,210
Registered Office: 9 Summerfield Road, Ealing, London, W5 1ND
Major Shareholder: Elaine Chi Kit Leung
Officers: Elaine Chi Kit Leung [1960] Director

The Natural Soap Company Limited
Incorporated: 4 October 2000
Net Worth Deficit: £164 Total Assets: £30,984
Registered Office: 2d Maryland, Wells-Next-The-Sea, Norfolk, NR23 1LY
Major Shareholder: Sara Elizabeth Phillips
Officers: Sara Phillips, Secretary; Max Phillips [1963] Director/Consultant; Sara Phillips [1959] Director/Designer

Naturali360 Limited
Incorporated: 3 February 2017
Net Worth: £1 Total Assets: £1
Registered Office: 88 Sherborne Court, London, SW5 0SU
Officers: Katia Bongermino [1981] Director [Italian]

Nature B Limited
Incorporated: 11 October 2017
Registered Office: Kemp House, 160 City Road, London, EC1V 2NX
Officers: Bruno Martin-Gilmore [1957] Director/Entrepreneur

Nature Spirits Limited
Incorporated: 15 February 2000 Employees: 6
Net Worth: £37,621 Total Assets: £50,438
Registered Office: Cullerne House, Findhorn, Moray, IV36 3YY
Major Shareholder: Marion Leigh
Officers: Iona Leigh Malcolm, Secretary/Singer/Artist; Marion Leigh [1951] Director; Iona Leigh Malcolm [1983] Director/Singer/Artist; Michael William Stoker [1978] Director/Sales Accounts Manager

Nature's Embrace Limited
Incorporated: 4 January 2017
Registered Office: 71-75 Shelton Street, London, WC2H 9JQ
Major Shareholder: Lucy Phillips
Officers: Lucy Phillips [1982] Director/Human Resources Officer

Naturoganik Limited
Incorporated: 19 November 2018
Registered Office: 26 Heathcotes, Crawley, W Sussex, RH10 7DN
Shareholders: Ouenadio Hyacinthe Mbemba; Jean Ferrand Ngot
Officers: Ouenadio Hyacinthe Mbemba [1965] Director; Jean Ferrand Ngot [1962] Director

Neal's Yard (Natural Remedies) Limited
Incorporated: 11 November 1981
Net Worth: £6,890,000 Total Assets: £24,280,000
Registered Office: Peacemarsh, Gillingham, Dorset, SP8 4EU
Officers: Elizabeth York, Secretary; Denise Anne Bonner [1955] Director; Anabel Kindersley [1971] Director; Barnabas Guy Kindersley [1970] Director; Peter David Kindersley [1941] Director/Publisher and Farmer; Alexander Ian Leach [1981] Sales Director; Timothy Alan Baylor Leach [1964] Director; Stephen Henry Tobitt [1965] Director/Chief Operating Officer; Susan Jane Winter [1960] Director/Product Development Manager

Nectar International Limited
Incorporated: 11 May 2001
Net Worth: £184,891 Total Assets: £304,139
Registered Office: 52 Berkeley Square, London, W1J 5BT
Officers: Robert Peter Smith, Secretary/Consultant; Mhd Anas Al Kasmi [1973] Director/Marketing [Syrian]; Robert Peter Smith [1939] Director; William Banks Waring [1950] Director

Neighbourhood Botanicals Ltd
Incorporated: 5 April 2016
Net Worth: £3,600 Total Assets: £3,600
Registered Office: 20-22 Wenlock Road, London, N1 7GU
Major Shareholder: Micaela Charlotte Nisbet
Officers: Micaela Nisbet [1986] Director [Australian]

Neptune Perfume Ltd
Incorporated: 18 February 2019
Registered Office: 15 Bruthwaite Green, Bedford, MK41 0NH
Major Shareholder: Neyonta Mamun
Officers: Neyonta Mamun [1994] Director/Officer

Neurocosmetics Limited
Incorporated: 2 October 2018
Registered Office: 9 Limes Road, Beckenham, Kent, BR3 6NS
Major Shareholder: Carmen Cutillas
Officers: Carmen Cutillas [1956] Director/Therapy Consultant [Spanish]

Neville Cut and Shave Limited
Incorporated: 14 August 2013
Registered Office: 72-74 Dean Street, London, W1D 3SG
Parent: Soho House Limited
Officers: Nicholas Keith Arthur Jones [1963] Director; Peter Jonathan McPhee [1975] Director [American]

New Vistas Avant Garde Limited
Incorporated: 23 March 2007
Net Worth: £23,797 Total Assets: £23,797
Registered Office: 90 Bradshaw Close, Wimbledon, London, SW19 8NL
Major Shareholder: Dale Lucas Philip Charles Richards
Officers: Dale Lucas Philip Charles Richards [1993] Director

Nihad A Rawi Limited
Incorporated: 23 March 2012
Net Worth: £821 Total Assets: £25,355
Registered Office: First Floor, 244 Edgware Road, London, W2 1DS
Major Shareholder: Nihad Razak
Officers: Nihad Razak, Secretary; Nihad Razak [1957] Director

Ninni Ltd
Incorporated: 11 March 2013
Previous: Koliox Ltd.
Net Worth Deficit: £52,636 *Total Assets:* £13,681
Registered Office: Highview House, Tattenham Crescent, Epsom, Surrey, KT18 5QJ
Major Shareholder: Katarina Maria Matilda Stetz
Officers: Katarina Maria Matilda Stetz [1978] Director/Management [Swedish]

Maya Njie Perfumes Limited
Incorporated: 3 June 2016
Net Worth Deficit: £4,940 *Total Assets:* £4,652
Registered Office: Unit 4 Block B, The Old Spratts Factory, 2 Fawe Street, London, E14 6PD
Major Shareholder: Marie Mariyama Njie
Officers: Marie Mariyama Njie [1980] Director/Perfume Designer [Swedish]

Nobell Group Ltd
Incorporated: 30 September 2016
Registered Office: Suite 12, 2nd Floor, Queens House, 180 Tottenham Court Road, London, W1T 7PD
Major Shareholder: Alex Nord
Officers: Alex Nord [1978] Director [Israeli]

Noblechart Cosmetic Ltd
Incorporated: 8 July 2014
Net Worth: £661 *Total Assets:* £4,333
Registered Office: 2nd Floor, 21-22 Great Castle Street, London, W1G 0HZ
Major Shareholder: David Levy
Officers: David Levy [1968] Director [French]

Northern Aromatics (Sales) Limited
Incorporated: 9 August 1974
Registered Office: Eton Hill Industrial Estate, Eton Hill Road, Radcliffe, Manchester, M26 2FR
Officers: John Morgan, Secretary; John Morgan [1955] Director/Accountant; Martin Christopher Francis Potts [1959] Director; Jeffrey Robert Slavin [1952] Director/Chartered Accountant

Nova Extraction Ltd
Incorporated: 26 January 2018
Registered Office: Flat 72, Anchorage Point, 42 Cuba Street, London, E14 8NF
Major Shareholder: Alexander Novitskiy
Officers: Dr Alexander Novitskiy [1984] Executive Director

NTM (UK) Limited
Incorporated: 18 October 2012 *Employees:* 2
Net Worth Deficit: £6,598 *Total Assets:* £34,835
Registered Office: 69 Bethel Street, Norwich, NR2 1NR
Major Shareholder: Anthony Graham Norton
Officers: Anthony Graham Norton [1944] Director/Salesman

Nutracrest Ltd
Incorporated: 19 February 2018
Registered Office: Unit 4l Lakesview International Business Park, Hersden, Canterbury, Kent, CT3 4JH
Shareholders: John Malcolm Tiley; Sandra Elizabeth Tiley
Officers: John Malcolm Tiley [1957] Director; Sandra Elizabeth Tiley [1951] Director

O Sable France Ltd
Incorporated: 28 August 2014
Net Worth: £18 *Total Assets:* £989
Registered Office: Enterprise House, Ocean Way, Southampton, SO14 3XB
Major Shareholder: Fania Bajot
Officers: Dr Fania Bajot [1974] Director [French]

Jaye O'Boye & Co Ltd
Incorporated: 6 July 2009
Registered Office: Flat 2, 16 Stanhope Terrace, London, W2 2SH
Officers: Jaiye Adebukola Ogboye [1970] Director

Odejo Limited
Incorporated: 12 August 2014
Net Worth Deficit: £101,690 *Total Assets:* £136,965
Registered Office: 155 Sutherland Avenue, London, W9 1ES
Officers: Timothy Seldon Blanks [1954] Director/Writer [New Zealander]

Old Park Farm Estate Limited
Incorporated: 20 July 2005
Net Worth Deficit: £28,688 *Total Assets:* £707
Registered Office: Third Floor, 20 Old Bailey, London, EC4M 7AN
Major Shareholder: Susan Jane Wells
Officers: Susan Jane Wells [1959] Director/Project Manager

Oleo Bodycare Limited
Incorporated: 27 July 2009
Net Worth: £44,272 *Total Assets:* £67,785
Registered Office: 9 New Zealand Farm Close, Bridport, Dorset, DT6 3FR
Major Shareholder: Olivia Kim Chapman
Officers: Olivia Kim Chapman, Secretary; Olivia Kim Chapman [1960] Director/Aromatherapist

Olfactive London Ltd
Incorporated: 10 July 2017
Registered Office: 18-20 High Street, Stevenage, Herts, SG1 3EJ
Major Shareholder: Michael Edwards
Officers: Michael Edwards [1963] Director

Olire Ltd
Incorporated: 20 February 2019
Registered Office: 417 Wick Lane, London, E3 2JJ
Shareholders: Jurate Raugale; Aleksandras Raugalis
Officers: Jurate Raugale [1985] Director/Manager [Lithuanian]; Aleksandras Raugalis [1984] Director/Stock Controller [Lithuanian]

A W Oliver & Co Ltd
Incorporated: 14 March 2018
Registered Office: 5 Oram Street, Bury, Lancs, BL9 6EN
Major Shareholder: Andrew William Oliver
Officers: Andrew William Oliver [1980] Director

Oliver & Taylor Ltd
Incorporated: 19 March 2018
Registered Office: 37 John Heywood Street, Manchester, M11 4EL
Major Shareholder: Andrew Oliver
Officers: Andrew Oliver [1980] Director/Perfumer

Ombotas Limited
Incorporated: 5 July 2016 *Employees:* 1
Net Worth Deficit: £4,574
Registered Office: 22 Crown Walk, Hemel Hempstead, Herts, HP3 9WS
Major Shareholder: Jacqueline Naana Kemp
Officers: Jacqueline Naana Kemp [1970] Director; Martin Paul Kemp [1964] Director

Omprus Limited
Incorporated: 12 November 2018
Registered Office: 338 Bristol Road, Birmingham, B5 7SN
Major Shareholder: Mohammed Fakhir Hashim Yassin
Officers: Mohammed Fakhir Hashim Yassin [1996] Director/Self Employed

One Green Lab Ltd
Incorporated: 12 January 2015
Net Worth: £40,801 *Total Assets:* £48,653
Registered Office: 77 High Street, Littlehampton, W Sussex, BN17 5AG
Shareholders: Peter Laszlo Takacs; Zsanett Kolonics
Officers: Peter Laszlo Takacs [1974] Director [Hungarian]

Onlyou Limited
Incorporated: 5 February 2018
Registered Office: 11 Briar Close, Cheshunt, Waltham Cross, Herts, EN8 9PN
Shareholders: Jonathan Andrew Cropper; Angela Cropper
Officers: Angela Cropper [1968] Director; Jonathan Andrew Cropper [1966] Director

Onyii's Cosmetics Ltd
Incorporated: 7 January 2019
Registered Office: 38 Salstar Close, Birmingham, B6 4PP
Major Shareholder: Onyinyechi Chimamaka Adannaya Udo-Chijioke
Officers: Dr. Onyinyechi Chimamaka Adannaya Udo-Chijioke [1990] Director/Researcher by Profession [Nigerian]

Onze Limited
Incorporated: 13 December 2018
Registered Office: 16 Hillside Gardens, Northwood, Middlesex, HA6 1RL
Shareholder: Jeeta Mona
Officers: Jeeta Mona [1976] Director

Organatural Ltd
Incorporated: 11 May 2006
Previous: The Green Chemyst Ltd
Net Worth Deficit: £87,157 *Total Assets:* £49,558
Registered Office: 9-13 High Street, Wells, Somerset, BA5 2AA
Major Shareholder: Barbara Olioso
Officers: Dr Barbara Olioso [1971] Director/Consultant [Italian]

The Organic Alchemist Ltd
Incorporated: 13 December 2016
Registered Office: 11 Yoxall Drive, Derby, DE22 3SF
Major Shareholder: Farwah Batool Kazmi
Officers: Dr Farwah Batool Kazmi [1991] Director/Doctor

Organic Basics Ltd
Incorporated: 10 December 2018
Registered Office: 71-75 Shelton Street, Covent Garden, London, WC2H 9JQ
Major Shareholder: Maria Isabel Alves Carneiro
Officers: Maria Isabel Alves Carneiro [1987] Director/Industrial Designer [Italian]

The Organic Fragrance Company Ltd
Incorporated: 21 June 2018
Registered Office: Badgemore House, Badgemore, Henley on Thames, Oxon, RG9 4NR
Major Shareholder: Frank Paul Julian Carter
Officers: Frank Paul Julian Carter [1947] Director

Organic Stuff Limited
Incorporated: 7 November 2017
Registered Office: International House, 24 Holborn Viaduct, London, EC1A 2BN
Shareholder: Irma Luotiene
Officers: Irma Luotiene [1968] Director [Lithuanian]

Organic Youth Limited
Incorporated: 25 May 2016
Registered Office: 110 Cheadle Road, Cheadle Hulme, Cheadle, Cheshire, SK8 5DP
Major Shareholder: Leanne Danielle Howell
Officers: Leanne Danielle Howell, Secretary; Leanne Danielle Howell [1981] Director/Nurse Advisor

Orikii Naturals Ltd
Incorporated: 7 January 2019
Registered Office: 28 Felipe Road, Chafford Hundred, Grays, Essex, RM16 6NE
Major Shareholder: Olubunmi Oyetoun Johnson
Officers: Olubunmi Oyetoun Johnson [1968] Director

Orion Independent Limited
Incorporated: 26 February 2019
Registered Office: 10 Martello Street, London, E8 3PE
Shareholder: Sarah Baker
Officers: Sarah Baker [1977] Director/Artist [American]; Andy Hsu [1971] Director/Artist [American]

Orton Limited
Incorporated: 3 July 2018
Registered Office: 27 Old Gloucester Street, London, WC1N 3AX
Major Shareholder: Hector Lucien Manthorpe
Officers: Hector Lucien Manthorpe [1992] Director

Ostens Limited
Incorporated: 7 February 2017
Net Worth Deficit: £150,981 *Total Assets:* £19,999
Registered Office: c/o Bryan Cave Leighton Paisner LLP, Adelaide House, London Bridge, London, EC4R 9HA
Shareholders: Christopher Yu; Frederic Jean Laurent Delafon
Officers: Frederic Jean Laurent Delafon [1974] Managing Director [French]; Christopher Yu [1975] Director/Solicitor

Ostera Limited
Incorporated: 2 July 2018
Registered Office: 49 Coronet Avenue, Northwich, Cheshire, CW9 8FX
Major Shareholder: Louise Margaret Halliday
Officers: Louise Margaret Halliday [1969] Director

Osunti Limited
Incorporated: 13 April 2018
Registered Office: Unit 4, 75 Kilbowie Road, Glasgow, G81 5LB
Officers: Tinu Petzke [1966] Director [Nigerian]

Otte Limited
Incorporated: 19 June 2018
Registered Office: 63 New Concordia Wharf, Mill Street, London, SE1 2BB
Major Shareholder: Lucy Ayla Hosmer
Officers: Lucy Ayla Hosmer [1988] Director

Ottimo Supplies Limited
Incorporated: 7 January 1980
Net Worth: £3,112 *Total Assets:* £248,284
Registered Office: 7 Livingstone Mills, Howard Street, Batley, W Yorks, WF17 6JH
Shareholders: Reginald Frank Harwood; Harry Edward Wilson
Officers: Harry Edward Wilson, Secretary; Zakir Hussain Chopdat [1984] Director; Reginald Frank Harwood [1956] Director; Dorothy Wilson [1943] Director; Harry Edward Wilson [1943] Director

Our Modern Lives Ltd
Incorporated: 28 July 2017
Net Worth: £100 *Total Assets:* £100
Registered Office: Unit 8 Issigonis House, Cowley Road, London, W3 7UN
Shareholders: Sarah McCartney; Nicholas Charles Rendell
Officers: Sarah McCartney [1960] Director; Nicholas Charles Rendell [1969] Director

Oyepitan and Okunniwa Limited
Incorporated: 6 September 2018
Registered Office: Midway House, Staverton Technology Park, Herrick Way, Staverton, Cheltenham, Glos, GL51 6TQ
Shareholders: Abiodun Oyepitan; Liha Okunniwa
Officers: Liha Okunniwa [1979] Director/Co-Founder; Abiodun Oyepitan [1979] Director/Co-Founder

P & H Natural Skincare Ltd
Incorporated: 25 January 2019
Registered Office: The Long Lodge, 265-269 Kingston Road, Wimbledon, London, SW19 3NW
Shareholder: Pavla Humpulova
Officers: Jiri Humpula [1978] Director [Czech]; Pavla Humpulova [1981] Director [Czech]

Paddy's Bathroom Limited
Incorporated: 20 March 2008
Net Worth: £406,612 *Total Assets:* £433,263
Registered Office: 82 St John Street, London, EC1M 4JN
Shareholders: Paul John Lindley; Alison Jane Lindley
Officers: Paul John Lindley [1966] Director

The Paisley Soap Company Ltd
Incorporated: 2 August 2018
Registered Office: 18 Kirkton Road, Neilston, Glasgow, G78 3HN
Major Shareholder: Marie Margaret Ballesteros
Officers: Marie Margaret Ballesteros [1964] Director/Businesswoman

Palm Bars Ltd
Incorporated: 2 January 2019
Registered Office: 23 Eisenberg Close, Baldock, Herts, SG7 6TA
Major Shareholder: Lindsey Jane Magee
Officers: Lindsey Jane Magee [1976] Director/Accountant

Pandorra Ltd.
Incorporated: 14 December 2015
Net Worth Deficit: £2,299
Registered Office: Tally Accountants Ltd, Top Floor, College House, 17 King Edwards Road, Ruislip, Middlesex, HA4 7AE
Major Shareholder: Daniel Wilhelm
Officers: Daniel Wilhelm, Secretary; Daniel Wilhelm [1974] Managing Director [German]

Papillon Perfumery Ltd
Incorporated: 19 July 2011
Net Worth: £1,533 *Total Assets:* £12,387
Registered Office: 26 York Street, London, W1U 6PZ
Shareholder: Simon Frank Oliver Goodland
Officers: Simon Frank Oliver Goodland [1979] Director

Paradoxical Solutions Limited
Incorporated: 11 November 2011
Net Worth: £18,851 *Total Assets:* £71,358
Registered Office: 6 Edward Street, Birmingham, B1 2RX
Shareholder: Robert Alan Baskerville
Officers: Robert Alan Baskerville [1967] Director; Thomas William Morgan Baskerville [1997] Director/Student

Parfums Bleu Limited
Incorporated: 26 October 1994 *Employees:* 4
Net Worth Deficit: £140,307 *Total Assets:* £202,656
Registered Office: St Stephen's House, Laburnum Avenue, Robin Hoods Bay, Whitby, N Yorks, YO22 4RR
Parent: Blazergold Limited
Officers: Seamus Foley, Secretary; Maurice Anthony Foley [1957] Director/Marketing Executive [Irish]; Seamus Foley [1957] Director; Timothy Bernard Foley [1950] Director/Marketing Consultant

Paromachem Limited
Incorporated: 10 August 2007
Net Worth: £16,256 *Total Assets:* £21,302
Registered Office: Meadowrise, Willington Lane, Clotton, Cheshire, CW6 0HQ
Major Shareholder: Steven Richard Pipe
Officers: Steven Richard Pipe, Secretary; Nicola Pipe [1962] Director/Teacher; Steven Richard Pipe [1958] Director/Consultant

Paz By Nature Ltd
Incorporated: 18 January 2019
Registered Office: 304b Ballards Lane, London, N12 0EY
Shareholders: Pazit Azoulay; Valerio Lupo
Officers: Pazit Azoulay [1988] Director/Therapist [Italian/Israeli]; Valerio Lupo [1992] Director [Italian]

Penny Price Aromatherapy Ltd
Incorporated: 21 May 2003
Net Worth: £260,240 *Total Assets:* £340,260
Registered Office: D3, Radius Court, Maple Way, Hinckley, Leics, LE10 3BE
Shareholders: Penelope Anne Stephen; Revd Dr Robert Stephen
Officers: Revd Dr Robert Stephen, Secretary; Penelope Anne Stephen [1957] Director/Aromatherapist; Revd Dr Robert Stephen [1963] Director/Teacher

Pepsyn Limited
Incorporated: 22 February 1996
Net Worth Deficit: £1,640,791 *Total Assets:* £175
Registered Office: William Russell House, The Square, Lightwater, Surrey, GU18 5SS
Parent: MSIF Limited
Officers: John Crispin Kirkman, Secretary; John Crispin Kirkman [1951] Director/Consultant; Dr John Arthur Smith [1948] Director/Lecturer

Perfair Limited
Incorporated: 25 May 2012
Registered Office: 31e Stoneleigh Street, Notting Hill, London, W11 4DU
Major Shareholder: David Robinson
Officers: David Robinson [1958] Managing Director

Perfance Limited
Incorporated: 17 January 2018
Registered Office: 6 Rhuddlan Court, Chester, CH4 8NH
Major Shareholder: Alona Holub
Officers: Alona Holub [1988] Director [Ukrainian]

Perfume By Design Ltd.
Incorporated: 7 August 1998 *Employees:* 1
Net Worth: £108,462 *Total Assets:* £112,444
Registered Office: 5 North Street, Hailsham, E Sussex, BN27 1DQ
Major Shareholder: Andrew James Kobus
Officers: Beverley Bayne, Secretary; Andrew James Kobus [1962] Director

The Perfume Studio Limited
Incorporated: 30 March 2002 *Employees:* 3
Net Worth: £73,591 *Total Assets:* £180,242
Registered Office: 17b Church Road, Tunbridge Wells, Kent, TN1 1HT
Shareholder: Judith Lynn Naake
Officers: Benjamin Janousek [1975] Director/Consultant; Judith Lynn Naake [1947] Director; John Nicholas Grant Warden [1956] Director

Persephone Bio Ltd
Incorporated: 14 July 2014
Net Worth Deficit: £2,050 *Total Assets:* £14,864
Registered Office: Bankside 300, Peachman Way, Broadland Business Park, Norwich, NR7 0LB
Shareholders: Catherine Rosemary Martin; Eugenio Butelli
Officers: Eugenio Butelli [1968] Director [Italian]; Dr Catherine Rosemary Martin [1955] Director

Pharmaco Group Limited
Incorporated: 6 April 2018
Registered Office: Kemp House, 160 City Road, London, EC1V 2NX
Shareholders: Roy Salmons; Nutresco Limited
Officers: Roy Salmons [1945] Director

Phoenix Fragrances Limited
Incorporated: 18 June 1987 *Employees:* 46
Net Worth: £1,862,198 *Total Assets:* £2,415,650
Registered Office: Unit 1 Chieftain Business Park, Morris Close, Park Farm Industrial Estate, Wellingborough, Northants, NN8 6XF
Shareholders: Alan Norman Parry; Anthony James Dallimore
Officers: Bryan Cecil de Beer, Secretary; Robert David Adderley [1950] Director/Accountant; Anthony James Dallimore [1949] Director/Perfumer; Alan Norman Parry [1947] Sales Director

Phytacol Limited
Incorporated: 24 February 2009 *Employees:* 1
Net Worth Deficit: £106,728 *Total Assets:* £152,552
Registered Office: 10 Station Road, Henley on Thames, Oxon, RG9 1AY
Major Shareholder: Michael John Allaway
Officers: Michael John Allaway, Secretary; Michael John Allaway [1947] Director

Phyto Pharm Limited
Incorporated: 12 October 2016
Registered Office: 5 Jupiter House, Calleva Park, Aldermaston, Reading, Berks, RG7 8NN
Major Shareholder: Laura Catherine Dewar
Officers: Laura Dewar [1957] Director

Phyto Pharma Limited
Incorporated: 13 October 2016
Registered Office: 5 Jupiter House, Calleva Park, Aldermaston, Reading, Berks, RG7 8NN
Major Shareholder: Laura Catherine Dewar
Officers: Laura Catherine Dewar [1957] Director

Pierre Precieuse Parfum UK Limited
Incorporated: 12 May 2017
Registered Office: Sussex Innovation Croydon, 12-16 Addiscombe Road, Croydon, Surrey, CR0 0XT
Officers: Mervyn Suresh Aranha, Secretary; Mervyn Suresh Aranha [1962] Director/Business Executive; Alwyn Hobert Stephen [1963] Director/Perfume Manufacturer and Distributor [Indian]; Aquillha Marietta Stephen [1978] Director/Businesswoman [Indian]

Pitt London Ltd
Incorporated: 19 February 2018
Registered Office: Flat 45, Dalehead, Harrington Square, London, NW1 2JL
Shareholders: Edward Alexander Currie; Andrew Shaun Coxon
Officers: Andrew Shaun Coxon [1988] Director/Actor; Edward Alexander Currie [1990] Director

Plant Department Ltd
Incorporated: 4 September 2018
Registered Office: Willow Court, Beeches Green, Stroud, Glos, GL5 4BJ
Officers: Oliver Geoffrey Bushnell [1987] Director; Richard John Hemelryk [1989] Director; Thomas Paul Hemelryk [1987] Director; Samuel William Vickers [1987] Director

Platinum Beards Ltd
Incorporated: 22 January 2019
Registered Office: 16 Coniston House, Wyndham Road, London, SE5 0UF
Major Shareholder: Mohamed Noor
Officers: Mohamed Noor [1992] Managing Director

Polka Lab Limited
Incorporated: 5 September 2018
Registered Office: Flat 8a, Bridge Street, Denbigh, LL16 3TF
Major Shareholder: Michalina Elzbieta Piekarska
Officers: Michalina Elzbieta Piekarska [1991] Director/Chemist [Polish]

Pools of Cleopatra Limited
Incorporated: 10 January 2019
Registered Office: 71-75 Shelton Street, London, WC2H 9JQ
Major Shareholder: Georgina Morgan
Officers: Georgina Morgan [1994] Director

Poseidon Skincare Limited
Incorporated: 20 April 2017
Registered Office: Lower Baybridge House, Owslebury, Winchester, Hants, SO21 1JN
Major Shareholder: George Adams
Officers: George Adams [1994] Director/Chief Executive Officer

Possibility of London Ltd
Incorporated: 21 August 2015 *Employees:* 4
Net Worth: £33,688 *Total Assets:* £170,395
Registered Office: 20-22 Wenlock Road, London, N1 7GU
Shareholders: Bridget Veronica Gaughan; Norah Gabrielle Gaughan
Officers: Bridget Veronica Gaughan [1957] Managing Director; Norah Gabrielle Gaughan [1964] Sales Director

Pot of Gold Cosmetics Limited
Incorporated: 25 May 2004 *Employees:* 3
Net Worth: £13,579 *Total Assets:* £30,438
Registered Office: 4 Akroyd Mill, Northgate, Halifax, W Yorks, HX1 1YH
Shareholders: Matthew Neil Wroot; Alexander Michael Oliver Myers
Officers: Matthew Neil Wroot [1965] Director/Cosmetic Manufacturer

Potions & Possibilities Limited
Incorporated: 2 February 2017
Registered Office: 10 Kindlewood Drive, Toton, Nottingham, NG9 6NE
Major Shareholder: Lu Wang
Officers: Lu Wang, Secretary; Lu Wang [1977] Director [Chinese]

Potter & Moore (Devon) Ltd
Incorporated: 12 February 2016 *Employees:* 104
Net Worth: £428,000 *Total Assets:* £3,267,000
Registered Office: 1210 Lincoln Road, Peterborough, PE4 6ND
Parent: Creightons PLC
Officers: Philippa Clark [1969] Marketing Director; Paul Forster [1958] Director/Chartered Accountant; Bernard James Mary Johnson [1945] Managing Director; William Oliver McIlroy [1945] Director/Company Investor; Nicholas O'Shea [1954] Director/Chartered Management Accountant; Martin Stevens [1961] Technical Director

Potter & Moore Innovations Limited
Incorporated: 22 January 2003 *Employees:* 266
Net Worth: £6,439,000 *Total Assets:* £14,846,000
Registered Office: 1210 Lincoln Road, Werrington, Peterborough, Cambs, PE4 6ND
Parent: Creightons PLC
Officers: Mary Teresa Carney [1953] Director/Tax Consultant; Philippa Clark [1969] Sales & Marketing Director; Paul Forster [1958] Director/Chartered Accountant; William Torrance Glencross [1946] Director/Marketing Consultant; Bernard James Mary Johnson [1945] Director/Management Consultant; William Oliver McIlroy [1945] Director; Nicholas Desmond John O'Shea [1954] Director/Management Consultant; Martin Stevens [1961] Technical Director

Precious Clothing & Beauty Ltd
Incorporated: 11 June 2018
Registered Office: International House, 142 Cromwell Road, Kensington, London, SW7 4EF
Major Shareholder: Peter Phillips
Officers: Peter Phillips [1968] Director/Entrepreneur

Premier Specialties Europe Limited
Incorporated: 23 April 2013
Registered Office: 5 Premus Coldharbour Way, Aylesbury, Bucks, HP19 8AP
Officers: Roger George Rich [1944] Director/Company Executive [American]

The Pretty Little Treat Company (Yorkshire) Ltd
Incorporated: 10 July 2017
Registered Office: 2 Western Street, Barnsley, S Yorks, S70 2BP
Major Shareholder: Victoria Helen Woodger
Officers: Victoria Helen Woodger [1976] Director

Prispens Limited
Incorporated: 4 March 2017
Net Worth Deficit: £16,150 *Total Assets:* £6,390
Registered Office: 16 Park Street, Crediton, Devon, EX17 3EQ
Shareholders: Jane Harding-Smolik; Jakub Harding-Smolik
Officers: Jakub Harding-Smolik [1981] Director [Czech]; Jane Harding-Smolik [1985] Director

Professional Beauty Systems (Holdings) Limited
Incorporated: 29 December 2006 *Employees:* 173
Net Worth: £21,322,632 *Total Assets:* £26,159,012
Registered Office: 3 Newmains Avenue, Inchinnan, Renfrew, PA4 9RR
Shareholder: Gerard Patrick Hegarty
Officers: Brian Aitken, Secretary/Accountant; Brian Aitken [1954] Director/Accountant; Generald Patrick Hegarty [1940] Director/Sales Executive; Colette Frances MacDonough [1967] Director; Stephen James MacDonough [1962] Director; Stephen McLaughlin [1974] Director/Accountant

Professional Beauty Systems Limited
Incorporated: 3 November 1982 *Employees:* 158
Net Worth: £18,599,196 *Total Assets:* £22,932,808
Registered Office: 3 Newmains Avenue, Inchinnan, Renfrew, PA4 9RR
Officers: Brian Aitken, Secretary; Brian Aitken [1954] Director/Accountant; Sheena Johnston Cunniffe [1972] Director/Commercial Manager; Generald Patrick Hegarty [1940] Director/Sales Executive; Colette Frances MacDonough [1967] Director; Stephen James MacDonough [1962] Director/Sales Executive; Stephen McLaughlin [1974] Director/Accountant; Simon McPartland [1961] Director/General Manager

Project Cosmetics Limited
Incorporated: 16 October 2017
Registered Office: Meadowcroft Mill, Bury Road, Rochdale, Lancs, OL11 4AU
Major Shareholder: Joy Elizabeth Howieson
Officers: Joy Howieson, Secretary; Joy Elizabeth Howieson [1990] Director/Cosmetics Manufacturer and Retailer

Project Renegades Ltd
Incorporated: 25 January 2016
Net Worth Deficit: £17,748 *Total Assets:* £252,270
Registered Office: Ground Floor, 5-6 Underhill Street, London, NW1 7HS
Major Shareholder: Geza Schoen
Officers: David John Welsh, Secretary; Paul Douglas White [1959] Director/Designer

Prophylaxis Ltd
Incorporated: 21 January 2019
Registered Office: Flat 4, 47 Fentiman Road, London, SW8 1LH
Shareholders: Anisha Gupta; Carly Marie Billing
Officers: Dr Carly Marie Billing [1989] Director/Dentist; Dr Anisha Gupta [1990] Director/Dentist

Prosody London Limited
Incorporated: 22 February 2017
Registered Office: Harben House, Harben Parade, Finchley Road, London, NW3 6LH
Parent: Prosody Group Holdings Limited
Officers: Kok SEN Teo [1970] Director/Brand Consultant [Singaporean]; Paul Vinogradoff [1959] Director/Brand Consultant

Protect Biosciences Ltd
Incorporated: 4 April 2009
Previous: Wild Organic Research Ltd
Net Worth Deficit: £44,621 *Total Assets:* £185,285
Registered Office: The Barn, 3 Red Brick Cottages, Old Bury Road, Palgrave, Diss, Norfolk, IP22 1AZ
Shareholder: Bruce Smith
Officers: Rita Brady [1947] Director/Retiree; Allison Wild [1962] Director/Writer

Providence Ventures Limited
Incorporated: 28 July 2009
Net Worth: £17,188 *Total Assets:* £19,950
Registered Office: 22 Tamar Way, London, N17 9HF
Shareholder: Oluwabunmi Omolara Samuel
Officers: Oluwabunmi Omolara Samuel [1966] Director/Accountant; Victoria Onola Samuel [1992] Director

Psyche Com & Merch Ltd
Incorporated: 2 November 2017
Registered Office: Flat 60, 2a St Luke's Avenue, London, SW4 7EA
Major Shareholder: Samantha Liart
Officers: Samantha Liart [1978] Director/Business Person [French]

Pur-D Natural Skin Care Ltd
Incorporated: 20 January 2017
Registered Office: 23 Lymington Road, Wallasey, Merseyside, CH44 3EG
Shareholders: Deborah Frances Usher; Geoffrey Rees
Officers: Geoffrey Rees [1945] Director; Deborah Frances Usher [1961] Director

Purdie's of Argyll Ltd
Incorporated: 31 January 2017
Net Worth: £100 *Total Assets:* £60,500
Registered Office: 6b Main Street West, Inveraray, Argyll & Bute, PA32 8TU
Shareholder: Gavin Ernest Purdie
Officers: Gavin Ernest Purdie [1962] Director

Pure English Cosmetics Limited
Incorporated: 3 January 2017
Net Worth: £100 *Total Assets:* £100
Registered Office: 27 Gateford Drive, Horsham, W Sussex, RH12 5FW
Major Shareholder: Cyril Francis Chresta
Officers: Cyril Francis Chresta, Secretary; Cyril Francis Chresta [1932] Director

Pure Fiji (EU) Limited
Incorporated: 16 February 2017
Registered Office: 24a Aldermans Hill, Palmers Green, London, N13 4PN
Shareholders: Andree Gaetane Austin; Gaetane Marie Austin
Officers: Andree Gaetane Austin [1962] Director [Fijian]; Gaetane Marie Austin [1941] Director [Fijian]

Pure Lakes Skincare Limited
Incorporated: 26 February 2014 *Employees:* 10
Net Worth: £42,664 *Total Assets:* £334,800
Registered Office: Unit 21 Staveley Mill Yard, Back Lane, Staveley, Kendal, Cumbria, LA8 9LR
Shareholders: Claire Nicole McKeever; Gareth McKeever
Officers: Claire Nicole McKeever [1980] Director; Gareth John McKeever [1975] Director

Pure Ohana Limited
Incorporated: 1 October 2018
Registered Office: 33 Avro House, 5 Boulevard Drive, London, NW9 5HF
Major Shareholder: Nureen Iqbal
Officers: Nureen Iqbal [1980] Director/Housewife

Purely Skincare Limited
Incorporated: 2 September 2016
Net Worth Deficit: £8,730 *Total Assets:* £2,450
Registered Office: Cherry Cottage, Ryeflatts Lane, Hatton, Derby, DE65 5ET
Shareholders: Malcolm John Haire; Antonita Charlene Haire
Officers: Dr Antonita Charlene Haire [1960] Director/Psychologist; Malcolm John Haire [1963] Director/Machinist

Purepure Limited
Incorporated: 9 June 2017
Net Worth Deficit: £2,731 *Total Assets:* £2,330
Registered Office: Colman House, Station Road, Knowle, Solihull, W Midlands, B93 0HL
Major Shareholder: Martin Leitner
Officers: Martin Leitner [1980] Director [Austrian]

Purplelilac Ltd
Incorporated: 16 December 2009
Net Worth Deficit: £30,846 *Total Assets:* £3,328
Registered Office: 45 High Street, Swanscombe, Kent, DA10 0AG
Major Shareholder: Delphina Kitson-Mills-Jones
Officers: Delphina Kitson-Mills-Jones [1972] Director

Q-Pack Limited
Incorporated: 16 September 1997 *Employees:* 2
Net Worth: £60,334 *Total Assets:* £126,611
Registered Office: 5 Martins Lane, Linton, Cambridge, CB21 4NG
Shareholders: Roy Webb; Barbara Webb
Officers: Roy Webb, Secretary; Barbara Webb [1949] Director; Roy Webb [1952] Director

Quality Analysis Limited
Incorporated: 9 October 1986 *Employees:* 6
Net Worth: £251,827 *Total Assets:* £817,683
Registered Office: Lambert Chapman, 3 Warners Mill, Silks Way, Braintree, Essex, CM7 3GB
Major Shareholder: Clive Lionel Bendon
Officers: Clive Lionel Bendon [1955] Director/Analytical Perfumer

Qualkem Ltd
Incorporated: 9 November 2018
Registered Office: Alextra Group Ltd, Macon Court, Unit 7-9 Herald Drive, Crewe, Cheshire, CW1 6EA
Shareholders: Ivan Anketell-Clifford; Rachael Louise Anketell-Clifford
Officers: Ivan Anketell-Clifford, Secretary; Ivan Anketell-Clifford [1968] Director; Rachael Louise Anketell-Clifford [1973] Director/Administrator

Queen Cosmetics Limited
Incorporated: 18 May 1949 *Employees:* 1
Net Worth: £70,856 *Total Assets:* £75,123
Registered Office: Unit 2 Hillsdown Farm, Twyford Lane, Birch Grove, Haywards Heath, W Sussex, RH17 7DH
Major Shareholder: David Stephen Lees
Officers: Catherine Lees, Secretary; David Stephen Lees [1940] Director

The Quint Essence Lab Ltd
Incorporated: 13 February 2019
Registered Office: Hova House, 1 Hova Villas, Hove, E Sussex, BN3 3DH
Shareholders: Agnes Renata Majoros; Attila Varro
Officers: Agnes Renata Majoros [1978] Director [Hungarian]; Attila Varro [1959] Director [Hungarian]

R.M. Investments Limited
Incorporated: 16 November 1988 *Employees:* 2
Net Worth: £372,775 *Total Assets:* £378,048
Registered Office: 22 Friars Street, Sudbury, Suffolk, CO10 2AA
Officers: Rosalie Mary Hood, Secretary; Alan Roger Hood [1950] Director/Chemist; Rosalie Mary Hood [1952] Director/Secretary

R.P.C. Midlands Ltd
Incorporated: 30 April 2007
Net Worth: £577,070 *Total Assets:* £1,362,793
Registered Office: McArthur, Alma Street, Smethwick, W Midlands, B66 2RL
Major Shareholder: Sajid Riaz
Officers: Sajid Riaz [1972] Director

Radiant Glow Beauty UK Ltd
Incorporated: 12 November 2018
Registered Office: 61 Bridge Street, Kington, Herefords, HR5 3DJ
Major Shareholder: Abiodun Olusesan
Officers: Abiodun Olusesan [1965] Commercial Director

Rasta Life Ltd
Incorporated: 6 November 2018
Registered Office: 71-75 Shelton Street, London, WC2H 9JQ
Major Shareholder: Darron Cousins
Officers: Darron Cousins [1975] Director

Raw Supremo Ltd
Incorporated: 9 August 2016
Registered Office: 62 Rothersthorpe Crescent, Northampton, NN4 8JD
Shareholders: Katy Tong; Barry Keith Tong
Officers: Barry Keith Tong [1977] Director; Katy Tong [1978] Director

Razias London Ltd
Incorporated: 15 June 2016
Net Worth Deficit: £30,680 *Total Assets:* £9,450
Registered Office: Cranford House, 24a Longley Road, Rainham, Gillingham, Kent, ME8 7RU
Officers: Razia Malik [1964] Director

Reesoaps.co.uk Ltd
Incorporated: 18 December 2018
Registered Office: 13a Heath Gap Road, Cannock, Staffs, WS11 6DY
Major Shareholder: Marie Ann Williams
Officers: Marie Ann Williams [1968] Director and Company Secretary

Regis Personal Care Ltd
Incorporated: 24 July 2017
Registered Office: Unit 16, Building 10, Central Park, Mallusk, Newtownabbey, Co Antrim, BT36 4FS
Major Shareholder: Richard Walsh
Officers: Dr Richard Walsh [1967] Director/Doctor

Relax Candle and Bath Company Limited
Incorporated: 21 February 2018
Registered Office: Usher Spiby & Co, Manchester Road, Denton, Manchester, M34 3PS
Major Shareholder: Jacqueline Ann Gilluley
Officers: Jacqueline Ann Gilluley [1966] Director

Renbow Haircare Limited
Incorporated: 27 May 2009
Registered Office: Unit 3 Newmains Avenue, Inchinnan Business Park, Renfrew, PA4 9RR
Officers: Brian Aitken, Secretary; Stephen James MacDonogh [1962] Director

Renewyou Cancertology UK Ltd
Incorporated: 16 August 2017
Registered Office: 45 Netherfield Avenue, Eastbourne, E Sussex, BN23 7BT
Officers: Jonathan Phillip Sorrell-Fleet [1953] Director

Renu Consultancy Ltd
Incorporated: 20 December 2011 *Employees:* 3
Net Worth: £9,455 *Total Assets:* £24,019
Registered Office: Full Stop Accounts, 25 Pen-Y-Lan Road, Cardiff, CF24 3PG
Major Shareholder: Clare Louise Anderson
Officers: Clare Louise Anderson [1975] Director

Revlon & Elie Healthcare Ltd
Incorporated: 14 September 2017
Registered Office: Unit 2 Block B, Scrabo Business Park, Jubilee Road, Newtownards, Co Down, BT23 4YH
Parent: Elie Consumer Care Ltd
Officers: Mary Stephen [1972] Director/Businesswoman

Zandra Rhodes Fragrances Limited
Incorporated: 27 February 1992
Registered Office: 5 The Square, Bagshot, Surrey, GU19 5AX
Major Shareholder: Dame Zandra Lindsey Rhodes
Officers: Dame Zandra Lindsey Rhodes [1940] Director/Fashion Designer

Riley & Sons Ltd
Incorporated: 17 July 2017
Registered Office: 57 High Street, Ballymena, Co Antrim, BT43 6DT
Major Shareholder: Charlotte Riley
Officers: Charlotte Riley [1974] Director/Businesswoman

Rimmel & Flynn Healthcare Ltd
Incorporated: 15 September 2017
Registered Office: Unit 41 Antrim Business Park, Enkalon Industrial Estate, Antrim, BT41 4LD
Parent: Flynn Group of Companies Ltd
Officers: Michael Bronson [1975] Director/Businessman

Ring in Ring Ltd
Incorporated: 9 November 2016
Registered Office: 3 Acres Gardens, Tadworth, Surrey, KT20 5LP
Major Shareholder: Behzad Gharehbaghi
Officers: Behzad Gharehbaghi [1971] Director [Iranian]

RMBeauty Limited
Incorporated: 25 June 2016
Net Worth Deficit: £169 *Total Assets:* £25
Registered Office: 19 Grasmere Court, Leeds, LS12 1LY
Officers: Rawaa Mahdi [1989] Director

Robertet (U.K.) Limited
Incorporated: 10 May 1971 *Employees:* 45
Net Worth: £8,519,296 *Total Assets:* £9,973,241
Registered Office: Kings Road, Haslemere, Surrey, GU27 2QU
Parent: Robertet SA
Officers: Vivienne Sandra Lawrence, Secretary; Stephanie Samantha Mackrell [1964] Managing Director; Christophe Maubert [1959] Director [French]; Olivier Maubert [1965] Director [French]; Brian McCandless [1951] Sales Director; Lionel Picolet [1956] Director/Secretary General [French]

Ethel Roberts Limited
Incorporated: 9 August 1954
Registered Office: 79 Marine Gate Mansions, Promenade, Southport, Merseyside, PR9 0EF
Parent: Laboratory Facilities Limited
Officers: Christopher Michael Holmes [1945] Director

Rodette International Limited
Incorporated: 26 September 1995
Net Worth Deficit: £131,427 *Total Assets:* £13,062
Registered Office: 19 Sturges Road, Ashford, Kent, TN24 8NE
Major Shareholder: Jean Stephanie Brown
Officers: Jean Stephanie Brown, Secretary/Teacher Retired; Jean Stephanie Brown [1939] Director/Teacher Retired

Rodriguez Corporation Ltd
Incorporated: 7 January 2019
Registered Office: 46 Baker Street, Northampton, NN2 6DJ
Major Shareholder: George Luis Vicente Rodriguez
Officers: George Luis Vicente Rodriguez [1976] Director [Bulgarian]

Royale Essance Ltd
Incorporated: 9 February 2015
Net Worth Deficit: £28,949 *Total Assets:* £17,215
Registered Office: 1a Ludlow Avenue, Luton, Beds, LU1 3RW
Major Shareholder: Aroosa Ali
Officers: Aroosa Neela Ali [1996] Director/Business Development Manager

Ru Si Lacquers Global Ltd.
Incorporated: 3 July 2018
Registered Office: Companies House, Default Address, Cardiff, CF14 8LH
Officers: Vidya Bhushan Goyal [1955] Director/Self Employed; Rushikesh Vishwanath Nashte [1995] Director/Businessman [Indian]

Rustic Blends Limited
Incorporated: 19 June 2017
Registered Office: 27 Old Gloucester Street, London, WC1N 3AX
Shareholder: Remecae Gordon
Officers: Remecae Gordon [1982] Director/Entrepreneur

Rutherford Bambury Ltd
Incorporated: 12 June 2018
Registered Office: Coachwerks, 19 Hollingdean Terrace, Brighton, BN1 7HB
Officers: Jasmine Bambury [1988] Director/Brand Owner/Manager/Manufacturer/Care Worker

S.R.S.Aromatics Limited
Incorporated: 28 September 1983 *Employees:* 9
Net Worth: £767,335 *Total Assets:* £2,054,031
Registered Office: Beodric House, 5 Boldero Road, Bury St Edmunds, Suffolk, IP32 7BS
Shareholders: Steven John Baker; Barbara Rose Baker
Officers: Jonathan Marc Baker, Secretary; Barbara Rose Baker [1956] Director; Jonathan Marc Baker [1980] Director/Commercial Manager; Lee John Baker [1977] Director/Financial Manager; Steven John Baker [1956] Director

Sabel Cosmetics Limited
Incorporated: 1 April 1997 *Employees:* 24
Net Worth: £1,584,273 *Total Assets:* £2,253,220
Registered Office: Mount Pellon Works, Pellon Lane, Halifax, W Yorks, HX1 4TZ
Parent: Sabel Cosmetics Holdings Limited
Officers: John Birrel Abel [1943] Director; Simon William Abel [1967] Operations Director

Sachets Limited
Incorporated: 30 November 1987 *Employees:* 32
Net Worth: £2,001,808 *Total Assets:* £4,853,222
Registered Office: 225 Market Street, Hyde, Cheshire, SK14 1HF
Major Shareholder: Andrew Cooper Ball
Officers: Richard Andrew Ball, Secretary; Christopher John Mellodew Ball [1969] Director

The Saints & Co London Ltd
Incorporated: 8 February 2018
Registered Office: 3 New Arcade, High Street, Uxbridge, Middlesex, UB8 1LG
Officers: Ekemezie Mbonu, Secretary; Ekemezie Mbonu [1968] Director [Nigerian]

Saisha Marra Ltd.
Incorporated: 6 November 2018
Registered Office: 71-75 Shelton Street, London, WC2H 9JQ
Major Shareholder: Namitha Muthukrishnan
Officers: Namitha Muthukrishnan [1987] Director [Indian]

Salix Moon Apothecary Ltd
Incorporated: 28 December 2018
Registered Office: Flat 3, Marlborough Court, 63 Woodfield Road, Leigh on Sea, Essex, SS9 1ES
Shareholders: Louise Kay Swain; Maxwell Ben Levy
Officers: Louise Kay Swain [1992] Director/Graphic Designer

Salopian Ltd
Incorporated: 10 July 2017
Registered Office: 15 Harlescott Barns, Harlescott Lane, Shrewsbury, Salop, SY1 3SZ
Shareholders: Jorg Alexander Richard Muschner; Jenny Muschner
Officers: Jenny Muschner [1966] Director; Jorg Alexander Richard Muschner [1962] Director

Saltaire Soap Ltd
Incorporated: 25 May 2017
Registered Office: Q20 Theatre, Creative Arts Hub, Dockfield Road, Shipley, W Yorks, BD17 7AD
Officers: Fiona Smith [1981] Director/Soap Maker

Sandine Zartaux Holding Ltd
Incorporated: 25 November 2014
Net Worth Deficit: £3,722 *Total Assets:* £3,544
Registered Office: 27 Old Gloucester Street, London, WC1N 3AX
Major Shareholder: Kyriaki Zartaloudi
Officers: Kyriaki Zartaloudi [1973] Director/Trader [Greek]

Sandwich Consultants Ltd
Incorporated: 19 September 2018
Registered Office: 22 Woodnesborough Road, Sandwich, Kent, CT13 0AA
Shareholders: Gopala Krishna Gosain; Rajendra Gosain
Officers: Gopala Krishna Gosain [1979] Director

Sanofi International Biotech Company Ltd.
Incorporated: 8 May 2017
Registered Office: 3/3, 4 Firpark Close, Glasgow, G31 2HQ
Officers: Zhanhong HE [1992] Director/Manager [Chinese]

Sansuraya Limited
Incorporated: 25 February 2019
Registered Office: 60 Gordon Road, Ilford, Essex, IG1 1SR
Major Shareholder: Bharti Vadher
Officers: Bharti Vadher [1986] Managing Director

Satellite Industries GB Limited
Incorporated: 22 December 1994 *Employees:* 6
Net Worth: £2,499 *Total Assets:* £202,499
Registered Office: Unit 1 Redhill Farm, Top Street, Appleby Magna, Swadlincote, Derby, DE12 7AH
Major Shareholder: Todd Loren Hilde
Officers: John Jacob Babcock, Secretary; Todd Hilde [1960] Director [American]; Georges Koller [1971] Managing Director [Luxembourger]

Savage Alchemy Limited
Incorporated: 3 January 2018
Net Worth Deficit: £7,462 *Total Assets:* £2,436
Registered Office: Ossington Chambers, 6-8 Castle Gate, Newark, Notts, NG24 1AX
Major Shareholder: Adam Watson
Officers: Adam Watson, Secretary; Adam Watson [1990] Director/Self Employed

Savillequinn Pty Ltd.
Incorporated: 5 June 2017
Net Worth Deficit: £42,941 *Total Assets:* £8,138
Registered Office: 101a Erlanger Road, London, SE14 5TQ
Officers: Dongfang Daniel Zhao [1994] Director [Chinese]

Savon de V Ltd
Incorporated: 6 November 2017
Registered Office: Meriton Foundry, Meriton Street, Bristol, BS2 0SZ
Major Shareholder: Veronika Korytakova
Officers: Veronika Korytakova [1981] Director [Czech]

Scence Ltd
Incorporated: 17 May 2018
Registered Office: Meaderville House, Wheal Buller, Redruth, Cornwall, TR16 6ST
Major Shareholder: Krista Louise Taylor
Officers: Krista Louise Taylor [1967] Director

Scent from Ireland Ltd
Incorporated: 29 July 2016
Net Worth: £2,310 *Total Assets:* £25,519
Registered Office: Unit 47c Innotec Drive, Balloo Road, Bangor, Co Down, BT19 7PD
Major Shareholder: Patrick Laurence Duggan
Officers: Patrick Laurence Duggan [1958] Director/Candle Manufacturer

The Scent Pod Company Limited
Incorporated: 19 January 2017
Registered Office: Hawthorn House, Upper Aston, Claverley, Wolverhampton, W Midlands, WV5 7EE
Major Shareholder: Tami Murray
Officers: Tami Maria Murray [1970] Director

Scent To Inspire Ltd
Incorporated: 26 May 2018
Registered Office: Mentone, Timsbury Road, High Littleton, Bristol, BS39 6HL
Major Shareholder: Richard Geoffrey Howard
Officers: Nigel Paul Dominic Bond [1959] Director/Accountant

Scents of Nature Ltd
Incorporated: 22 January 2018
Registered Office: Gardeners Cottage, Rectory Farm, Finchampstead, Berks, RG40 4JY
Major Shareholder: Jonathan David Chapman
Officers: Jonathan David Chapman [1972] Director

Scentz of Smell Ltd
Incorporated: 9 February 2017
Net Worth: £224 *Total Assets:* £2,391
Registered Office: 72 Borough Road, Middlesbrough, Cleveland, TS1 2JH
Shareholder: Safraz Hussain
Officers: Debbie Coulson [1981] Director; Safraz Hussain [1986] Director

Science for Skin Ltd.
Incorporated: 12 June 2015
Net Worth: £1,660 *Total Assets:* £1,660
Registered Office: 7a Ramore Street, Portrush, Co Antrim, BT56 8BD
Shareholders: Johanne Brolly; James Davies
Officers: Dr Johanne Brolly [1979] Director; James Davies [1980] Director

Scots Mist Ltd
Incorporated: 22 May 2015
Registered Office: 240 Old Castle Road, Cathcart, Glasgow, G44 5EZ
Major Shareholder: Matthew Wilson
Officers: Matthew Wilson [1982] Director/Warehouse Operative

Barbara Scott Aromatics Ltd
Incorporated: 27 April 2017
Net Worth: £9,454 *Total Assets:* £14,162
Registered Office: Unit 17a, Pineapple Business Park, Salwayash, Bridport, Dorset, DT6 5DB
Officers: Barbara Scott [1957] Director

Scrubbingtons Limited
Incorporated: 12 September 2014
Net Worth Deficit: £63,250 *Total Assets:* £81,078
Registered Office: Team House, 1 Fairview Estate, Henley on Thames, Oxon, RG9 1HE
Shareholders: Emma Cranstoun; Karen Waring
Officers: Emma Cranstoun [1975] Director; Mark John Simon Cranstoun [1971] Director; David William Waring [1963] Director/Wine Merchant; Karen Waring [1972] Director

Scrummy U Health Ltd
Incorporated: 7 February 2018
Registered Office: 37 Elgood Avenue, Northwood, Middlesex, HA6 3QR
Shareholder: Hilda Wright
Officers: Daryl Olutoye Wright [1980] Director; Hilda Wright [1980] Director

SE & SA Limited
Incorporated: 5 April 2017
Registered Office: 245 Sherrard Road, London, E12 6UG
Shareholders: Fulya Salur; Gizem Ezgi Senturk
Officers: Fulya Salur [1983] Director/Sales [Turkish]; Gizem Ezgi Senturk [1985] Director/Finance [Turkish]

Sears UK Ltd
Incorporated: 7 January 2008 *Employees:* 1
Net Worth Deficit: £49,175 *Total Assets:* £29,318
Registered Office: 42 Cranbourne Gardens, London, NW11 0HP
Major Shareholder: Damini Sharma
Officers: Damini Sharma [1977] Director/Analyst [Australian]

Seilich Limited
Incorporated: 12 November 2018
Registered Office: 7 Tyneholm Cottages, Pencaitland, Tranent, E Lothian, EH34 5AD
Major Shareholder: Sally Gouldstone
Officers: Dr Sally Gouldstone [1980] Director/Botanist

Sensa Personal Care Limited
Incorporated: 6 August 2013 *Employees:* 9
Net Worth Deficit: £86,031 *Total Assets:* £213,727
Registered Office: 12a Fleet Business Park, Sandy Lane, Church Crookham, Fleet, Hants, GU52 8BF
Shareholders: Patricia Winyard; Simon Andrew Winyard
Officers: John Streeton Ward OBE [1933] Director; Patricia Winyard [1948] Director; Simon Andrew Winyard [1973] Director

Sensapeel Ltd
Incorporated: 11 February 2013 *Employees:* 5
Net Worth Deficit: £184,699 *Total Assets:* £20,597
Registered Office: Norton Hill Lodge, Norton Hill, Snettisham, Norfolk, PE31 7LZ
Shareholder: Paul Courtney Bishopp
Officers: Paul Courtney Bishopp [1957] Director/Sales Manager; Valerie Joy Bishopp [1947] Director/Accountant; David William Carter [1946] Director/Marketing; Michael James Fox [1951] Director/Engineer; David Ian Walker [1980] Director

Sensora Limited
Incorporated: 24 February 2014 *Employees:* 1
Net Worth: £16,736 *Total Assets:* £20,800
Registered Office: 35 Stamford New Road, Altrincham, Cheshire, WA14 1EB
Shareholders: Eric Steven Reed; Sharon Naomi Reed
Officers: Eric Steven Reed [1959] Director

Sharakkas United Kingdom Limited
Incorporated: 28 February 2017
Registered Office: 71-75 Shelton Street, Covent Garden, London, WC2H 9JQ
Major Shareholder: Amr Sharaka
Officers: AMR Sharaka [1977] Director [Egyptian]

Sharrier Beauty Incorporated Limited
Incorporated: 6 July 2011
Net Worth: £100 *Total Assets:* £100
Registered Office: Blue House Farm Office, Brentwood Road, West Horndon, Essex, CM13 3LX
Major Shareholder: Colin Meredith Barthelmy
Officers: Colin Meredith Barthelmy [1961] Managing Director; Roxanne Sharrier [1987] Sales Director

Shaw & Company Business Ltd
Incorporated: 4 July 2013
Net Worth: £49,033 *Total Assets:* £53,656
Registered Office: 2 Chancery Place, Writtle, Chelmsford, Essex, CM1 3DY
Major Shareholder: Karen Louise Marsh
Officers: Karen Louise Marsh [1969] Director

Shea Natural Skincare Limited
Incorporated: 2 November 2018
Registered Office: 5 Little Onn Road, Church Eaton, Stafford, ST20 0AY
Shareholders: Louise Emma Charlotte McLintock-Peasley; Patrick James Paul McLintock
Officers: Patrick James Paul McLintock [1949] Director; Louise Emma Charlotte McLintock-Peasley [1978] Director

Sheabynature Ltd
Incorporated: 14 March 2017
Net Worth Deficit: £7,000 *Total Assets:* £4,000
Registered Office: 4 Victorian Crescent, Doncaster, S Yorks, DN2 5BW
Major Shareholder: Chinwe Mercy Russell
Officers: Chinwe Mercy Russell [1970] Director

Shifting London Ltd
Incorporated: 15 November 2018
Registered Office: 22 Queen Street, Gravesend, Kent, DA12 2EE
Major Shareholder: Angelo Mancuso
Officers: Angelo Mancuso [1961] Director [Italian]

Shinso Skin Care Limited
Incorporated: 16 February 2011 *Employees:* 1
Net Worth Deficit: £13,017 *Total Assets:* £36,413
Registered Office: 17 Cavendish Square, London, W1G 0PH
Parent: Shinso Skin Care Inc
Officers: Naoteru Tsuruta [1970] Director/Self Employed [Japanese]

Sikania Ltd
Incorporated: 26 January 2017
Net Worth: £357 *Total Assets:* £1,447
Registered Office: 50 Mayfield Road, Gosport, Hants, PO12 1RA
Major Shareholder: Consolazione Ranno
Officers: Consolazione Ranno [1979] Director/Chemist [Italian]

Silyn Products Ltd
Incorporated: 21 May 2012
Net Worth: £815 *Total Assets:* £68,264
Registered Office: 205 Well Street, London, E9 6QU
Shareholders: Simon Bailey; Linda Rose O'Neill
Officers: Margaret Trotter, Secretary; Lynda Rose O'Neill [1960] Director/Manufacturer

Simply Ewe Limited
Incorporated: 10 April 2017
Net Worth Deficit: £331 *Total Assets:* £69
Registered Office: 5 Targetts Mead, Tisbury, Salisbury, Wilts, SP3 6SR
Major Shareholder: Clare Brunton
Officers: Clare Brunton [1983] Director

Simply Seaweed Limited
Incorporated: 19 April 2017
Registered Office: 19b Kings Road, Belfast, BT5 6JF
Major Shareholder: Pauline Black
Officers: Pauline Black [1963] Director

Since Six Ltd
Incorporated: 28 December 2017
Registered Office: 7 Devonshire House, 1 Walford Road, London, N16 8EW
Major Shareholder: Hannah George
Officers: Hannah George [1987] Director/Cosmetic Consultant

Sipro (UK) Ltd
Incorporated: 1 July 2013
Net Worth Deficit: £567 *Total Assets:* £1,002
Registered Office: Pentax House, South Hill Avenue, South Harrow, Middlesex, HA2 0DU
Shareholders: Abdullah Soltan Talib; Noraini Binti Soltan Talib
Officers: Abdul Rahman Soltan Talib [1966] Director [Malaysian]; Abdullah Soltan Talib [1953] Director [Malaysian]; Noraini Binti Soltan Talib [1961] Director [Malaysian]

Skin Defence Limited
Incorporated: 22 December 2014
Registered Office: 88 The Martlets, Rustington, Littlehampton, W Sussex, BN16 2UF
Major Shareholder: Richard Patrick Sinnott
Officers: Richard Patrick Sinnott [1993] Director

Skin Intuition Ltd
Incorporated: 25 January 2019
Registered Office: 36 Brecon Lodge, 2 Wintergreen Boulevard, West Drayton, Middlesex, UB7 9GJ
Shareholders: Yvonne Ile; David Thomas
Officers: Yvonne Ile [1995] Director/Student; David Thomas [1997] Director/Student

Skin Nectar Ltd
Incorporated: 21 February 2018
Registered Office: 20-22 Wenlock Road, London, N1 7GU
Major Shareholder: Venita Machnicki
Officers: Venita Machnicki, Secretary; Venita Machnicki [1979] Director/Aromatherapist

The Skin Specialist Limited
Incorporated: 24 August 2010 *Employees:* 2
Net Worth Deficit: £259,864 *Total Assets:* £13,293
Registered Office: The French Quarter, 114 High Street, Southampton, SO14 2AA
Shareholders: John Mountney; Neena Nayak
Officers: Dr John Mountney [1966] Director/Doctor; Dr Neena Nayak [1970] Director

Skincare Laboratories Ltd
Incorporated: 5 April 2018
Registered Office: International House, 24 Holborn Viaduct, London, EC1A 2BN
Major Shareholder: Muhammad Khyber
Officers: Muhammad Khyber [1980] Director

Skinirvana Limited
Incorporated: 18 July 2017
Registered Office: Basement Flat 1, 8 Lansdowne Road, Hove, E Sussex, BN3 1FF
Major Shareholder: Mary-Rose Lobo
Officers: Mary-Rose Lobo [1980] Director

Skinsence Ltd
Incorporated: 16 November 2018
Registered Office: 11 Droxford Crescent, Tadley, Hants, RG26 3BA
Shareholders: Alan Crawford; Sheila May Dandy Crawford
Officers: Alan Crawford [1944] Sales Director; Sheila May Dandy Crawford [1950] Financial Director

Skyn Deep Ltd
Incorporated: 7 August 2017
Net Worth Deficit: £1,672 *Total Assets:* £685
Registered Office: Kemp House, 152-160 City Road, London, EC1V 2NX
Major Shareholder: Deniz Altinoluk
Officers: Deniz Altinoluk [1989] Director/Massage Therapist & Mindfulness Teacher

Slavikk Ltd
Incorporated: 24 January 2019
Registered Office: 55 Petworth Court, Bath Road, Reading, Berks, RG1 6PH
Shareholders: Lucie Sediva; Julia Komornikova
Officers: Julia Komornikova [1984] Director [Slovak]; Lucie Sediva [1975] Director [Czech]

Sloane Home Ltd
Incorporated: 14 November 2013
Net Worth Deficit: £3,650 *Total Assets:* £37,320
Registered Office: The Rectory, Llandow, Cowbridge, Vale of Glamorgan, CF71 7NT
Major Shareholder: Leanne Peta Johns
Officers: Leanne Peta Johns [1971] Director

Smelliz Ltd
Incorporated: 15 February 2019
Registered Office: 2 Factory Way, Chorley, Lancs, PR7 3FH
Shareholders: Sarah Christina Stewart; Emma Jayne Lewis
Officers: Emma Jayne Lewis [1998] Managing Director; Sarah Christina Stewart [1987] Managing Director

So Skincare Limited
Incorporated: 10 January 2019
Registered Office: 15 Leach Road, Aylesbury, Bucks, HP21 8LG
Shareholders: Olivia Frances Kilburn; Serena Ann Cuthbert
Officers: Serena Ann Cuthbert [1983] Director; Olivia Frances Kilburn [1987] Director

Soak Rochford Ltd
Incorporated: 12 December 2018
Registered Office: 10 Tongue End, Spalding, Lincs, PE11 3JJ
Major Shareholder: Jason Robert Rochford
Officers: Jason Robert Rochford [1989] Director

The Soap Cellar Limited
Incorporated: 11 July 2016
Registered Office: 9 South Town, Dartmouth, Devon, TQ6 9BX
Major Shareholder: Daniel Khoo
Officers: Daniel Khoo, Secretary; Daniel Khoo [1980] Director [Malaysian]

The Soap Legacy Ltd
Incorporated: 15 May 2018
Registered Office: 40c Preston New Road, Blackburn, BB2 6AH
Shareholders: Muhammad Mobeen-Ul-Anwar Ismail; Husnabanu Patel
Officers: Muhammad Mobeen-Ul-Anwar Ismail [1987] Director; Husnabanu Patel [1982] Director

The Soap People Ltd
Incorporated: 2 October 2018
Registered Office: Chapel Grange, Chapel Lane, East Chiltington, Lewes, E Sussex, BN7 3BA
Major Shareholder: Helen Louise Munier
Officers: Helen Louise Munier, Secretary; Helen Louise Munier [1974] Director/Graphic Designer

The Soap Souk Ltd
Incorporated: 23 August 2017
Net Worth Deficit: £602 *Total Assets:* £370
Registered Office: 41 Quinton Road, Coventry, Warwicks, CV3 5FE
Major Shareholder: Marria Jeena
Officers: Marria Jeena [1992] Director/Accountant

Soapberries Ltd
Incorporated: 25 April 2018
Registered Office: 20-22 Wenlock Road, London, N1 7GU
Shareholders: Valerie Anne Humphrey; Sophie Louise Humphrey
Officers: Sophie Louise Humphrey [1996] Marketing Director; Valerie Anne Humphrey [1963] Director

Soapy Skin Limited
Incorporated: 18 April 2013
Net Worth Deficit: £22,049 *Total Assets:* £13,866
Registered Office: 1 Springwater Close, Bolton, Lancs, BL2 4NT
Shareholders: David Gordon Shorrocks; Janet Marie Shorrocks
Officers: Janet Shorrocks, Secretary; Janet Marie Shorrocks [1968] Director

Softme Beauty Ltd
Incorporated: 8 November 2018
Registered Office: Charles Mugagga, 25 Washington Avenue, Manor Park, London, E12 5JA
Shareholders: Catherine Nakato; Rachael Bassey
Officers: Rachael Bassey, Secretary; Rachael Bassey [1995] Director/Economist [Nigerian]; Catherine Nakato [1984] Director/Accounts [Ugandan]

Solab Group Limited
Incorporated: 16 April 2012 *Employees:* 166
Previous: Hampshire Cosmetics Limited
Net Worth: £1,323,332 *Total Assets:* £9,265,814
Registered Office: Brambles House, Waterberry Drive, Waterlooville, Hants, PO7 7UW
Officers: Wayne Stuart Humphreys [1961] Director/Chartered Accountant; Julien Philippe Noel Henry Laporte [1979] Director [French]; Mark Polding [1963] Director; Michael John Ward [1963] Director/Board Chairman

Solar Cosmetics International Limited
Incorporated: 6 November 1996
Net Worth: £75,176 *Total Assets:* £75,176
Registered Office: Unit 3 Heads of The Valley Industrial Estate, Rhymney, Tredegar, Gwent, NP22 5RL
Parent: Richards and Appleby Limited
Officers: Dilip Raichand Shah, Secretary/Director; Mitchell Lawrence Field [1952] Director

The Somerset Toiletry Company Limited
Incorporated: 8 April 1999 *Employees:* 44
Net Worth: £2,109,195 *Total Assets:* £3,623,954
Registered Office: Unit 15 Clutton Hill Farm Estate, Clutton, Bristol, BS39 5QQ
Major Shareholder: Sakina Bowhay
Officers: Robert Taylor, Secretary; Sakina Buoy [1960] Director/Chairman

Sonyah Adan Limited
Incorporated: 5 November 2018
Registered Office: 74 Dudley Road, London, IG1 1ET
Major Shareholder: Chomba Mulundika
Officers: Chomba Mulundika [1973] Director/Accountant [Zambian]

Sophrina Gos Limited
Incorporated: 4 June 2018
Registered Office: Room 58, Lime Tree House, North Castle Street, Alloa, Clackmannanshire, FK10 1EX
Major Shareholder: Oboratare Tracy Inije
Officers: Oboratare Tracy Inije [1976] Fashion Director [British/Nigerian]

South West Aesthetics Ltd
Incorporated: 19 September 2017 *Employees:* 2
Net Worth: £203,297 *Total Assets:* £204,073
Registered Office: Suite 128, Pegaxis House, 61 Victoria Road, Surbiton, Surrey, KT6 4JX
Shareholders: Chafic Kaedbey; Kamel Malek Jonblat
Officers: Kamel Malek Jonblat [1973] Managing Director [Lebanese]; Dr Chafic Kaedbey [1974] Director of Product Development and Operations [Lebanese]

Sphere 7 Lab Ltd
Incorporated: 13 August 2018
Registered Office: Unit 10, Studio 20, Elizabeth Industrial Estate, Juno Way, London, SE14 5RW
Major Shareholder: Maxamillion Henry
Officers: Maxamillion Henry [1983] Director

Spiezia Organics Limited
Incorporated: 16 May 2003
Net Worth Deficit: £183,731 *Total Assets:* £157,594
Registered Office: Whyfield, Building A, Truro Business Park, Threemilestone, Truro, Cornwall, TR4 9LF
Major Shareholder: Amanda Jane Vivian Winwood
Officers: Amanda Jane Vivian Winwood, Secretary/Hotelier; Amanda Jane Vivian Winwood [1962] Director/Hotelier

Spirit of The Isle Ltd.
Incorporated: 26 February 2013
Net Worth Deficit: £14,488 *Total Assets:* £14,584
Registered Office: Penrhiw Bach, Bryngwran, Holyhead, Anglesey, LL65 3RD
Officers: Nia Jones [1967] Director/Housewife; Tony Wyn Jones [1962] Director/Local Government Officer

Splash Cosmetics Ltd
Incorporated: 27 September 2018
Registered Office: 15 Beach Road, Westgate-on-Sea, Kent, CT8 8AD
Shareholders: Hannah Wild; Fredrick Wild
Officers: Fredrick Wild [1992] Director; Hannah Wild [1992] Director

Spots & Stripes Products Ltd
Incorporated: 14 May 2018
Registered Office: The Hatch, High Street, Seend, Melksham, Wilts, SN12 6NW
Major Shareholder: Charlotte-Anne Field Fidler
Officers: Charlotte-Anne Field Fidler [1965] Director

Squeaky Clean Queen Ltd
Incorporated: 5 July 2018
Registered Office: 74 Southfield Road, Worthing, W Sussex, BN14 9EQ
Officers: Laura Vaughan-Field [1983] Director

Squires and Trelawny Ltd
Incorporated: 19 October 2017
Registered Office: 2 Zulu Mews, London, SW11 2BQ
Major Shareholder: Michael Marshall-Clarke
Officers: Michael Marshall-Clarke [1968] Director

Stantondown Limited
Incorporated: 2 February 1984 *Employees:* 13
Net Worth: £593,894 *Total Assets:* £686,153
Registered Office: Shafton Lane, Leeds, LS11 9QY
Officers: Lee Jason Smith, Secretary; Lee Jason Smith [1967] Director/Production Manager; Stewart Leslie Smith [1965] Director/Production Manager; Terence Smith [1937] Director/General Manager

Lauren Stone Limited
Incorporated: 7 June 2016
Net Worth Deficit: £51,025 *Total Assets:* £19,037
Registered Office: McLintock Chartered Accountants, 2 Hilliards Court, Chester Business Park, Chester, CH4 9PX
Major Shareholder: Lauren Belinda Simon
Officers: Lauren Belinda Simon [1972] Director

Storey Enterprises Limited
Incorporated: 7 October 2013 *Employees:* 2
Net Worth: £19,007 *Total Assets:* £31,525
Registered Office: 19 Quernstone Lane, Northampton, NN4 8UN
Shareholders: Suzanna Sujantha Storey; Daniel Christopher Storey
Officers: Daniel Storey [1980] Director; Suzanna Sujantha Storey [1985] Director

Stormfree Holdings Ltd
Incorporated: 24 July 2013
Previous: Hive Originals Limited
Net Worth Deficit: £38,572 *Total Assets:* £18,302
Registered Office: 38-42 Newport Street, Swindon, Wilts, SN1 3DR
Major Shareholder: Claire Elizabeth Barker
Officers: Claire Elizabeth Barker [1974] Director

Strathpeffer Spa Soap Company Limited
Incorporated: 3 March 2004
Registered Office: Woodside, Heights of Inchvannie, Strathpeffer, Ross & Cromarty, IV14 9AE
Shareholders: John Thomas Fulton; Elizabeth Brock Kendall
Officers: Elizabeth Brock Kendall, Secretary/Teacher [American]; John Thomas Fulton [1952] Director/Technician; Elizabeth Brock Kendall [1957] Director/Teacher [American]

H.E. Stringer (Perfurmery) Limited
Incorporated: 3 July 1962
Registered Office: c/o H E Stringer Ltd, Icknield Way, Tring, Herts, HP23 4JZ
Parent: H. E. Stringer Limited
Officers: Stephen David Baxter, Secretary; Gwendoline Harriette Baxter [1946] Director/Businesswoman; Stephen David Baxter [1952] Director/Consultant

Stunning Fragrance Ltd
Incorporated: 10 October 2018
Registered Office: c/o 18 Hall Street, Bury, Lancs, BL8 1RY
Shareholders: Paul Mainwaring; Barbara Allen
Officers: Barbara Allen [1943] Director; Paul Mainwaring [1958] Director

Sub Tropic Limited
Incorporated: 21 August 1995
Registered Office: 27 Connaught Street, Port Talbot, W Glamorgan, SA13 1ET
Officers: John Allan Simonson, Secretary; James Alexander Simonson [1989] Director/Student; John Allan Simonson [1939] Director/Consultant

Sultan Pasha Artisanal Perfumery Ltd
Incorporated: 17 May 2017
Net Worth: £2,633 *Total Assets:* £14,455
Registered Office: 20-22 Wenlock Road, London, N1 7GU
Major Shareholder: Sultan Zabir Hossain
Officers: Sultan Zabir Hossain [1978] Director

Sundarak Ltd
Incorporated: 11 October 2018
Registered Office: Flat 4, 34 Elm Park Gardens, London, SW10 9NZ
Shareholders: Kate Wilson; Kathleen Adams Kingsford Weber
Officers: Kathleen Adams Kingsford Weber [1973] Director/Producer [American]; Kate Wilson [1969] Director/Producer

Sunshapers Limited
Incorporated: 25 August 2018
Registered Office: 71-75 Shelton Street, London, WC2H 9JQ
Shareholders: Rosa Gardella Trias; Gemma Louise Clarke; Charles Edward Turpin
Officers: Gemma Louise Clarke, Secretary; Gemma Louise Clarke [1962] Director; Rosa Gardella Trias [1979] Director [German]; Charles Edward Turpin [1973] Director

Superfine Manufacturing Limited
Incorporated: 9 January 1963 *Employees:* 20
Net Worth: £3,607,568 *Total Assets:* £4,200,140
Registered Office: Orchard Bank, Glamis Road, Forfar, Angus, DD8 1TD
Major Shareholder: Nigel John Archer
Officers: Julie Patricia Philip, Secretary; Gemma Louise Archer [1984] Director; Lyn Archer [1981] Director; Maureen Archer [1956] Director; Nigel John Archer [1956] Managing Director

Superfood Beauty Limited
Incorporated: 19 November 2018
Registered Office: 69 Moorside North, Newcastle upon Tyne, NE4 9DU
Major Shareholder: Sarah Upendo Hannah Taylor
Officers: Sarah Upendo Hannah Taylor [1974] Director

Surefil Beauty Products Limited
Incorporated: 20 February 1980 *Employees:* 72
Net Worth: £2,401,510 *Total Assets:* £3,569,123
Registered Office: The Bedford Centre, Bedford Street, St Helens, Merseyside, WA9 1PN
Parent: Surefil Investments Limited
Officers: Catherine Jeanette Critchley, Secretary; Catherine Jeanette Critchley [1968] Director/Accountant; Paul Barry Critchley [1969] Director; James MacAvoy [1952] Director

Swallowfield PLC
Incorporated: 7 January 1986 *Employees:* 593
Net Worth: £26,943,000 *Total Assets:* £60,490,000
Registered Office: Swallowfield House, Station Road, Wellington, Somerset, TA21 8NL
Officers: Matthew Gazzard, Secretary; Edward John Beale [1960] Director/Chief Executive; Franklin Pinhas Berrebi [1943] Director [French]; Jane Fletcher [1967] Director/Sales & Marketing; Matthew Gazzard [1971] Group Financial Director; Brendan Hynes [1960] Director; Roger Steven McDowell [1955] Director; Timothy James Perman [1962] Director

Swanny's Ltd.
Incorporated: 22 May 2017
Registered Office: The Cottage, 26 Wolverhampton Road, Pattingham, Wolverhampton, W Midlands, WV6 7AF
Shareholders: Noi Swan; Brian Michael Swan
Officers: Brian Michael Swan [1936] Director; Noi Swan [1965] Director

Swaziboy Limited
Incorporated: 18 March 2013
Net Worth: £89,138 *Total Assets:* £184,132
Registered Office: c/o Breckman & Company, 49 South Molton Street, London, W1K 5LH
Shareholders: Joan Esterhuysen; Richard Grant-Esterhuysen
Officers: Joan Esterhuysen [1946] Director/Dialect Coach; Richard Grant-Esterhuysen [1957] Actor, Writer, Director

Sweet Arabian Ltd
Incorporated: 9 October 2018
Registered Office: 20-22 Wenlock Road, London, N1 7GU
Shareholder: Bogdan Stefanidis-Vlad
Officers: Bogdan Stefanidis-Vlad [1987] Director/Marketing Specialist [Romanian]

Swiss Pharma Dynamic Ltd
Incorporated: 18 February 2016
Registered Office: 27 Old Gloucester Street, London, WC1N 3AX
Major Shareholder: Kiriaki Zartaloudi
Officers: Kyriaki Zartaloudi [1973] Director [Greek]

T & H Marketing Limited
Incorporated: 11 August 2000 *Employees:* 24
Net Worth: £442,749 *Total Assets:* £633,155
Registered Office: Unit 5 Ventura Centre, Factory Road, Upton, Poole, Dorset, BH16 5SL
Shareholders: Christopher Rogerson; Louise Harris
Officers: Christopher Rogerson, Secretary; Louise Harris [1964] Managing Director

TAC Perfumes & Cosmetics (UK) Ltd
Incorporated: 12 February 2018
Registered Office: Kemp House, 160 City Road, London, EC1V 2NX
Shareholders: Khandoker Choudhury; Tasbirul Ahmed Choudhury
Officers: Khandoker Choudhury, Secretary; Tasbirul Choudhury, Secretary; Khandoker Choudhury [1976] Director [Bangladeshi]; Tasbirul Ahmed Choudhury [1966] Managing Director [Bangladeshi]

Tahmasso Limited
Incorporated: 26 March 2018
Registered Office: Old Gunn Court, North Street, Dorking, Surrey, RH4 1DE
Major Shareholder: Souad Malik
Officers: Souad Malik [1973] Director/Artisan [French/British]

Eve Taylor (London) Limited
Incorporated: 29 July 1968 *Employees:* 21
Net Worth: £632,366 *Total Assets:* £1,049,308
Registered Office: Unit 1 Mallard Business Centre, Bretton, Peterborough, Cambs, PE3 8YR
Shareholders: Raymond Neil Taylor; Alan Leslie Taylor; Christopher Mark Taylor
Officers: Evelyn May Taylor OBE, Secretary; Alan Leslie Taylor [1952] Director/Export Manager; Christopher Mark Taylor [1963] Marketing Director; Evelyn May Taylor OBE [1932] Director

TCJ Treatments Limited
Incorporated: 3 May 2018
Registered Office: 204 Horton Road, Datchet, Berks, SL3 9HL
Officers: Dean Van Elkan, Secretary; Amanda Van Elkan [1979] Director

Tea & Therapy Ltd
Incorporated: 10 April 2018
Registered Office: Whyfield, Building A, Green Court, Truro Business Park, Threemilestone, Truro, Cornwall, TR4 9LF
Major Shareholder: Amanda Jane Vivian Barlow
Officers: Amanda Jane Vivian Barlow [1962] Director

Teknord Limited
Incorporated: 18 February 1999 *Employees:* 1
Net Worth: £1,059,704 *Total Assets:* £1,266,151
Registered Office: Unit B, 1B Crimple Court, Hornbeam Park, Hookstone Road, Harrogate, N Yorks, HG2 8PB
Shareholders: Nader Iskander; Medhat Iskander
Officers: Graham Edward Hindmarsh, Secretary; Graham Edward Hindmarsh [1947] Director/Food Technologist; Medhat Iskander [1954] Director/Engineer [Egyptian]; Nader Iskander [1951] Director/Engineer [Egyptian]

Terra Mater Ltd
Incorporated: 20 June 2018
Registered Office: 2d Berwick Road, Port Glasgow, Inverclyde, PA14 5QN
Major Shareholder: Simone Accolla
Officers: Simone Accolla [2001] Director/Entrepreneur [Italian]

TH / Edition Ltd
Incorporated: 15 January 2014
Previous: Edition Perfumes Limited
Net Worth: £65,587 *Total Assets:* £75,004
Registered Office: Acre House, 11-15 William Road, London, NW1 3ER
Major Shareholder: Timothy Han
Officers: Timothy Han [1971] Director/Designer [Canadian]

Thatcompany Limited
Incorporated: 7 April 2009
Registered Office: 5-6 Underhill Street, London, NW1 7HS
Officers: David John Welsh, Secretary; Timothy Seldon Blanks [1954] Director/Writer [New Zealander]; Jeff Blaine Lounds [1966] Director/Sales Executive [Canadian]

THC Effect Ltd
Incorporated: 22 April 2014 *Employees:* 1
Net Worth Deficit: £127,746 *Total Assets:* £70,024
Registered Office: 4 Exchange Place, Middlesbrough, Cleveland, TS1 1DR
Major Shareholder: Scott Morgan
Officers: Scott Morgan [1971] Director

Thebubblebar Ltd
Incorporated: 11 February 2019
Registered Office: 62 Ullswater Avenue, Nuneaton, Warwicks, CV11 6HS
Major Shareholder: Anissa Boumecid-Thompson
Officers: Anissa Boumecid-Thompson [1995] Director [British/Algerian]

TheManeCompany Ltd
Incorporated: 26 September 2018
Registered Office: 14 Portland Road, Great Sankey, Warrington, Cheshire, WA5 8DR
Major Shareholder: Sean Antony Cosgrave
Officers: Sean Antony Cosgrave [1988] Director

This Wode Company Ltd
Incorporated: 11 April 2014
Net Worth: £11,183 *Total Assets:* £105,103
Registered Office: 5-6 Underhill Street, London, NW1 7HS
Officers: Zowie Broach [1966] Director/Designer; Susan Irvine [1961] Director/Writer; Brian Kirkby [1965] Director/Designer; Jeff Blaine Lounds [1966] Director [Canadian]; Paul Douglas White [1959] Director/Designer

Thiscompany Limited
Incorporated: 7 April 2009 *Employees:* 4
Net Worth: £12,180,033 *Total Assets:* £20,047,952
Registered Office: 5-6 Underhill Street, London, NW1 7HS
Shareholders: Escentric Molecules Ug; Jeff Blaine Lounds
Officers: David John Welsh, Secretary; Hugh Gerard Devlin [1962] Director/Consultant; Jeff Blaine Lounds [1966] Director/Sales Executive [Canadian]

Thomas Andy Ltd.
Incorporated: 8 September 2017
Registered Office: 3rd Floor, 207 Regent Street, London, W1B 3HH
Officers: Thomas Andy Branson [1987] Director/General Manager [Croatian]

Thread and Co UK Limited
Incorporated: 26 February 2018
Registered Office: Kemp House, 160 City Road, London, EC1V 2NX
Major Shareholder: Charmilla Herath
Officers: Charmilla Herath, Secretary; Charmilla Herath [1978] Director [Australian]

Three Fizzy Pigs Ltd
Incorporated: 21 November 2017
Registered Office: 38 Farmdale Grove, Rednal, Birmingham, B45 9NA
Major Shareholder: Laura Plimmer
Officers: Laura Plimmer [1997] Director/Owner

Three Organics Ltd
Incorporated: 12 September 2017
Registered Office: 71-75 Shelton Street, Covent Garden, London, WC2H 9JQ
Major Shareholder: Hameed Alam
Officers: Roszella Ibrahim, Secretary; Hameed Alam [1967] Director/Finance Manager; Sagira Hussain [1968] Director/Teacher

Tiger Lily Soapery Ltd
Incorporated: 27 September 2017
Registered Office: 8 Westhorpe Close, King's Lynn, Norfolk, PE30 3WB
Major Shareholder: Michele Leagh Beard
Officers: Michele Leagh Beard [1974] Director/Tiger Lily Soapery [American]

Toddle Born Wild Limited
Incorporated: 31 August 2016
Net Worth: £12,600 *Total Assets:* £12,600
Registered Office: Wrexham Enterprise Hub, 11-13 Rhosddu Road, Wrexham, Clwyd, LL11 1AT
Major Shareholder: Hannah Saunders
Officers: Ian David Gale [1970] Director/RAF Officer; Deri Green [1980] Director/Investor; Martyn James Hogg [1956] Investor Director Toddle; Sophie Maunder [1986] Director/Buyer; Samantha Marie Oxford [1979] Director; Hannah Saunders [1985] Director; Maxime Daniel Philippe Wibaux [1986] Director/Student [French]

Tom's Garden Limited
Incorporated: 16 May 2017
Registered Office: 17 St Peters Place, Fleetwood, Lancs, FY7 6EB
Major Shareholder: Rachael Louise Wheeldon
Officers: Rachael Louise Wheeldon [1979] Managing Director

Tranquility Cosmetics Limited
Incorporated: 23 October 2017
Registered Office: 26 Ashton Road, Denton, Manchester, M34 3EX
Shareholders: Kimberley Lindop; Jacob Paul Lindop
Officers: Jacob Paul Lindop [1990] Director; Kimberley Lindop [1995] Director

Travik Chemicals (UK) Limited
Incorporated: 8 November 2010 *Employees:* 10
Net Worth: £300,620 *Total Assets:* £380,966
Registered Office: Unit 24-26 Maitland Road, Lion Barn Business Park, Needham Market, Suffolk, IP6 8NS
Shareholders: Carl John Climpson; Kim Joy Climpson
Officers: Carl John Climpson [1963] Director; Kim Joy Climpson [1961] Director; Laura Climpson [1988] Director; Robert James Climpson [1990] Director

Trees of Beauty Ltd
Incorporated: 20 December 2018
Registered Office: 71-75 Shelton Street, London, WC2H 9JQ
Major Shareholder: Cendesse Zidi
Officers: Cendesse Zidi [1979] Director/Manager [French]

Tresaigh Ltd
Incorporated: 14 May 2018
Registered Office: 5 Eccleston House, Tulse Hill, London, SW2 2HP
Major Shareholder: Tracy Schouburgh
Officers: Tracy Schouburgh [1970] Director/Local Government Officer

Triblaz Limited
Incorporated: 25 March 2010
Registered Office: 72 Burghley Road, Peterborough, Cambs, PE1 2QE
Officers: Ayotunde Adetokunbo Adekaiyero [1966] Director/Chemist

Geo. F. Trumper (Perfumer and Products) Limited
Incorporated: 27 January 1923 *Employees:* 18
Net Worth: £1,307,793 *Total Assets:* £1,759,021
Registered Office: 166 Fairbridge Road, London, N19 3HT
Major Shareholder: Paulette Bersch
Officers: Paulette Bersch, Secretary; Paulette Bersch [1949] Director; Sebastian Cherchi Bersch [1980] Director/Manager

Tsaka Limited
Incorporated: 5 April 2016
Net Worth Deficit: £43,382 *Total Assets:* £7,395
Registered Office: 2 Twynes Meadow, Hook, Hants, RG27 9UG
Major Shareholder: Celmira Taju Amade
Officers: Celmira Taju Amade [1990] Director [Mozambican]

The Top UK Perfume and Toilet Preparations Manufacturers dellam

TWC Products Limited
Incorporated: 8 April 2016 Employees: 2
Net Worth Deficit: £59,570 Total Assets: £854,136
Registered Office: St Bride's House, 10 Salisbury Square, London, EC4Y 8EH
Officers: Lars Soren Sorensen [1956] Director [Danish]

Twelve Beauty Ltd
Incorporated: 9 February 2015
Net Worth: £20,890 Total Assets: £55,560
Registered Office: 12 Wyndham House, 24 Bryanston Square, London, W1H 2DS
Major Shareholder: Pedro Juan Catala Moncho
Officers: Pedro Juan Catala Moncho [1974] Director/Pharmacist [Spanish]

UK Pandora Fairy Skin Beautiyfying Co., Ltd
Incorporated: 11 December 2018
Registered Office: 9 Pantygraigwen Road, Pontypridd, Mid Glamorgan, CF37 2RR
Major Shareholder: Qingye Ruan
Officers: Qingye Ruan [1979] Director [Chinese]

Ulu Botanicals Ltd
Incorporated: 3 December 2018
Registered Office: 71-75 Shelton Street, London, WC2H 9JQ
Shareholder: Charity Mutonga Mauluka
Officers: Charity Mutonga Mauluka, Secretary; Charity Mutonga Mauluka [1964] Director/Speech and Language Therapy Assistant

Umma Therapy Ltd.
Incorporated: 24 February 2014
Registered Office: 215 Lymington Avenue, London, N22 6JL
Major Shareholder: Georgina Donoghue
Officers: Georgina Donoghue [1975] Director/Complementary Therapist

Un Air D'Antan Limited
Incorporated: 11 May 2017
Net Worth: £141,321 Total Assets: £149,946
Registered Office: 9 Harley House, Brunswick Place, London, NW1 4PR
Shareholders: Sophie Christine Laporte; Julien Philippe Noel Henry Laporte
Officers: Julien Philippe Noel Henry Laporte [1974] Director [French]; Sophie Christine Laporte [1977] Director [French]

Uncareditional Ltd
Incorporated: 3 September 2018
Registered Office: 71-75 Shelton Street, London, WC2H 9JQ
Major Shareholder: Luisa Chirac
Officers: Luisa Chirac [1980] Director/Student [Romanian]

Ungerer Limited
Incorporated: 29 May 1959 Employees: 138
Net Worth: £29,897,000 Total Assets: £35,211,000
Registered Office: Sealand Road, Chester, CH1 4LP
Officers: John Graham Percy, Secretary/Director; John Graham Percy [1960] Director; Kenneth Garretson Voorhees III [1963] Sales Director [American]; Kenneth Garretson Voorhees Jr [1938] Director/President Ungerer & Company [American]

Unique Relaxation Specialist Limited
Incorporated: 17 September 2018
Registered Office: 35 Hollands Avenue, Folkestone, Kent, CT19 6PN
Officers: Corrina Bristow [1978] Director; Jannet Bristow [1956] Director

United Beauty Products Limited
Incorporated: 7 January 2005 Employees: 10
Net Worth: £166,144 Total Assets: £1,487,894
Registered Office: 4th Floor, Imperial House, 8 Kean Street, London, WC2B 4AS
Major Shareholder: Hugh Vincent Cooke
Officers: Robert Douglas Wilson, Secretary [American]; Hugh Vincent Cooke [1950] Director [Irish]; Victoria Sophie Cooke [1990] Director [American]; Robert Douglas Wilson [1959] Director/Lawyer [American]

Universal Chemicals Limited
Incorporated: 24 February 1986 Employees: 4
Net Worth: £3,348 Total Assets: £29,102
Registered Office: Radnor House, Greenwood Close, Cardiff Gate Business Park, Pontprennau, Cardiff, CF23 8AA
Shareholders: Malcolm David Shepherd; Ryan David Shepherd
Officers: Brenda Jean Shepherd, Secretary; Daryl Paxton Shepherd [1974] Director; Malcolm David Shepherd [1948] Managing Director; Ryan David Shepherd [1978] Director

Universal Toiletries Corporation Limited
Incorporated: 27 October 1999 Employees: 7
Net Worth: £779,298 Total Assets: £1,933,357
Registered Office: Unit 7 Bermer Place, Imperial Way, Watford, Herts, WD24 4AY
Major Shareholder: Dinesh Shah
Officers: Mahendra Kanabar, Secretary; Dinesh Chhabildas Shah [1958] Director; Jayshree Dinesh Shah [1963] Director; Karan Shah [1988] Director

Urban Nymph Limited
Incorporated: 10 October 2013
Registered Office: The Design Studio, Royd Ings Avenue, Keighley, W Yorks, BD21 4BZ
Major Shareholder: Julia Margaret Fikkert
Officers: Julia Margaret Fikkert [1971] Managing Director

Urembo Naturally Ltd
Incorporated: 20 March 2018
Registered Office: 83 Ducie Street, Manchester, M1 2JQ
Major Shareholder: Debora Dwamena
Officers: Debora Dwamena [1988] Director/Financial Accountant

Uyumbu Limited
Incorporated: 4 February 2019
Registered Office: Flat 24, Hornsey Road, London, N7 7NL
Major Shareholder: Ngongo Uyumbu Berekad Tongomo
Officers: Ngongo Uyumbu Berekad Tongomo [1996] Director/Businessman

Uzu Ltd
Incorporated: 21 February 2018
Registered Office: 9 Bank Street, Glasgow, G12 8JQ
Major Shareholder: Gael Lambie
Officers: Gael Lambie [1971] Director/Perfumer

Valencia Vanna Ltd.
Incorporated: 8 August 2018
Registered Office: 2 Allied Close, Coventry, Warwicks, CV6 6GN
Major Shareholder: Amanpreet Bajwa
Officers: Amanpreet Bajwa [1996] Director/Cosmetics

Valorem Bespoke Ltd
Incorporated: 31 July 2018
Registered Office: 16 West Way, Carshalton, Surrey, SM5 4EW
Parent: Valorem Holdings Ltd
Officers: David Adrian Crisp [1958] Director

Vaunt Limited
Incorporated: 1 June 2018
Registered Office: 68 Hillier Road, London, SW11 6AU
Shareholders: Lorenzo James Vasini; Ryan Gordon Hall
Officers: Lorenzo James Vasini [1975] Director

Veloskin Limited
Incorporated: 28 May 2016
Net Worth Deficit: £14,162 *Total Assets:* £18,452
Registered Office: 14c Westfield Court, Mirfield, W Yorks, WF14 9PT
Shareholders: Chrisotpher Lewis Bairstow; Tanya Ann Michaela Bairstow
Officers: Christopher Lewis Bairstow [1982] Director; Tanya Ann Michaela Bairstow [1981] Director

Verde London Ltd.
Incorporated: 11 September 1991
Net Worth: £3,578 *Total Assets:* £42,392
Registered Office: Doshi Accountants Ltd, 6th Floor, Amp House, Dingwall Road, Croydon, Surrey, CR0 2LX
Major Shareholder: Ruby Susan Anne Cook
Officers: Ruby Susan Anne Cook [1948] Director

Very Good Vegan Company Limited
Incorporated: 9 August 2018
Registered Office: 114 Cambrian Way, Basingstoke, Hants, RG22 5AL
Shareholders: Ash Paul Dobrock; Hannah Faye Dobrock
Officers: Ash Paul Dobrock [1983] Director/Civil Servant; Hannah Faye Dobrock [1986] Director/Manager

Vetivert & Co Ltd
Incorporated: 9 March 2017
Net Worth Deficit: £884 *Total Assets:* £146
Registered Office: 156 Mandeville Road, Enfield, Middlesex, EN3 6SG
Major Shareholder: Aanuoluwa Oduyemi
Officers: Aanuoluwa Oduyemi [1989] Director/Student [Nigerian]

Villa Sauod Ltd
Incorporated: 1 November 2018
Registered Office: Premier Business Centre, 47-49 Park Royal Road, London, NW10 7LQ
Major Shareholder: Abdulazeez Althefeeri
Officers: Abdulazeez Althefeeri [1979] Director [Kuwaiti]

Village Barber Skin Products Ltd
Incorporated: 2 December 2013
Net Worth Deficit: £2,830 *Total Assets:* £2,279
Registered Office: 47c Front Street, Langley Park, Co Durham, DH7 9XB
Shareholders: Iain Wilson Kane; Sharon Kane
Officers: Iain Wilson Kane [1962] Director/Barber; Sharon Kane [1961] Director/Secretary

Vinculum Ltd
Incorporated: 2 October 2015
Registered Office: 5-6 Underhill Street, London, NW1 7HS
Officers: David John Welsh, Secretary; Paul Douglas White [1959] Director/Designer

Viraj Organics Ltd
Incorporated: 12 July 2017
Registered Office: 69 High Street, London, N14 6LD
Officers: Viraj Saksena [1977] Director/Self Employed [American]

Virtue Botanicals Limited
Incorporated: 22 June 2018
Registered Office: 62 Park Mead, Sidcup, Kent, DA15 9PJ
Major Shareholder: Villana Charles
Officers: Villana Charles [1983] Director [Trinidadian]

Washworks Bodycare Limited
Incorporated: 11 April 2013
Net Worth Deficit: £125,821 *Total Assets:* £51,509
Registered Office: 207 Regent Street, London, W1B 3HH
Shareholder: Alexandra Louise Turner
Officers: Tejal Ajay Ramnathkar [1981] Director/Entrepreneur [Indian]; Alexandra Louise Turner [1975] Director/Entrepreneur

Waterman Corporate Enterprises Limited
Incorporated: 10 July 2012
Net Worth: £43,246 *Total Assets:* £514,087
Registered Office: Unit 12F-12G, Lidget Lane Industrial Estate, Albion Drive, Thurnscoe, Rotherham, S Yorks, S63 0BA
Major Shareholder: Matt Luca Waterman
Officers: Gail Marie Waterman [1972] Director/Chief Financial Officer (CFO); Matt Luca Waterman [1974] Managing Director/CEO

Wayus Limited
Incorporated: 25 July 2018
Registered Office: 6 Newark Street, Reading, Berks, RG1 2SR
Officers: Angkit Gurung [1993] Director; Dihnesh Gurung [1992] Director; Pukar Gyawali [1992] Director

Wheesht Ltd
Incorporated: 29 August 2018
Registered Office: Summit House, 4-5 Mitchell Street, Edinburgh, EH6 7BD
Major Shareholder: Kelly Ford
Officers: Kelly Ford [1978] Director

Whole International Limited
Incorporated: 2 August 2018
Registered Office: Unit 5 Price Street Business Centre, Birkenhead, Merseyside, CH41 4JQ
Officers: Alison MacKenzie [1963] Commercial Director; Vivien Woerdenweber [1961] Director/Creative Manager

Wicked Vicky Company Limited
Incorporated: 14 August 2018
Registered Office: 39 Watling Street, Brownhills, Walsall, W Midlands, WS8 7PT
Major Shareholder: Viktorija Cerniauskiene
Officers: Dr Viktorija Cerniauskiene [1973] Director/Doctor [Lithuanian]

Wickham Soap Co. Ltd
Incorporated: 17 September 2018
Registered Office: 18 Green Walk, Fareham, Hants, PO15 6AZ
Major Shareholder: Darron Stephen Barnes
Officers: Darron Stephen Barnes [1971] Director

Wild & Organic Bioactive Essentials Limited
Incorporated: 26 July 2007
Net Worth Deficit: £302,508 *Total Assets:* £742
Registered Office: The Barn, 3 Red Brick Cottages, Old Bury Road, Palgrave, Diss, Norfolk, IP22 1AZ
Shareholders: Bruce Smith; Allison Wild
Officers: Bruce William Leo Smith [1952] Director/Chartered Quantity Surveyor; Allison Wild [1962] Director/Writer

The Top UK Perfume and Toilet Preparations Manufacturers

The Wild Bathing Company Ltd
Incorporated: 9 January 2019
Registered Office: 1 Kathleen Avenue, Helens Bay, Bangor, Co Down, BT19 1LF
Major Shareholder: Stephanie Renee Dunlop
Officers: Stephanie Renee Dunlop [1982] Director/Entrepreneur

Wilde Beauty Limited
Incorporated: 25 February 2011
Net Worth: £207,145 *Total Assets:* £245,762
Registered Office: Alexandra House, St Johns Street, Salisbury, Wilts, SP1 2SB
Major Shareholder: Susanne Willis
Officers: Susanne Willis [1966] Director

The Wildsmith Collection Limited
Incorporated: 8 April 2016 *Employees:* 2
Net Worth Deficit: £620,581 *Total Assets:* £373,484
Registered Office: St Bride's House, 10 Salisbury Square, London, EC4Y 8EH
Officers: Lars Soren Sorensen [1956] Director [Danish]

Winterpark Paris Parfums Limited
Incorporated: 13 June 2003
Net Worth Deficit: £181,302
Registered Office: 28 Rosslyn Hill, Hampstead, London, NW3 1NH
Major Shareholder: Nadeem Saifi
Officers: Nadeem Saifi [1954] Director; Sultana Nadeem Saifi [1957] Director [Indian]

Wist and Wonder Limited
Incorporated: 23 August 2017
Registered Office: 135 Engadine Street, London, SW18 5DU
Major Shareholder: Katharine Bryce
Officers: Katharine Bryce [1982] Director/Brand Development

Wonder and Wild Ltd
Incorporated: 16 March 2018
Registered Office: 10 D'Abernon Drive, Stoke D'Abernon, Cobham, Surrey, KT11 3JD
Shareholders: Lucy Mary Hey; Oliver Felstead
Officers: Oliver Felstead [1981] Director; Lucy Mary Hey [1982] Director

Wrath Cosmetics Limited
Incorporated: 10 February 2018
Registered Office: Office 010, Upper Wortley Business Centre, 127 Upper Wortley Road, Leeds, LS12 4JG
Shareholders: Samuel Hague; Michelle Hague
Officers: Michelle Hague [1966] Director; Samuel Hague [1995] Director

Wrimes Cosmetics Ltd
Incorporated: 12 May 2014
Net Worth: £498,210 *Total Assets:* £1,250,000
Registered Office: Unit 1 Access Business Park, Gunnels Wood Road, Stevenage, Herts, SG1 2GR
Shareholders: Lewis Drew Ames; Lee Steven Wright
Officers: Lewis Drew Ames [1989] Director; Lee Steven Wright [1990] Director

WT Limited
Incorporated: 15 September 2005
Registered Office: The Dairy, Manor Courtyard, Aston Sandford, Aylesbury, Bucks, HP17 8JB
Officers: Augusto Loannilli [1955] Director [Italian]

XDC Limited
Incorporated: 3 February 2014
Registered Office: The Pines, Chalk Lane, East Horsley, Leatherhead, Surrey, KT24 6TH
Major Shareholder: Michael Alexander Stuart-Matthews
Officers: Helena Danuta Stuart-Matthews [1955] Director

The Yellow Can Company Limited
Incorporated: 27 June 1989
Registered Office: Swallowfield House, Station Road, Wellington, Somerset, TA21 8NL
Officers: Jane Fletcher [1967] Director/Sales & Marketing; Matthew Gazzard [1971] Group Financial Director; Timothy James Perman [1962] Director

Yess Essentials Limited
Incorporated: 17 January 2001
Net Worth: £22,355 *Total Assets:* £22,355
Registered Office: 82 Felixstowe Road, London, SE2 9QH
Shareholders: Oluyemisi Olabisi Shode; Olufemi Olukayode Shode
Officers: Babatunde Oladipo Obisesan, Secretary; Dr. Olufemi Olukayode Shode [1953] Director/Chemist; Dr Oluyemisi Olabisi Shode [1954] Director/Chemist

Yin Yang Natural Sciences Limited
Incorporated: 31 October 2007
Net Worth Deficit: £39,538
Registered Office: The Courtyard, River Way, Uckfield, E Sussex, TN22 1SL
Parent: Agronomy Capital Advisors Limited
Officers: Douglas George Hawkins [1951] Director/Farmer [New Zealander]

Yverman Ltd
Incorporated: 9 February 2009
Previous: Studio XN Limited
Net Worth: £4,751 *Total Assets:* £28,803
Registered Office: Winton House, Winton Square, Basingstoke, Hants, RG21 8EN
Shareholder: Neville John Aubrey Phillips
Officers: Mary Kathleen Keable [1965] Director/Teacher; Neville John Aubrey Phillips [1964] Director

E. Zabari Holdings UK Limited
Incorporated: 19 February 2019
Registered Office: c/o Fladgate LLP, 16 Great Queen Street, London, WC2B 5DG
Major Shareholder: Erez Zabari
Officers: Erez Zabari [1966] Director [Israeli]

Zaeda Alexia Limited
Incorporated: 4 July 2017
Registered Office: Nottingham One Tower, 156 Canal Street, Nottingham, NG1 7HG
Major Shareholder: Alexia Okoye
Officers: Alexia Okoye [1994] Director/Student [Nigerian]; Odera Okoye [1992] Director/Student [Nigerian]

Zahrat Alqurashi Ltd
Incorporated: 13 June 2017
Registered Office: 11-13 Ellesmere Road, Sheffield, S4 7JA
Officers: Qasem Qasem Mohammed Al-Ahmadi [1960] Director [Yemeni]; Gamal Ali Hussein Al-Esaei [1962] Director

Zelenci Natural Health Ltd
Incorporated: 5 November 2018
Registered Office: Kemp House, 160 City Road, London, EC1V 2NX
Major Shareholder: Shelley McGuire
Officers: Shelley McGuire [1972] Director/Solicitor

Zidac Laboratories Ltd
Incorporated: 14 February 2017 *Employees:* 12
Net Worth Deficit: £706,870 *Total Assets:* £164,028
Registered Office: Brambles House, Waterberry Drive, Waterlooville, Hants, PO7 7UW
Shareholder: Solab Group Limited
Officers: Wayne Stuart Humphreys [1961] Director/Chartered Accountant

Zodiac International (London) Limited
Incorporated: 11 October 1999 *Employees:* 3
Net Worth: £584,157 *Total Assets:* £966,878
Registered Office: Zodiac House, 363 Kenton Road, Harrow, Middlesex, HA3 0XS
Major Shareholder: Mohammad Nia
Officers: Minoo Nia, Secretary; Mohammad Nia [1952] Director

Zoe Lane Ltd
Incorporated: 12 December 2018
Registered Office: 590 Kingston Road, London, SW20 8DN
Major Shareholder: Waclaw Deren
Officers: Waclaw Deren [1965] Director [Polish]

Index of Directorships

Stegemann, Barbara Ann Sarah
The 7 Virtues Beauty Ltd

Aba, John Edo
Chaud Solutions Limited
J2NR Ltd

Abdul, Ambreen
Eabir Ltd

Abdul-Rauf, Haroon
Fragrantia Limited

Abel, John Birrel
Sabel Cosmetics Limited

Abel, Simon William
Sabel Cosmetics Limited

Abramson, David
Natural Products Factory Ltd

Abu, Abike
Bixie Group Ltd

Accolla, Simone
Terra Mater Ltd

Adams, George
Poseidon Skincare Limited

Adderley, Robert David
Phoenix Fragrances Limited

Adekaiyero, Ayotunde Adetokunbo
Triblaz Limited

Agarwal, Ripul
Ayuroma Limited

Agoro, Zaynab Adenrele
Adunni Ori Limited

Ahajiou, Zakaria
Karamat Collection Ltd

Ahmad, Kashif Ijaz
Cheshire Fragrances Limited

Ahmed, Almas Khawar, Dr
Acarrier Limited

Aitken, Brian
Beauty Essentials (Scotland) Ltd
Beauty Exchange Limited
Professional Beauty Systems (Holdings)
Professional Beauty Systems Ltd

Ajmal, Mohammed Amiruddin
Ajmal Perfume (UK) Limited

Ajmal, Mohammed Fakhruddin
Ajmal Perfume (UK) Limited

Ajmal, Mohammed Sirajuddin
Ajmal Perfume (UK) Limited

Akhtar, Sahdia
Lucidlure Ltd

Akhter, Lalarukh, Dr
L.A Life Limited

Akinola, Dola Alika
Aspire Eden Ltd

Akoto, Adwoa Kuffour
AA Group Holdings Ltd

Al Asfoor, Mohammed
Designer Shaik Limited

Al Damegh, Saleh Abdullah
Infinity Global Corporation & Investment - IGCI

Al Harkan, Saleh Mohammad
Infinity Global Corporation & Investment - IGCI

Al Kasmi, Mhd Anas
Nectar International Limited

Al-Ahmadi, Qasem Qasem Mohammed
Zahrat Alqurashi Ltd

Al-Ayoubi, Omar
Aswad P.S.S Ltd

Al-Esaei, Gamal Ali Hussein
Zahrat Alqurashi Ltd

Al-Rubeyi, Saeed Muayad
Chirps London Ltd

Alam, Hameed
Three Organics Ltd

Albakour, Yamen Muneer
Alkaiser Perfumes Ltd

Alcide, Leigh-Marie
A Natural Treat Limited

Ali, Aroosa Neela
Royale Essance Ltd

Ali, Nasir
Cheshire Fragrances Limited

Ali, Vinisha
Advanced Aesthetics Training Academy

Aljadawi, Mai Abdulatif
Iam By Nature Ltd.

Alkury, Riyadh Ahmad Mohammed
Natural Looks Trading Limited

Alkury, Wendy Helen
Natural Looks Trading Limited

Allan, Samara
Meek and Mild Essentials Ltd

Allaway, Michael John
Phytacol Limited

Allen, Barbara
Stunning Fragrance Ltd

Alleyne, Latoya Makayla
Calibria Ltd

Illingworth-Dennis, William
The Ally Dog Co Ltd

Abdelkarim, Rihab Alteraifi, Dr
Ray Alteraifi Limited

Althefeeri, Abdulazeez
Kehal Ltd
Villa Sauod Ltd

Altinoluk, Deniz
Skyn Deep Ltd

Alvarez, Vilma
Intradicted Ltd

Alves Carneiro, Maria Isabel
Organic Basics Ltd

Amade, Celmira Taju
Tsaka Limited

Ames, Lewis Drew
Wrimes Cosmetics Ltd

Amoah, Lillian
Aventual Ltd

Amure, Felicity Nyekpunwo
Black Gem Cosmetics Ltd

Anderson, Clare Louise
Renu Consultancy Ltd

Anderson, Damien Kurt Scott
Leviticus 19:27 Beard Co Ltd

Anderton, Philip John
Credence Hair Venture Limited

Andrean, Danielle
Aura Organics Limited

Andrean, Elizabeth Ann
Aura Organics Limited

Ankersoe, Kirsten
IAP Cosmetics International Ltd

Anketell-Clifford, Ivan
Qualkem Ltd

Anketell-Clifford, Rachael Louise
Qualkem Ltd

Anunta, Augustine
83 Associates Limited

Appleton, Anthony Joseph
Gillette U.K. Limited

Apte, Deepa, Dr
Ayurveda Pura Ltd

Apte, Vasudev Raju Ravindra
Ayurveda Pura Ltd

Aranha, Mervyn Suresh
Pierre Precieuse Parfum UK Ltd

Archer, Gemma Louise
Superfine Manufacturing Ltd

Archer, Lyn
Superfine Manufacturing Ltd

Archer, Maureen
Superfine Manufacturing Ltd

Archer, Nigel John
Superfine Manufacturing Ltd

Arnold, Kevin Eric, Dr
Legendes Products Ltd

Asante, Eunice
Glory Skin Ltd

Ashley, Laura, Prof
Elliott Nutrition Ltd
Nars & Elliott Healthcare Ltd

Ashley, Matilda Elvira
Double Take Limited

Ashraf, Antony Paul
Essential Gent Ltd

Aspinall, Williams
Eifelcorp Consumer Care Ltd

Aujla, Charnjit Singh
Convoy Fragrances Ltd

Austin, Andree Gaetane
Pure Fiji (EU) Limited

Austin, Gaetane Marie
Pure Fiji (EU) Limited

Auteri, Simona
Midnight Apothecary Limited

Aydin, Alptekin
Cosmos Cosmetics Limited

Aysan, Umran
Mast - Art Group Limited

Azoulay, Pazit
Paz By Nature Ltd

Backstrom, Mikael Tage Valentin
Female Balance Shop Limited

Baines, Helen
Cocoa Lime Limited

Bairstow, Christopher Lewis
Veloskin Limited

Bairstow, Tanya Ann Michaela
Veloskin Limited

Bajot, Fania, Dr
O Sable France Ltd

Bajwa, Amanpreet
Valencia Vanna Ltd.

Baker, Barbara Rose
S.R.S.Aromatics Limited

Baker, Jonathan Marc
S.R.S.Aromatics Limited

Baker, Lee John
S.R.S.Aromatics Limited

Baker, Sarah
Orion Independent Limited

Baker, Steven John
S.R.S.Aromatics Limited

Baldwin, Luke Thomas
All Good Skincare Limited

Ball, Christopher John Mellodew
Sachets Limited

Balle, Palo William
Bill & Artisans Ltd

Bambury, Jasmine
Rutherford Bambury Ltd

Baransananiye, Aime Moses
Koze Limited

Barfull Giralt, Jaume
Bluhans Ltd

Barham, Edward
KPSS (UK) Limited
Kao (UK) Limited

Barker, Claire Elizabeth
Stormfree Holdings Ltd

Barlow, Amanda Jane Vivian
Tea & Therapy Ltd

Barnes, Darron Stephen
Wickham Soap Co. Ltd

Barstow, Megan Heather
Banyan Skincare Ltd

Barthelmy, Colin Meredith
Lip Sync Beauty Limited
Sharrier Beauty Incorporated Ltd

Barton, Mark
Brigantia Personal Care Ltd
Ladd Cosmetics Ltd

Baskerville, Robert Alan
Paradoxical Solutions Limited

Baskerville, Thomas William Morgan
Paradoxical Solutions Limited

Bassey, Rachael
Softme Beauty Ltd

Bauwens, Marc
Baum of London Limited

Bawden, Keith William David
Muir Events Ltd

Beadle, Amanda
Bedeaux Ltd

Beale, Edward John
Swallowfield PLC

Beard, Michele Leagh
Tiger Lily Soapery Ltd

White, Paul Douglas
The Beautiful Mind Series Ltd

Field, Mitchell Laurence
The Beauty Alliance International

Beckett, Elizabeth
Elibec Limited

Beever, Stephen Colin
Beever Retail Limited

Begg, Tahir Masood
Bloom Aromatics Limited

Bejenar, Ksenia
Hoc Parfum Ltd

Belhassen, David
Miller Harris Limited

Bell, Jon
Bell & Loxton Innovations Ltd

Bendon, Clive Lionel
Abendana Enterprises Limited
Aromaherb Limited
Everlasting Youth Limited
Quality Analysis Limited

Bennett, Paul Nigel Robert
Linden and Lime Limited

Berrebi, Franklin Pinhas
Swallowfield PLC

Beyls, Pieter-Jan
Coriungo Limited

Bhuta, Soab
Adam Michaels Group Ltd

Bianchi, Lucrecia Silvana
LU Aromatherapy Ltd

Bibb, Matthew
Happy Products Limited

Bibb, Suzanne
Happy Products Limited

Biles, Philippa Jane
Arco England Limited

Biles, Roger John
Arco England Limited

Billing, Carly Marie, Dr
Prophylaxis Ltd

Bird, Rowena Jaqueline
Lush Ltd.

Birkmyre, David William Lawton
Costradis Limited

Bishop, Marta
Evocativ Limited

Bishop, Thomas
Evocativ Limited

Bishopp, Paul Courtney
Sensapeel Ltd

Bishopp, Valerie Joy
Sensapeel Ltd

Bissmire, Jennifer Mary
B.S. Eurochem Limited

Black, John Francis
Aroma Trading Limited

Black, Pauline
Simply Seaweed Limited

Black, Sharon Margaret
Aroma Trading Limited

Blackhurst, Lily May
L.E.C.(L'pool) Limited

Blanks, Timothy Seldon
Odejo Limited
ThatCo Ltd

Blatchford-Tagg, Tobias Julian
Lukas Products Limited

Bloxham, Roger Mark
Ferndale Pharmaceuticals Ltd

Boakye, Donald Nyampong
Buachi Limited

Bolton, Jan
Hypothesis One Ltd

Bond, Nigel Paul Dominic
Scent To Inspire Ltd

Bongermino, Katia
Naturali360 Limited

Bonner, Denise Anne
Neal's Yard (Natural Remedies) Ltd

Borshchev, Andrei
Barony Universal Products PLC

Boselli, Tommaso
Boselli Europe Ltd

Bouchard, Elodie Josiane
Firmenich Holdings (UK) Ltd
Firmenich UK Limited
Firmenich Wellingborough (UK) Ltd

Boujarwa, Walid
Dareen London Ltd.

Boulos, Mark
LJSP Ltd

Boumecid-Thompson, Anissa
Thebubblebar Ltd

Bourne, Antoinette Stephanie
Es-Ssentially Yours Ltd

Borissoff, Constantine Leo
Andre Boyard Perfumes Limited

Rughani, Ameet Chandubhai
Andre Boyard Perfumes Limited

Bracher, Verity Kate
Meadow Farm Friends Ltd

Brady, Karren, Dr
Clarins & Felix Healthcare Ltd
Felix Medical Group Ltd

Brady, Rita
Protect Biosciences Ltd

Branson, Thomas Andy
Thomas Andy Ltd.

Brearley, Ray Anthony
Grace & Hartland Ltd

Brinkenhoff, Michael Curt, Dr
Athena Cosmetics Limited

Brinton, Evaleen
Blackbird and Rain Limited

Bristow, Corrina
Unique Relaxation Specialist Ltd

Bristow, Jannet
Unique Relaxation Specialist Ltd

Broach, Zowie
This Wode Co Ltd

Brockhus, Eric Anthonius
Molton Brown Limited

Brodie, Arizona
Arizona Botaniq Limited

Brolly, Johanne, Dr
Science for Skin Ltd.

Bronson, Michael
Flynn Group of Companies Ltd
Rimmel & Flynn Healthcare Ltd

Broomfield, Chantel Latoya
Kylah K Skincare Ltd

Brown, Tari-Ere Belinda Osoru
Belinda Brown Limited

Brown, Elizabeth
Liza.B. Glow Actives Ltd

Brown, Jean Stephanie
Rodette International Limited

Brown, Kim
Anyki Ltd

Browne, Crystal Dale
Natural Sheaness Ltd

Brownless, Kenneth Derek
K.K. Toiletries Limited

Brunton, Clare
Simply Ewe Limited

Bryce, Katharine
Wist and Wonder Limited

Buckland, Richard Mark
Get Lucky Inc Ltd

Buckthorp, Alexander George
Gillette U.K. Limited

Burgess, Susan Elizabeth
Artisane Aromatherapy Limited

Burgin, Rebecca Louise
Kropp & Hem Ltd

Burns, Michael John, Doctor
Ferndale Pharmaceuticals Ltd

Burrell, Antonia
Gracetree Ltd

Burton, Luissa
Luissa Burton Limited

Burton, Max Richard Leslie
Hamiltons of Canterbury Ltd

Burton, Sarah Kate
Canco Candles Limited

Bushnell, Oliver Geoffrey
Plant Department Ltd

Bustamante, Eliseo
LU Aromatherapy Ltd

Butelli, Eugenio
Persephone Bio Ltd

Bye, Geoff
Jubilee Capital (UK) Ltd

Bygrave, Karl Joseph
Lush Ltd.

Byrne, Wayne Thomas
Emerald Kalama Chemical Ltd

Cain, Christian Miles
In Line Health and Beauty Ltd

Caldwell, Amanda Frances Louise
Mibelle Ltd

Caldwell, Teodora Georgieva
Dermafood Limited

Caley, Judy
Caley's of Exeter Ltd

Cambray-Smith, Ian John
Fragrant Earth International Ltd

Camp, Stephen William
Elsan Limited

Campbell, Edward
Esensi Skincare Ltd

Campbell, Leanna Natasha
Cutelovelee Limited

Canham, Louisa, Dr
La-Eva Limited

Carden, Elizabeth Anne
Esensi Skincare Ltd

Carnes Ellis, Michele
Act of Kindness Organics Ltd

Carney, Mary Teresa
Creightons PLC
Potter & Moore Innovations Ltd

Carr, Angela Rosemary
Body & Face St. Cyrus Limited

Carr, William Milne Ritchie
Body & Face St. Cyrus Limited

Carter, Barbara
Fragrance Oils (International) Ltd

Carter, David William
Sensapeel Ltd

Carter, Frank Paul Julian
Aroma Design Ltd
Artemis Oils Ltd
Natural Science Aromas Ltd

Cassell, Josephine, Dr
Little Green Beehive Ltd

Castro Romero, Paloma
Hanan Pacha Ltd

Catala Moncho, Pedro Juan
Twelve Beauty Ltd

Catlin, Andrew Philip
Frosts of London Limited

Catlin, Katie
Frosts of London Limited

Cerniauskiene, Viktorija, Dr
Wicked Vicky Co Ltd

Cestaro, Michael Anthony
Caldey Island Estate Co Ltd

Cetin, Esra
MAC Professional Haircare Ltd

Cetin, Ilhan
MAC Professional Haircare Ltd

Chapman, Jonathan David
Scents of Nature Ltd

Chapman, Olivia Kim
Oleo Bodycare Limited

Charles, Kim Christopher
Indult Paris Ltd

Charles, Villana
Virtue Botanicals Limited

Chen, Aie
Lumine Beauty Ltd

Childs, Ben Geoffrey
Caldey Island Estate Co Ltd

Chinnery, Samantha Ophelia
Magpie's Ocean Ltd

Chirac, Luisa
Uncareditional Ltd

Chitty, Luke Stephen James
Lukas Products Limited

Chopdat, Zakir Hussain
Ottimo Supplies Limited

Choudhury, Khandoker
TAC Perfumes & Cosmetics (UK) Ltd

Choudhury, Tasbirul Ahmed
TAC Perfumes & Cosmetics (UK) Ltd

Chresta, Cyril Francis
CC Business Limited
Pure English Cosmetics Limited

Christian, Joshua
Auli London Ltd

Chumburidze, Maria
Hoc Parfum Ltd

Chung Kee Mew, Marie Francoise Krin Chin
Faces Cosmetics Limited

Cita, Natalie
Mbikudi Ltd

Clare, Laurence John
L.E.C.(L'pool) Limited

Clark Headley, Annette Yvonne
Almond & Avocado Ltd

Clark Prakash, Preyanka Jayanti
Bloomtown Ltd

Clark, Philippa
Creightons PLC
Potter & Moore (Devon) Ltd
Potter & Moore Innovations Ltd

Clarke, Gary Brian
Mibelle Ltd

Clarke, Gemma Louise
Sunshapers Limited

Clifton, Nicola Grace
Grace & Hartland Ltd

Clifton, Sheila Mary
Grace & Hartland Ltd

Climpson, Carl John
Travik Chemicals (UK) Limited

Climpson, Kim Joy
Travik Chemicals (UK) Limited

Climpson, Laura
Travik Chemicals (UK) Limited

Climpson, Robert James
Travik Chemicals (UK) Limited

Coates, Timothy William
K.K. Toiletries Limited

Coleman, Carol Ann
Designer Fragrances Limited
Jean Christian Perfumes Ltd

Coleman, Thomas Martin
Designer Fragrances Limited
Jean Christian Perfumes Ltd

Collins, Mandy
5 Senses Healthcare Ltd

Collins, Michelle
M.C Skin Truth Ltd

Collins, Nicholas John Heywood
Dr. Organic Limited

Colovic, Zagorka
Beauty Handmade Limited

Combe-Shetty, Keech
Combe International Limited

Connock, Elizabeth
A. & E. Connock (Perfumery & Cosmetics)

Connock, Rosemary Diana
A. & E. Connock (Perfumery & Cosmetics)

Connock, Tim
A. & E. Connock (Perfumery & Cosmetics)

Constantine, Jack
Lush Ltd.

Constantine, Margaret Joan
Lush Ltd.
Lush Manufacturing Limited

Constantine, Mark
Lush Ltd.

Conway, Craig
Heidi J Naturals Limited

Cook, Ruby Susan Anne
Verde London Ltd.

Cooke, Hugh Vincent
United Beauty Products Limited

Cooke, Victoria Sophie
United Beauty Products Limited

Cooper, Lynn
La Parfumerie Anglaise Limited

Coote, John Lindsay
Jubilee Capital (UK) Ltd

Copeman, Chioma Esther
Concept: Skin Limited

Copeman, James Edward
Concept: Skin Limited

Cornwall, Randy Lindo
Lese & Lista Ltd

Cosgrave, Sean Antony
TheManeCo Ltd

Costantini, Massimiliano
Mibelle Ltd

Cotsford-Dolden, Reena
Hi Energy Healing Limited

Coulson, Debbie
Scentz of Smell Ltd

Cousins, Darron
Rasta Life Ltd

Coveva, Tony
G and B Beauty Products Ltd

Covey Jr, William Edward
Hair Systems Europe Limited

Cowdery, Marianne Jennifer
Marsh Organics Limited

Coxon, Andrew Shaun
Pitt London Ltd

Craig, Shane Paul
Ink of Coco Skincare Ltd

Crane, Linda
House of Unique Parfum Limited

Cranstoun, Emma
Scrubbingtons Limited

Cranstoun, Mark John Simon
Scrubbingtons Limited

Crawford, Alan
Skinsence Ltd

Crawford, Sheila May Dandy
Skinsence Ltd

Crisp, David Adrian
Valorem Bespoke Ltd

Critchley, Catherine Jeanette
Surefil Beauty Products Ltd

Critchley, Paul Barry
Surefil Beauty Products Ltd

Cropper, Angela
Onlyou Limited

Cropper, Jonathan Andrew
Onlyou Limited

Cross, Stephen James
Gotvox Limited

Crumblehulme, Steven John
LTSC Ltd

Crush, Verity Elizabeth
Ecocrushuk Ltd

Culmer, Medwin John
Bloomtown Ltd

Cunniffe, Sheena Johnston
Professional Beauty Systems Ltd

Currie, Edward Alexander
Pitt London Ltd

Cuthbert, Serena Ann
So Skincare Limited

Cutillas, Carmen
Neurocosmetics Limited

Dallimore, Anthony James
Phoenix Fragrances Limited

Daly, Stephen Charles
L.E.C.(L'pool) Limited

Damian, Valentin
Blackbird and Rain Limited

Datema, Marili
Aroma Body Treats Limited

Dattani, Keval
KD Trading (UK) Limited

Dattani, Kunal
KD Trading (UK) Limited

Dattani, Savan
KD Trading (UK) Limited

Davies, James
Science for Skin Ltd.

Davies, Rachel Angharad, Dr
Kisu Skincare Ltd

Davies, Sem Lloyd
Ferndale Pharmaceuticals Ltd

Dawson, Karena Dawn
Aroma Amour Ltd

Day, Alison Claire
Make-Up Art Cosmetics (U.K.) Ltd

Day, Robert
Bonita Lou Ltd

De Brauwere Brozler, Anastasia
Creative Perfumers London Ltd

De Valcy, Chloe Pressoir
Bleu D'Argan Skincare Limited

Wood, Debra Ann
J Deboy & Co Limited

Wood, Joy Beverley
J Deboy & Co Limited

Deegan, Robert Anthony
Cool Gell Limited

Degutyte, Ruta
Art de Parfum Ltd.

Delafon, Frederic Jean Laurent
Ostens Limited

Denner, Laura Elizabeth
Itaconix (U.K.) Limited

Deren, Waclaw
Zoe Lane Ltd

Devlin, Hugh Gerard
ThisCo Ltd

Dewar, Laura Catherine
Phyto Pharma Limited

Dewar, Laura
Phyto Pharm Limited

Dicker, Jasper Elliot
JLP Cosmetics Ltd

Dimichele, Maria
Ginger & Vanilla Ltd

Morrison-MacLeod, Margaret
The Divine Hag Ltd

Dobrock, Ash Paul
Very Good Vegan Co Ltd

Dobrock, Hannah Faye
Very Good Vegan Co Ltd

Dodds, Robert Cecil Gifford
Cosmetics a la Carte Limited

Donald, Nichola Delita
Missy D Collection Limited

Donoghue, Georgina
Umma Therapy Ltd.

Donovan, Tara Gail
La-Eva Limited

Dore, Stephen
Flo Ventures Ltd

Dos Santos Rita de Jesus, Ieva
Leum Skin Care Ltd

Douglas, Jennifer
Jenni Douglas Limited
London Goddess Limited

Downing, Adrian
AD Fragrances Ltd

Dragicevic, Martina
Molecula Ltd

Draper, Jonathan Wolfgang
Glad Gent Ltd

Cockton, Peter Drew George
Owen Drew Luxury Candles Ltd

Drosou, Kyriaki
Kisens Ltd

Duggan, Patrick Laurence
Scent from Ireland Ltd

Dunbar, Oriele Anne
Elemis Limited

Duncan-Lajewski, Kimberleen
Libhairation Ltd

Dunkley, Miles Spencer Maitland
Get Lucky Inc Ltd

Dunseath, Philip Alexander
Myroo Ltd

Dunseath, Rachael
Myroo Ltd

Durant, Mauro Barazarte
Dr Jackson Ltd

Dwamena, Debora
Urembo Naturally Ltd

Dwyer, Deborah Diane
L.E.C.(L'pool) Limited

Counsell, Rosemary Frances
Liz Earle Beauty Co. Limited

Murphy, Anne Louise
Liz Earle Beauty Co. Limited

Waller, David
Liz Earle Beauty Co. Limited

Eastabrook, David Stephen
Elmbronze Limited

Eastabrook, Winifred
Elmbronze Limited

Easton, Gary James
Eastwing Grooming Co. Limited

Ebrahim, Marwa Sayed Ahmed Ebrahim Hashem
Atypical Cosmetics Ltd

Edgerton, Graham John
Molton Brown Limited

Edwards, Elaine
Beauty 4 Me Ltd

Edwards, Michael
Olfactive London Ltd

Effiom, Stephanie Efefiong
Mayen Velvaere Limited

El-Bacha, Amine
Al-Jazeera Perfumes Ltd

Element, Jessica Grace
Green Jiva Ltd

Eleuterio, Julio Marcel Brugos
Eleuthere Ltd

Ellacott, John
Geltec Limited

Ellingworth - Hutley, Sian Elizabeth
Lobal Ltd

Ergas, Shaari
Dr Jackson Ltd

Erich, Bjorn
KPSS (UK) Limited
Kao (UK) Limited

Esterhuysen, Joan
Swaziboy Limited

Eustace, Desmond Charles
Clover Chemicals Limited

Evans, Anthony Ian
Evans Vanodine International PLC

Evans, Christopher John
Evans Vanodine International PLC

Evans, Derek Anthony
Evans Vanodine International PLC

Evans, Peter David
Evans Vanodine International PLC

Ezigboh, Kaosochi
Kaira Luchi Ltd

Duchesne, Frederic Marie
Pierre Fabre Limited

Danon, Michael Frederic
Pierre Fabre Limited

Benoist, Xavier Pierre Marie
Pierre Fabre Limited

McMullin, Laura Adele
Pierre Fabre Limited

Guiraud-Chaumeil, Vincent Henri Francois
Pierre Fabre Limited

Fahey, Samuel James
Claycoco Limited

Fallon, Christopher Charles
Baylis & Harding PLC

Farrington, Nicola
Elemental Beauty Limited

Faull, Odile Marie Francoise
Continental Fragrances Limited

Felstead, Oliver
Wonder and Wild Ltd

Fidler, Charlotte-Anne Field
Spots & Stripes Products Ltd

Shipman, Marc Jason
Daniel Field Purity Project Ltd

Shipman, Jonathan David
Daniel Field Purity Project Ltd

Field, Mitchell Lawrence
Cyclax Limited
Solar Cosmetics International Ltd

Fields, Mia
Cinsce Ltd

Fikkert, Julia Margaret
Fikkerts Limited
Urban Nymph Limited

Fikkert, Richard Nigel
Fikkerts Limited

Filiatre, Gregoire
Mibelle Ltd

Findley, Emma Louise
Bearface Industries Limited

Clarke, Gemma
The Fitzrovia Centre Ltd

Turpin, Charles Edward
The Fitzrovia Centre Ltd

Harrison, Jason General
The Fizzy Thistle Ltd

Fletcher, Jane
Atlas Group Limited
Swallowfield PLC

Foad, LeOne Rachel
Foad Wax Limited

Foad, Patt
Foad Wax Limited

Fofana, Mona
Honey Corn Limited

Foley, Maurice Anthony
Blazergold Limited
Parfums Bleu Limited

Foley, Seamus
Blazergold Limited
Parfums Bleu Limited

Foley, Timothy Bernard
Blazergold Limited
Parfums Bleu Limited

Forbes, Bruce
CPL Aromas (Holdings) Limited
CPL Aromas Limited

Ford, Kelly
Wheesht Ltd

Ford, Stephen Kelsey
Dr. Organic Limited

Foreman, Katie
By Kathryn Ltd

Forster, Paul
Creightons PLC
Potter & Moore (Devon) Ltd
Potter & Moore Innovations Ltd

Forte, Irene Alisea
Forte Organics Ltd

Fouracre, Philip Anthony
Black Cat Manufacturing Ltd

Fox, Brian Harry
Anyone Limited

Fox, Michael James
Sensapeel Ltd

Fraisse, Jean Pierre
Fillcare Limited

Frederick, Katherine Victoria
Hands Organic Ltd

Fulton, John Thomas
Strathpeffer Spa Soap Co Ltd

Gabriel, Noella
Elemis Limited

Gage, Alan Thomas Michael, Reverend
Caldey Island Estate Co Ltd

Gagnon, Beth
Gagnon Essentials Limited

Gale, Ian David
Toddle Born Wild Limited

Gallemore, John Andrew
Acheson & Acheson Limited
Mama Mio Distribution Limited

Gardella Trias, Rosa
Sunshapers Limited

Gardner, Philip Jonathan
CPL Aromas (Holdings) Limited
CPL Aromas Limited

Garfinkel, Joseph Warden
Bespoke Natural Health Ltd

Garthwaite, Nicholas James
Clover Chemicals Limited

Gasior, Michal
Body Candy Ltd.

Gatongi, Francis Nderitu
MWK Cosmetics (UK) Ltd

Gaughan, Bridget Veronica
Possibility of London Ltd

Gaughan, Norah Gabrielle
Possibility of London Ltd

Gazzard, Matthew
Atlas Group Limited
Swallowfield PLC

Gborigi, Abubakara Ademola
Incoplex Limited

Gedman, Paul Jonathan
Mama Mio Distribution Limited

Davis, Quentin Peter
M.S. George Limited

Davis, Mark Simon
M.S. George Limited

George, Hannah
Since Six Ltd

George, Mark John David
Mrs Greens Hemp Remedies Ltd

Gharehbaghi, Behzad
Ring in Ring Ltd

Giannandrea, Mark
KPSS (UK) Limited

Gibbs, Benjamin
G & G Skincare Ltd
Man Mask Ltd

Gibson, Emily McEwan
EMC Botanica Limited

Gill, Martin James Edgerton
Culpeper Limited

Gilland Robinson, Christine
Ko. Essentials Ltd.

Gilluley, Jacqueline Ann
Relax Candle and Bath Co Ltd

Girven, Mark
G & G Skincare Ltd
Man Mask Ltd

Glanville-Blackburn, Jo
Jogb Limited

Glencross, William Torrance
Creightons PLC
Potter & Moore Innovations Ltd

Godlington, Kevin
Calmen Lifestyle Co Ltd

Golding, Jasmine
Contour and More London Ltd

Gong, Xue
Cambridge Genefit Technologies Ltd

Good, Miriam Alexandra, Rev
De La Baie Arctic Skincare Ltd

Goodland, Simon Frank Oliver
Papillon Perfumery Ltd

Goodson, Kevin Joseph
Mono Naturoils Ltd

Goodson, Tracy
Mono Naturoils Ltd

Gopalakini, Veena
Ayurveda Wellness Ltd

Gordon, Peter William
Dr Jackson Ltd

Gordon, Remecae
Rustic Blends Limited

Gordon-Smith, Heidi
11:11 Limited

Gosain, Gopala Krishna
Sandwich Consultants Ltd

Fry, Matthew Peter
John Gosnell & Co Ltd

Tickner, Nicola Lesley
John Gosnell & Co Ltd

Warner, Christopher Robert
John Gosnell & Co Ltd

Warner, David Alan
John Gosnell & Co Ltd

Goswell, Rebecca Louise
Bex London Ltd

Gouldstone, Sally, Dr
Seilich Limited

Goyal, Vidya Bhushan
Ru Si Lacquers Global Ltd.

Grant, Alan
Aromabar (Scotland) Ltd

Grant, Catherine
Aromabar (Scotland) Ltd

Grant-Esterhuysen, Richard
Swaziboy Limited

Grayson, Collin
Ava Corporations Ltd
Lamer & Ava Healthcare Ltd

Green, Bruce
Little House of Wild Ltd

Green, Deri
Toddle Born Wild Limited

Green, Rachel Michelle
Clay Club Skincare Limited

Greene-Smith, Donniece
Eden's Legends Limited

Griffith, Sharon
Hair Systems Europe Limited

Groden, Steven David
Barony Universal Products PLC

Gupta, Anisha, Dr
Prophylaxis Ltd

Gurung, Angkit
Wayus Limited

Gurung, Dihnesh
Wayus Limited

Gyawali, Pukar
Wayus Limited

Hadleigh, Thomas
Body Station Limited

Hague, Michelle
Wrath Cosmetics Limited

Hague, Samuel
Wrath Cosmetics Limited

Haire, Antonita Charlene, Dr
Purely Skincare Limited

Haire, Malcolm John
Purely Skincare Limited

Hall, Marie Elizabeth
Bloom Remedies Ltd

Hall, Stephen Richard
Bloom Remedies Ltd

Halliday, Louise Margaret
Ostera Limited

Hamidi, Fazel
Ahwaz Ltd

Hamilton, John
Essentially Yours Limited

Hamilton, Jordan Ward
Care By Jords Ltd

Han, Timothy
TH / Edition Ltd

Handley, Alfred
Image Hub Limited

Handley, Juliet Anne
Image Hub Limited

Hann, Catherine
Gellure Ltd

Hanouna, Eytan
Miller Harris Limited

Hanson, Faith Elizabeth
Ethical House Ltd

Harding-Smolik, Jakub
Prispens Limited

Harding-Smolik, Jane
Prispens Limited

Haringman, Michael Stephan
Elemis Limited

Harman, Gabriella Bethany Tamsin
Dermamaitre Ltd.

Harpham, Andrew Harpham Dennis
Carapoll Chemicals Ltd

Harrington, Sean
Elemis Limited

Harris, Louise
T & H Marketing Limited

Hart, Dean Anthony
Hart Enterprise Limited

Harte, James Richard
Beard Oil Co Ltd

Harvey, Matthew James Richard
Dr. Organic Limited

Harwood, Reginald Frank
Ottimo Supplies Limited

Hatefi Mofrad, Robert
DBI Innovations Group Limited

Haughton, Ruth
Good Mela Ltd

Hawkins, Douglas George
Yin Yang Natural Sciences Ltd

He, Lili
Lily Her Limited

He, Zhanhong
Sanofi International Biotech Co Ltd.

Hegarty, Generald Patrick
Professional Beauty Systems (Holdings)
Professional Beauty Systems Ltd

Helpap, Karen Elsbeth
Mayla Skincare Ltd

Helt, Holly Anne
11:11 Limited

Hemelryk, Richard John
Plant Department Ltd

Hemelryk, Thomas Paul
Plant Department Ltd

Turner, Robert
The Hemp Garden Ltd

Henry, Maxamillion
Sphere 7 Lab Ltd

Henry, Phillip Jorge
Aexents Ltd

Herath, Charmilla
Thread and Co UK Limited

Herrmann, Nigel Kurt
Herrmann + Herrmann Limited

Herrmann, Susan
Herrmann + Herrmann Limited

Hetherington, Eleanor Lunaria
Magpie's Ocean Ltd

Hey, Lucy Mary
Wonder and Wild Ltd

Hicks, Oliver
Dr Jackson Ltd

MacDonald, Angus Francis
The Highland Soap Co. Limited

MacDonald, Archibald Sven
The Highland Soap Co. Limited

Parton, Emma
The Highland Soap Co. Limited

Hilde, Todd
Satellite Industries GB Ltd

Hili, Pauline, Doctor
Natural Products Factory Ltd

Hindle, Sharon Elizabeth
K.K. Toiletries Limited

Hindmarsh, Graham Edward
Teknord Limited

Hocaoglu, Funda
Cosmos Cosmetics Limited

Hodge, Jonathan
Mavala (U.K.) Limited

Hogan, Malcolm Charles
Fragrance Oils (International) Ltd
Fragrance Oils (Purchasing) Ltd

Hogan, Paul Lawrence
Emerald Kalama Chemical Ltd

Hogg, Martyn James
Toddle Born Wild Limited

Holloway, Daniel James
Bamboobar Online Ltd

Holman-Schmidt, Kerstin Birgit
Marine Beauty Care Limited

Holmes, Catherine
Laboratory Facilities Limited

Holmes, Christopher Michael
Laboratory Facilities Limited

Holmes, Patricia Ann
Laboratory Facilities Limited

Holtom, George Philip
Irregular Cosmetics Co Ltd

Holub, Alona
Perfance Limited

Hood, Alan Roger
R.M. Investments Limited

Hood, Derek Nairn
Kairn Holding Limited

Hood, Rosalie Mary
R.M. Investments Limited

Hosmer, Lucy Ayla
Otte Limited

Hossain, Sultan Zabir
Sultan Pasha Artisanal Perfumery Ltd

Houghton, Ginina
Aromatherapy Infusions Ltd

Howard, Richard Geoffrey
Arcania Apothecary Ltd

Howard-Macdonald, Anna Louise
Milo and James Limited

Howell, Leanne Danielle
Organic Youth Limited

Howieson, Joy Elizabeth
Haych Cosmetics Limited
Project Cosmetics Limited

Hsu, Andy
Orion Independent Limited

Huber, Walter Cornelio
Mibelle Ltd

Huggett, Tracey
Miller Harris Limited

Humphrey, Sophie Louise
Soapberries Ltd

Humphrey, Valerie Anne
Soapberries Ltd

Humphreys, Wayne Stuart
Solab Group Limited
Zidac Laboratories Ltd

Humpula, Jiri
P & H Natural Skincare Ltd

Humpulova, Pavla
P & H Natural Skincare Ltd

Hunniford, Brian Alexander
Archem (N.I.) Ltd

Hunniford, Lynne Diane Dorothy Joan
Archem (N.I.) Ltd

Hunter, Andrew Christopher
Green Jiva Ltd

Hurst, Joanne Sarah
Ecopel Corporation Limited
Foltex Hair Technology Limited

Huse, Katalin
Hkka Limited

Hussain, Safraz
Scentz of Smell Ltd

Hussain, Sagira
Three Organics Ltd

Hutchinson, Diane
Icilda's Ltd

Hutchinson, Lynda June
Charles Jordi Limited

Hynes, Brendan
Swallowfield PLC

Ibie, Chidinma Udegbunam, Dr
Dach Cosmeceutics Limited

Ibrahim, Ayesha
Honey Corn Limited

Ile, Yvonne
Skin Intuition Ltd

Indzhov, Vladislav Mihaylov
Elinor-UK Ltd

Inije, Oboratare Tracy
Sophrina Gos Limited

Iordanidis, Kleanthis
Fragrance and Glamour Ltd

Iqbal, Nureen
Pure Ohana Limited

Ireland, Sarah Louise
Sarah Ireland Perfumes Ltd

Irvine, Susan
This Wode Co Ltd

Iskander, Medhat
Teknord Limited

Iskander, Nader
Teknord Limited

Ismail, Amir
Aim8 Limited

Issa, Safiya
Atmosy Ltd

Marfo-Jackson, Agnes
Agnes Jackson Limited

Jackson, Deborah
Astarra Ltd

Jackson, John
Braw Beard Oils Ltd

Jacobs, Peter Jonathan
CPL Aromas (Holdings) Limited
CPL Aromas Limited

Jain, Nikita
Avenge Skincare Limited

Jain, Vikas
Ayurveda Pura Ltd

Jamal, Mohammed Sadik
Jamal London Ltd

Ingram, Alan David
Nicholas James (UK) Limited

Liversidge, Peter Eric
Nicholas James (UK) Limited

Mottram, Paul
Nicholas James (UK) Limited

Mottram, Susan
Nicholas James (UK) Limited

Schofield, Paul Richard
Nicholas James (UK) Limited

Jangaria, Jamila
Dermaplaning Pro Official Ltd
Kyoka Pro Ltd

Jarman, Alexander David
Hunk Grooming Ltd

Jarvis, Adam
Greatest of All Time Soapworks Ltd

Jarvis, Daphne Joy
Jarvis Cosmetic Developments Ltd.
Kingsmill Cosmetic Preparations Ltd

Jarvis, Peter Arthur Watson
Jarvis Cosmetic Developments Ltd.
Kingsmill Cosmetic Preparations Ltd

Jarvis, Quentin
Jarvis Cosmetic Developments Ltd.
Kingsmill Cosmetic Preparations Ltd

Jarvis, Sarah
Greatest of All Time Soapworks Ltd

Jeeves, Emily Victoria
Emily Victoria Candles Limited

Jeffs, Matthew David
Askett & English Ltd

Johns, Leanne Peta
Sloane Home Ltd

Johnson, Bernard James Mary
Creightons PLC
Potter & Moore (Devon) Ltd
Potter & Moore Innovations Ltd

Johnson, Mark Paul
L.E.C.(L'pool) Limited

Johnson, Mark
Molton Brown Limited

Johnson, Miles Stanley Clewley
Miller Harris Limited

Johnson, Olubunmi Oyetoun
Orikii Naturals Ltd

Johnson, Phillip
Elegant Boss Ltd

Jolley, Stuart Paul
Lukas Products Limited

Jonblat, Kamel Malek
South West Aesthetics Ltd

Jones, Christopher Andrew
Inspired Health & Beauty Products

Jones, Daniel Christopher
Inspired Health & Beauty Products

Jones, Harry William
Lukas Products Limited

Jones, Hilary Anita
Lush Ltd.

Jones, Janet Elizabeth
Inspired Health & Beauty Products

Jones, Lauren
Cocobubble Ltd

Jones, Natalie
Hairs & Graces Cosmetics Ltd

Jones, Nia
Spirit of The Isle Ltd.

Jones, Nicholas Keith Arthur
Neville Cut and Shave Limited

Jones, Richard Mansel
Chuckling Goat Limited

Jones, Shann Erin
Chuckling Goat Limited

Jones, Thomas, Prof
Julie's Natural Health Ltd

Jones, Tony Wyn
Spirit of The Isle Ltd.

Jones, Zena Patricia
Fragrances UK Limited

Juszczak, Henry Darroch
Costradis Limited

Kadiri, Amina
Kadiricosmetics Ltd

Kaedbey, Chafic, Dr
South West Aesthetics Ltd

Kalkowska, Patrycja
Cosmetic Hooligans Ltd

Kalukenda, Sara Ntumba
Mbikudi Ltd

Kanchwala, Alham
Ark Perfumeries Limited

Kanchwala, Manulla
Ark Perfumeries Limited

Kandohla, Ravinder
Madre Skincare Limited

Kane, Iain Wilson
Village Barber Skin Products Ltd

Kane, Sharon
Village Barber Skin Products Ltd

Kanyog, Adam
Hkka Limited

Kapoor, Sunita
JST Exports (UK) Ltd

Karlo, Anna Vanessa
Khali Min Limited

Kaur, Baljot
Bath Candy Ltd

Keable, Mary Kathleen
Yverman Ltd

Keet, Aloysius Nicolass
Caldey Island Estate Co Ltd

Kekiene, Aiste
Lathersmith Ltd

Kelly, Rachel Elizabeth
Earth Mother Soul Sister Ltd

Kelly-Morris, Joanna Helen
Earth Mother Soul Sister Ltd

Kemp, Jacqueline Naana
Ombotas Limited

Kemp, Martin Paul
Ombotas Limited

Kendall, Elizabeth Brock
Strathpeffer Spa Soap Co Ltd

Khan, Mohsin
BLVNCO Limited

Khan, Muhammad Mohsin
Lofty Gardens Ltd

Khandwala, Hafiz Anver
Aqua Natural Limited

Khandwala, Noor Hafiz
Aqua Natural Limited

Khandwala, Rosemeen Hafiz
Aqua Natural Limited

Khandwala, Tayab Hafiz
Aqua Natural Limited

Khyber, Muhammad
Skincare Laboratories Ltd

Kiernan, Kirsten
Happy Melon Skin Care Limited

Kilburn, Olivia Frances
So Skincare Limited

Killick, Douglas
Kairn Holding Limited

Kimbell, James Alexander
Awake Organics Ltd

Kimbell, Melissa
Awake Organics Ltd

Kindersley, Anabel
Neal's Yard (Natural Remedies) Ltd

Kindersley, Barnabas Guy
Neal's Yard (Natural Remedies) Ltd

Kindersley, Peter David
Neal's Yard (Natural Remedies) Ltd

King, Sasha
Insensed Ltd

Kirkby, Brian
This Wode Co Ltd

Kirkman, John Crispin
Pepsyn Limited

Kitson-Mills-Jones, Delphina
Purplelilac Ltd

Kobus, Andrew James
Perfume By Design Ltd.

Koller, Georges
Satellite Industries GB Ltd

Komornikova, Julia
Slavikk Ltd

Korytakova, Veronika
Savon de V Ltd

Kosmala, Tomasz
Thomas Kosmala Parfums Ltd

Koziol, Gillian
Arriva Fragrances Limited

Koziol, Stanley Peter
Arriva Fragrances Limited
Arrivatech Limited

Kozlova, Marina
MK Design & Art Direction Ltd

Krakowska, Aleksandra Ewa
Bubble-Bubble Ltd

Kruger, Anya
Anyki Ltd

Kumar Arya, Kiran
Ekstaze London Limited

Kumar, Ajay, Dr
Herc Ltd.

Kumar, Narinder
Herc Ltd.

Kumar, Vivek
Ikaa Cosmetics Limited

Kusmirek, Jan Brian
Fragrant Earth International Ltd

Kwiecinski, Tomasz
Holistic Plant Technologies Ltd

Akhter, Lalarukh, Dr
The L A Partnership Limited

Labbe, Daniel
M.88 Fragrances Ltd

Laing, Jacqueline Annetta
Lovefro Ltd.

Lamb, Terence
East China Sourcing Ltd

Lambie, Gael
Uzu Ltd

Landreth-Smith, Joseph
Ko. Essentials Ltd.

Landreth-Smith, Megan
Ko. Essentials Ltd.

Laporte, Julien Philippe Noel Henry
Un Air D'Antan Limited
Solab Group Limited

Laporte, Sophie Christine
Un Air D'Antan Limited

Larmour, Gordon Alexander
Beard Armour Limited

Laskaris, Panagiotis
Fysifarm Limited

Macpherson, Vicki Helen
Thomas Laurie Naturals Limited

Le, Trang Huyen Thi
Eifelcorp Consumer Care Ltd
Elie Consumer Care Ltd

Leach, Alexander Ian
Neal's Yard (Natural Remedies) Ltd

Leach, Timothy Alan Baylor
Neal's Yard (Natural Remedies) Ltd

Leak, Malcolm Allan
MLC Parfum & Oudh Ltd

Ledes, Leslie Bayly
Fashion Fragrances & Cosmetics UK Ltd

Lee, Nikki, Dr
Little Green Beehive Ltd

Lees, David Stephen
Queen Cosmetics Limited

Leigh, Marion
Nature Spirits Limited

Leitner, Martin
Purepure Limited

Leppinen, David, Dr
Garnier & Hemo Healthcare Ltd
Hemo Bioscience Ltd

McDonald, Nadeane
Nadeane Letisha Ltd

Leung, Elaine Chi Kit
Natural Skincare London Ltd

Levy, David
Noblechart Cosmetic Ltd

Lewis, Denise Frances Louise
Claes Heavenly Therapies and Aromas Ltd

Lewis, Emma Jayne
Smelliz Ltd

Liart, Samantha
Psyche Com & Merch Ltd

Lightowlers, Michael Henryk
Dr. Organic Limited

Lim, Seng Koon
Aroma Cosmetics Laboratory Ltd

Lincoln, Adebimpe Titilope, Doctor
Christian Lincoln Enterprise Ltd

Lindley, Paul John
Paddy's Bathroom Limited

Lindop, Jacob Paul
Tranquility Cosmetics Limited

Lindop, Kimberley
Tranquility Cosmetics Limited

Linell, David Michael
Fragrance du Bois (UK) Limited

Little, Stephanie
Meiyume (UK) Limited

Liu, Xiangrong
Fragrant Spa Limited

Lloyd, Anthony Ewart
CPL Aromas (Holdings) Limited
CPL Aromas Limited

Loannilli, Augusto
WT Limited

Lobashkov, Victor
Barony Universal Products PLC

Lobo, Mary-Rose
Skinirvana Limited

Loday, Sylvie
Maison Ex Nihilo UK Limited

Lounds, Jeff Blaine
ThatCo Ltd
This Wode Co Ltd
ThisCo Ltd

Lovett, Jennifer Margaret
Dermapharm Skincare Limited

Lovett, Timothy James
Dermapharm Skincare Limited

Low, Elizabeth
Divine Earth Ltd

Luengo, Daniela Maria
Aroma Body Treats Limited

Lulat, Zuber
Adam Michaels Group Ltd

Luotiene, Irma
Organic Stuff Limited

Lupo, Valerio
Paz By Nature Ltd

Lynton, Michael Mark
Islestarr Holdings Limited

Lyrae, Velma Claire
Astroscent Ltd

Maat, Hubert Willem
Inovair Limited

MacAvoy, James
Surefil Beauty Products Ltd

MacDonald, Ross
Milo and James Limited

MacDonogh, Stephen James
Renbow Haircare Limited

MacDonough, Colette Frances
Professional Beauty Systems (Holdings)
Professional Beauty Systems Ltd

MacDonough, Stephen James
Beauty Essentials (Scotland) Ltd
Beauty Exchange Limited
Professional Beauty Systems (Holdings)
Professional Beauty Systems Ltd

MacGregor, Rosemary
Arbar Ltd

MacKenzie, Alison
Whole International Limited

MacKenzie, Caroline
Above Beyond Group Ltd

MacLeod, Martin
Ishga Ltd

MacRae, Malcolm Robert
Ishga Ltd

Machnicki, Venita Machnicki
Skin Nectar Ltd

Mackrell, Stephanie Samantha
Robertet (U.K.) Limited

Magee, Lindsey Jane
Palm Bars Ltd

Mahdi, Rawaa
RMBeauty Limited

Mahony, Desmond, Rev
Caldey Island Estate Co Ltd

Mainwaring, Paul
Aromatic Scents Ltd
Stunning Fragrance Ltd

Makangu, Hermine
Mbikudi Ltd

Malcolm, Iona Leigh
Nature Spirits Limited

Malek, Shahid
Adam Michaels Group Ltd

Malik, Raghav
Ayuroma Limited

Malik, Razia
Razias London Ltd

Malik, Souad
Tahmasso Limited

Mallory-Skinner, Joe Jai
Above Beyond Group Ltd

Malone, John Anthony
Excel (GS) Limited

Malone, Paul Andrew
Excel (GS) Limited

Mamun, Neyonta
Neptune Perfume Ltd

Mancuso, Angelo
Shifting London Ltd

Manderson, Stephen
Calmen Lifestyle Co Ltd

Mangat, Rupinder Singh
H H Formulations Ltd

Morris, Zarina Zarina
The Manhattan Group Ltd.

Manocha, Amit
Faces Cosmetics Limited

Manthorpe, Hector Lucien
Orton Limited

McTiernan, Victoria
Victoria March Skincare Ltd

Marei, Jehan
Khali Min Limited

Markovic Ho, Zala
House of 18 Ltd

Marret, Cecile
Gallivant Perfumes Limited

Marsh, Karen Louise
Shaw & Company Business Ltd

Marshall-Clarke, Michael
Squires and Trelawny Ltd

Martin, Catherine Rosemary, Dr
Persephone Bio Ltd

Martin, Michelle Imelda
Icaro Sana Limited

Martin, Patricia Eleanor
Morgan's Pomade Co Ltd

Martin, Paul William John
Mob Fragrances Ltd.

Martin-Gilmore, Bruno
Nature B Limited

Masters, Christine
Modernista London Limited

Masters, John Edward
Modernista London Limited

Mather, Elaine
Dreamweave Products Ltd

Mather, Steven
Dreamweave Products Ltd

Matytsine, Alexandre
Barony Universal Products PLC

Maubert, Christophe
Robertet (U.K.) Limited

Maubert, Olivier
Robertet (U.K.) Limited

Mauluka, Charity Mutonga
Ulu Botanicals Ltd

Maunder, Sophie
Toddle Born Wild Limited

Maute, Hans August
Mavala (U.K.) Limited

Butts, Christina Juliet
Christina May Limited

Butts, Courtenay Arthur Robert
Christina May Limited

Butts, Oliver Courtenay Richard
Christina May Limited

Mbemba, Ouenadio Hyacinthe
Naturoganik Limited

McAllister, Vincent Patrick Glen
Man Mountain Beard Care Ltd

Rattigan, David Thomas
Robert McBride Ltd

Smith, Christopher Ian Charles
Robert McBride Ltd

Vos, Rik Jean Pierre Dora Albert De
Robert McBride Ltd

McCall, Euan David
Jorum of Scotland Limited

McCallum, Iain William
Kensa Chemicals Limited
McCallum Manufacturing Limited

McCandless, Brian
Robertet (U.K.) Limited

McCartney, Sarah
4160 Tuesdays Limited
Our Modern Lives Ltd

McCoulough, Ruth Elizabeth
Macks Wax Ltd

McDowell, Roger Steven
Swallowfield PLC

McGuire, Shelley
Zelenci Natural Health Ltd

McIlroy, William Oliver
Creightons PLC
Potter & Moore (Devon) Ltd
Potter & Moore Innovations Ltd

McIntyre, Archibald Dincan Ogilvie
Ebex International Limited

McKay, Craig
Biologico Cosmetics Limited

McKeever, Claire Nicole
Pure Lakes Skincare Limited

McKeever, Gareth John
Pure Lakes Skincare Limited

McLaughlin, Stephen
Professional Beauty Systems (Holdings)
Professional Beauty Systems Ltd

McLintock, Patrick James Paul
Shea Natural Skincare Limited

McLintock-Peasley, Louise Emma Charlotte
Shea Natural Skincare Limited

McMillan II, James Thayer
Ferndale Pharmaceuticals Ltd

McPartland, Simon
Professional Beauty Systems Ltd

McPhee, Peter Jonathan
Neville Cut and Shave Limited

Meekings, Angela Marie
Fragrances UK Limited

Megjhi, Ghulam Abbas
Fragrances and Cosmetics Ltd

Megoran, Tracy
Green Ladies N.I Ltd

Mehmood, Asim
AS Manufacturing Ltd

Mehta, Dilesh Bhogilal
Mayfair Perfumes Limited

Mehta, Hitesh Bhogilal
Mayfair Perfumes Limited

Meloni, Alberto
Coty Manufacturing UK Limited

Merrifield, Amanda Ruth
Cactus Skincare Limited

Miah, Runu
Karaama Fragrances Ltd

Michaels, Doris Mary Edema
Doris Michaels Cosmetics Ltd

Harris, Carolyn
Lyn Michel Limited

Michel, Christophe Francois Henri
Lyn Michel Limited
Miller Harris Limited

Midha, Jatinder
Midha Limited

Miezitis, Edgars
Beard Nature Limited

Miladinovic-Delic, Jelena
Beauty Core Limited

Miller, Grant Dean
Designer IP (2) Ltd
Eyegenius Ltd

Millington, Roy David
La Riche Limited

Mills, Heather Anne
HMMT Holdings Ltd.

Mitchell, Carrie
Mitchell London Limited

Mitchell, Jonathan Dominic
Mitchell and Peach Limited

Collins, Alexandra
The Model Handmade Limited

Collins, Harley
The Model Handmade Limited

Moeglin, Emmanuelle
Experimental Perfume Club Ltd

Molli Boulock, Richard
Haromatic Ltd

Van Bekkum, Laurent
Susan Molyneux Cosmetics Ltd

Mona, Jeeta
Onze Limited

Montague, Sarah Louise
Daughters of Circe Ltd

Morgan, Callum
Contour and More London Ltd

Morgan, Georgina
Pools of Cleopatra Limited

Morgan, John
Fragrance Oils (International) Ltd
Fragrance Oils (Purchasing) Ltd
Northern Aromatics (Sales) Ltd

Morgan, Lara
Activbod Limited

Morgan, Scott
THC Effect Ltd

Moritz, Michael Jonathan
Islestarr Holdings Limited

Morris, Paul
Gelspa Limited

Morrow, Leslie John
Irregular Cosmetics Co Ltd

Morrow, Rachel Lesley
Irregular Cosmetics Co Ltd

Mortimer, Andrew John
BCM Limited
Fillcare Limited

Morton, Angie Frances
Irregular Cosmetics Co Ltd

Mosbacher, Janet Elizabeth
L'Ocean Limited

Moss, Sara Ellen
Make-Up Art Cosmetics (U.K.) Ltd

Mudanohwo, Ese Ejiro
EEM Botanicals Limited

Muhammad, Raechel
Lana-Rae Ltd Ltd

Muller, David Jason
Lush Manufacturing Limited

Mulundika, Chomba
Sonyah Adan Limited

Mumvadi, Mata Marielle
Mata Labs Cosmetics Ltd

Murakami, Yoshihiro
Molton Brown Limited

Murdoch, Brian Ernest
International Toiletries & Cosmetics

Murdoch, Linda Margaret, Mrs
International Toiletries & Cosmetics

Mursaleen, Hamza
Majestic Company London Ltd

Muschner, Jenny
Salopian Ltd

Muschner, Jorg Alexander Richard
Salopian Ltd

Muthukrishnan, Namitha
Saisha Marra Ltd.

Timmer, Joy Myfanwy
Joy Myfanwy Limited

Nagarajan, Ravi Kumar
Ikaa Cosmetics Limited

Nakato, Catherine
Softme Beauty Ltd

Naqvi, Sam
BLVNCO Limited

Nashte, Rushikesh Vishwanath
Ru Si Lacquers Global Ltd.

Hooper, Laurie Clare
The Natural Deodorant Co Ltd

Sanders, Brett David
The Natural Deodorant Co Ltd

Phillips, Max
The Natural Soap Co Ltd

Phillips, Sara
The Natural Soap Co Ltd

Nazafi, Ayazali
4RM Ltd

Nazer, Zeina
Jardins D'Eden Ltd

Neale, Stephen
Maskalin Ltd

Neela Ali, Aroosa
Essancy Limited

Nelson, Gary Charles
Firmenich UK Limited

Nelson, Natalee
Madalyn and Rose Ltd

Ngot, Jean Ferrand
Naturoganik Limited

Nia, Mohammad
Zodiac International (London) Ltd

Nicholls, Simon George
Lush Ltd.

Nisbet, Micaela
Neighbourhood Botanicals Ltd

Njie, Marie Mariyama
Maya Njie Perfumes Limited

Nkemena, Obiechina
Balance By Nora Limited

Nogueira, Paulo Sergio Menoita
Firmenich UK Limited

Noor, Abdulaziz Omar
Atmosy Ltd

Noor, Mohamed
Platinum Beards Ltd

Nord, Alex
Nobell Group Ltd

Norton, Anthony Graham
NTM (UK) Limited

Nouri, Sam
Maskologist Ltd

Novitskiy, Alexander, Dr
Nova Extraction Ltd

Ogboye, Jaiye Adebukola
Jaye O'Boye & Co Ltd

O'Malley, Tara Louise
Good By Nature Ltd

O'Neill, Lynda Rose
Silyn Products Ltd

O'Shea, Nicholas Desmond John
Creightons PLC
Potter & Moore Innovations Ltd

O'Shea, Nicholas
Potter & Moore (Devon) Ltd

O'Sullivan, Evbi
Berry Inc Ltd

Ocampo, Edman Relox
Ed N' Grace Ltd

Oduyemi, Aanuoluwa
Vetivert & Co Ltd

Ogden, Mark Peter
Fragrance Oils (International) Ltd

Ogden, Natalie Jane
Alchemy Skin and Soul Ltd.

Okafor, Vivienne
Hypha Cosmetics Ltd

Okeke, Nneoma Chibudibia, Dr
Freshly Whip'd Limited

Okoye, Alexia
Zaeda Alexia Limited

Okoye, Odera
Zaeda Alexia Limited

Okunniwa, Liha
Oyepitan and Okunniwa Limited

Oldham, Lucy
La Maison Hedonique Limited

Olioso, Barbara, Dr
Organatural Ltd

Oliver, Andrew William
A W Oliver & Co Ltd

Oliver, Andrew
Oliver & Taylor Ltd

Olusesan, Abiodun
Radiant Glow Beauty UK Ltd

Omara, Sean
Icebox Brands EU Limited

Omoyele, Emmanuel
Mr Vanguard Limited

Orbell, Joseph
Cool Gell Limited

Kazmi, Farwah Batool, Dr
The Organic Alchemist Ltd

Carter, Frank Paul Julian
The Organic Fragrance Co Ltd

Osuobeni, Ebi Peniella
Department Health & Beauty Ltd

Oxford, Samantha Marie
Toddle Born Wild Limited

Oyepitan, Abiodun
Oyepitan and Okunniwa Limited

Pacey, Simon Clifford
Elemental Beauty Limited

Ballesteros, Marie Margaret
The Paisley Soap Co Ltd

Panda, Anil Kumar
Lum Lifestyle Ltd.

Pankova, Tatiana
Jove London Ltd

Pardoe, Laura Jane
Field Fresh Skincare Ltd

Parmar, Bhupendra
Fragrance Selection (UK) Ltd

Parry, Alan Norman
Phoenix Fragrances Limited

Partridge, Naomi Joy
Ko. Essentials Ltd.

Partridge, Thomas Michael
Ko. Essentials Ltd.

Patel, Abdul Ebrahim
Freshorize Ltd

Patel, Dipty Hasmukh
Hod Perfumes Limited

Patel, Nasim Akhtar
Adam Michaels Group Ltd

Payne, George
International Toiletries & Cosmetics

Payne, Shelagh Margaret
International Toiletries & Cosmetics

Pearson, Deborah Frances
Morgan's Pomade Co Ltd

Peart, Meranda-Jade
Lucayan Limited

Pedrocchi, Luigi, Dr
Mibelle Ltd

Percy, John Graham
Ungerer Limited

Janousek, Benjamin
The Perfume Studio Limited

Naake, Judith Lynn
The Perfume Studio Limited

Warden, John Nicholas Grant
The Perfume Studio Limited

Perman, Timothy James
Atlas Group Limited
Swallowfield PLC

Petras, Christophe
BCM Limited

Petrovich, Christian
Argos International Fragrances Ltd

Pettitt, Daniel John
Heaven Scent Incense Limited

Pettitt, Mark Thomas
Heaven Scent Incense Limited

Petzke, Tinu
Osunti Limited

Phillips, Dominic Beavis Blake
Lola's Apothecary Ltd

Phillips, Grania Tiffany
Lola's Apothecary Ltd

Phillips, Lucy
Nature's Embrace Limited

Phillips, Neville John Aubrey
Yverman Ltd

Phillips, Peter
Precious Clothing & Beauty Ltd

Phillips, Simon Blake
Lola's Apothecary Ltd

Piasecka, Monika Ewa
Eco Labyrinth Limited

Pickthall, Christopher
CPL Aromas (Holdings) Limited
CPL Aromas Limited

Pickthall, Francis
CPL Aromas (Holdings) Limited
CPL Aromas Limited

Pickthall, Nicholas
CPL Aromas (Holdings) Limited
CPL Aromas Limited

Pickthall, Terence
CPL Aromas (Holdings) Limited
CPL Aromas Limited

Picolet, Lionel
Robertet (U.K.) Limited

Pictet, Laetitia Christabel
Firmenich UK Limited

Piekarska, Michalina Elzbieta
Polka Lab Limited

Pinsent, Demetra Aikaterini, Lady
Islestarr Holdings Limited

Pipe, Nicola
Paromachem Limited

Pipe, Steven Richard
Paromachem Limited

Plackett-Smith, Hannah Rose
My Life But Greener Limited

Plange, Ngozi
Alchemy Botanics Ltd

Plimmer, Laura
Three Fizzy Pigs Ltd

Pochin, James Patrick
Acheson & Acheson Limited

Polding, Mark
Hampshire Cosmetics Limited
Solab Group Limited

Popov, Sergei
Barony Universal Products PLC

Popple, Alex
Flowery Whiff Limited

Popple, Carolyn
Flowery Whiff Limited

Potts, Martin Christopher Francis
Fragrance Oils (International) Ltd
Fragrance Oils (Purchasing) Ltd
Northern Aromatics (Sales) Ltd

Pozniak, Adrian
HE FE Ltd

Presswell, James Stephen
Ecopel Corporation Limited
Foltex Hair Technology Limited

Presswell, June Linda
Ecopel Corporation Limited
Foltex Hair Technology Limited

Presswell, Roy Henry
Ecopel Corporation Limited
Foltex Hair Technology Limited

Woodger, Victoria Helen
The Pretty Little Treat Company (Yorkshire)

Price, Stephen Ronald
Dr. Organic Limited

Priestley, Charlotte
Balm House Limited

Prokhorova, Svetlana
Ainsel Limited

Purdie, Gavin Ernest
Purdie's of Argyll Ltd

Quinn, Elizabeth
Mary Jean Limited

Quinn, Leslie Thomas
Mary Jean Limited

Majoros, Agnes Renata
The Quint Essence Lab Ltd

Varro, Attila
The Quint Essence Lab Ltd

Qureshi, Nausheen
Elequra Limited

Radovic, Jacqueline
Fragrance Oils (International) Ltd

Rait, Cameron Alexander
Just Skincare Limited

Rall, Surinder Kaur
Khushi Skincare Limited

Ramnathkar, Tejal Ajay
Washworks Bodycare Limited

Ramshaw, Philip Neil
Castlefields Cosmetics Ltd.

Randell, Nicholas Charles
Our Modern Lives Ltd

Ranno, Consolazione
Sikania Ltd

Raugale, Jurate
Olire Ltd

Raugalis, Aleksandras
Olire Ltd

Raymond, Gerard Jan
Meiyume (UK) Limited

Razak, Nihad
Nihad A Rawi Limited

Rea, Kathryn Caroline Bennett
I Love Myself Ltd

Reddyhoff, Adam
Hoff Beards Limited

Reed, Eric Steven
Sensora Limited

Rees, Geoffrey
Pur-D Natural Skin Care Ltd

Regal, Ava
Above Beyond Group Ltd

Relph, David Charles John
Charmpits Ltd

Relph, Nicola Anne, Dr
Charmpits Ltd

Rhodes, Zandra Lindsey, Dame
Zandra Rhodes Fragrances Ltd

Rhouila, Kareem
Magma London Ltd

Riaz, Sajid
R.P.C. Midlands Ltd

Rice, Neil
AC Packing Ltd

Rich, Roger George
Premier Specialties Europe Ltd

Richards, Carol Elizabeth
Herbfarmacy Ltd

Richards, Dale Lucas Philip Charles
New Vistas Avant Garde Limited

Richards, Dean
AD Fragrances Ltd

Richards, Gordon Paul
Herbfarmacy Ltd

Richards, Jane Sharon
Karma Cosmetics Co Ltd

Richardson, Stephen John
Castlefields Cosmetics Ltd.

Ricketts, Lesley
BL Cosmetics Limited

Ricketts, William Paul
BL Cosmetics Limited

Riley, Charlotte
Benefit & Riley Healthcare Ltd
Riley & Sons Ltd

Ripley, Levi
Lick Labs Limited

Rissmann, Hans Hermann
Ishga Ltd

Rix, Deborah
Kao (UK) Limited

Holmes, Christopher Michael
Ethel Roberts Limited

Roberts, Julie Susan
Clover Chemicals Limited

Robinson, David
Perfair Limited

Robinson-Price, Keston
Indult Paris Ltd

Rochell, Luke Daniel
B Luxury Scents Ltd

Rochford, Jason Robert
Soak Rochford Ltd

Rodriguez, George Luis Vicente
Rodriguez Corporation Ltd

Rogers, Thomas Karl
Eco Earth Limited

Rohrbach, Francois Paul
Firmenich Holdings (UK) Ltd
Firmenich Wellingborough (UK) Ltd

Rosa Da Silva, Nilza
Naticuma Limited

Rose-Innes, Susannah
Hope and Rose Limited

Rosewarne, Ross Anthony
Lick Labs Limited

Ross, Gavin Innes
Dolphin Eco Ltd

Ross, Steven Arthur
Get Lucky Inc Ltd

Rossey, Jan Leon
Caldey Island Estate Co Ltd

Rossi, Susan Lynne
B.S. Eurochem Limited

Rotheram, Sarah
Miller Harris Limited

Routley, Shirley May
Fragrant Earth International Ltd

Royer, Philip
Millicent and Snob Limited

Royere, Olivier
Maison Ex Nihilo UK Limited

Ruan, Qingye
UK Pandora Fairy Skin Beautiyfying Co.,

Rueger, Sarah
Amaranthine Beauty Ltd

Rufino Dos Santos, Rosa Maria
Naticuma Limited

Rupasinghe, Dona Anushika Madhuwanthi
Earth Aroma Limited

Rushworth, Christopher
Carrie Wilson Limited

Russell, Chinwe Mercy
Sheabynature Ltd

Russell, Robin Christopher
First Natural Brands Ltd
First Natural Limited
Natural Aromatics Limited

Russon-Taylor, Imogen
Kingdom Scotland Limited

Rutherford-Mills, Katy
Chirps London Ltd

Saifi, Nadeem
Winterpark Paris Parfums Ltd

Saifi, Sultana Nadeem
Winterpark Paris Parfums Ltd

Mbonu, Ekemezie
The Saints & Co London Ltd

Saksena, Viraj
Viraj Organics Ltd

Salama, Mona Mahmoud Saad
Evoiq International Ltd

Salih, Abdulla
Glamoessence Ltd

Salman, Chachar
Credo Felix Ltd

Salmons, Roy
Pharmaco Group Limited

Salur, Fulya
SE & SA Limited

Salvage, Simon Paul
B.S. Eurochem Limited

Sambrook, Celia
La Riche Limited

Sambrook, Michael John
La Riche Limited

Samuel, Oluwabunmi Omolara
Providence Ventures Limited

Samuel, Victoria Onola
Providence Ventures Limited

Sanders, Hermione Lynne Cecilia
Cosmetics a la Carte Limited

Sanders, Mark
House of Sanders Limited

Sandhu, Jagat Ram
Butterbur and Sage Limited

Sanson, Edward Alexander
11:11 Limited

Saunders, Hannah
Toddle Born Wild Limited

Saurin, Amanda Jane
A.S Apothecary Limited

Sayed, Mohammed Ali
AM Fragrances Limited

Scaramuzza, Catarina
CS Holistic Therapy Products Ltd

Murray, Tami Maria
The Scent Pod Co Ltd

Schouburgh, Tracy
Tresaigh Ltd

Scott, Barbara
Barbara Scott Aromatics Ltd

Sczerbyna, Herve
HBNatura Ltd

Searle, Deborah Jane
Groomers Limited

Searle, Graham
Groomers Limited

Sediva, Lucie
Slavikk Ltd

Seewald-Butzerin, Alexandre
Axwood Limited

Senturk, Gizem Ezgi
SE & SA Limited

Serra, Massimo
Farasha-Cosmetics Ltd

Shah, Dilip Raichand
Cyclax Limited

Shah, Dinesh Chhabildas
Eden Classics Limited
Freestyle Beauty Products Ltd
Universal Toiletries Corporation Ltd

Shah, Jayshree Dinesh
Eden Classics Limited
Freestyle Beauty Products Ltd
Universal Toiletries Corporation Ltd

Shah, Karan
Freestyle Beauty Products Ltd
Universal Toiletries Corporation Ltd

Shah, Sanam
First Natural Brands Ltd
First Natural Limited
Natural Aromatics Limited

Shanab, Reemah
Lucidly Ltd

Sharaka, Amr
Sharakkas United Kingdom Ltd

Sharma, Aakanksha
Auli London Ltd

Sharma, Damini
Sears UK Ltd

Sharp, Andrew Martin
Mibelle Ltd

Sharpe, Frederick Augustus Fenton
Blank Factory Limited

Sharpe, Robert Adrian
Meiyume (UK) Limited

Sharrier, Roxanne
Sharrier Beauty Incorporated Ltd

Shaw, John Roger
Itaconix (U.K.) Limited

Shen, Ing-Nan Nancy
Miller Harris Limited

Shepherd, Daryl Paxton
Universal Chemicals Limited

Shepherd, Malcolm David
Universal Chemicals Limited

Shepherd, Ryan David
Universal Chemicals Limited

Shetty, Akshay Anand
Combe International Limited

Shipton, Brad
Luxury Personal Care Ltd

Shipton, Bradley John
Luxurious Personal Care Ltd

Shipton, James
Luxurious Personal Care Ltd
Luxury Personal Care Ltd

Shode, Olufemi Olukayode, Dr
Yess Essentials Limited

Shode, Oluyemisi Olabisi, Dr
Yess Essentials Limited

Shorrocks, Janet Marie
Soapy Skin Limited

Shukla, Rajev
Faces Cosmetics Limited

Siedlecki, Eugeniusz
IQ-Area Ltd

Siklawi, Samuel
Affinity Organics Limited

Silva, Joanna Wiktoria
Elan Skincare Ltd

Simonson, James Alexander
Sub Tropic Limited

Simonson, John Allan
Sub Tropic Limited

Simpson, Kevin Gordon, Rev
Caldey Island Estate Co Ltd

Sinclair, Margaret
Nadarra Cosmetics Ltd

Singh, Baljit Arora
Midha Limited

Sinnott, Richard Patrick
Skin Defence Limited

Sitlani, Vijay Indroo
Gillette U.K. Limited

Siwak, Waldemar
Aube Laboratories Ltd

Mountney, John, Dr
The Skin Specialist Limited

Nayak, Neena, Dr
The Skin Specialist Limited

Slater, Adrian David
Baylis & Harding PLC

Slater, Tania Angelina
Baylis & Harding PLC

Slavin, Jeffrey Robert
Fragrance Oils (International) Ltd
Fragrance Oils (Purchasing) Ltd
Northern Aromatics (Sales) Ltd

Smit, Christopher Willem
Inari Skincare Ltd

Smith, Andrew James
Moyy Limited

Smith, Bruce William Leo
Wild & Organic Bioactive Essentials

Smith, Elizabeth Kate
Lush Manufacturing Limited

Smith, Fiona
Saltaire Soap Ltd

Smith, Graham Robert
Emerald Kalama Chemical Ltd

Smith, John Arthur, Dr
Pepsyn Limited

Smith, Lee Jason
Stantondown Limited

Smith, Matthew Nathaniel
Eden's Legends Limited

Smith, Nancy Tanscia
B. Silki Naturally Ltd

Smith, Robert Peter
Nectar International Limited

Smith, Steven
Dilecta Cosmetics Limited

Smith, Stewart Leslie
Stantondown Limited

Smith, Terence
Stantondown Limited

Sneath, Anthony David
Balm House Limited

Khoo, Daniel
The Soap Cellar Limited

Ismail, Muhammad Mobeen-Ul-Anwar
The Soap Legacy Ltd

Patel, Husnabanu
The Soap Legacy Ltd

Munier, Helen Louise
The Soap People Ltd

Jeena, Marria
The Soap Souk Ltd

Sohpal, Sunil
Carefree Toiletries Limited

Soltan Talib, Abdul Rahman
Sipro (UK) Ltd

Soltan Talib, Abdullah
Sipro (UK) Ltd

Soltan Talib, Noraini Binti
Sipro (UK) Ltd

Buoy, Sakina
The Somerset Toiletry Co Ltd

Soremekun, Mobolaji
Adunni Ori Limited

Sorensen, Lars Soren
TWC Products Limited

Sorrell-Fleet, Jonathan Phillip
Renewyou Cancertology UK Ltd

Spaticchia, Katie
Inspired Diffusing Ltd

Spencer, Peter
Mechmark Ltd

Standring, Steven Alistair
Its All About The Skin Limited

Stanton, James Raymond
Jogb Limited

Starr, Barry
Fragrance Oils (International) Ltd

Stead Deegan, Chloe
Cool Gell Limited

Stead Deegan, Hannah
Cool Gell Limited

Stead, Martin
Cool Gell Limited

Steele, Sheila Joyce
Mint Julip Ltd

Steers, Michelle Wendy
Body Thyme Limited

Stefanidis-Vlad, Bogdan
Sweet Arabian Ltd

Steinhardt, Xenia
Earthwhile Ltd

Stephen, Alwyn Hobert
Pierre Precieuse Parfum UK Ltd

Stephen, Aquillha Marietta
Pierre Precieuse Parfum UK Ltd

Stephen, Mary
Elie Consumer Care Ltd
Revlon & Elie Healthcare Ltd

Stephen, Penelope Anne
Penny Price Aromatherapy Ltd

Stephen, Robert, Revd Dr
Penny Price Aromatherapy Ltd

Stetz, Katarina Maria Matilda
Ninni Ltd

Stevens, Martin
Creightons PLC
Potter & Moore (Devon) Ltd
Potter & Moore Innovations Ltd

Stevenson, Molly
Littlemore Candle Co Ltd

Steward, Nicholas John
Gallivant Perfumes Limited

Stewart, Sarah Christina
Smelliz Ltd

Steyer, Ingo
Fumarette Ltd

Still, Marie
Alice in Perfume Limited

Stoker, Michael William
Nature Spirits Limited

Simon, Lauren Belinda
Lauren Stone Limited

Storey, Daniel
Storey Enterprises Limited

Storey, Suzanna Sujantha
Storey Enterprises Limited

Storp, Andreas, Dr
Drom International UK Limited

Storp, Ferdinand, Dr
Drom International UK Limited

Stride, Belinda Mary
General Flavours & Fragrances Ltd

Baxter, Gwendoline Harriette
H.E. Stringer (Perfurmery) Ltd

Baxter, Stephen David
H.E. Stringer (Perfurmery) Ltd

Strug, Margaret
Bahoma Limited

Stuart-Matthews, Helena Danuta
XDC Limited

Sturgis, Judy Lynn
Banyan Skincare Ltd

Subramaniam, Karunakaran
Anuvaayum Ltd

Sumner, Jonathan
LJSP Ltd

Sumner, Robert Bird
LJSP Ltd

Swaby, Daniel
Bespoke Natural Health Ltd

Swain, Louise Kay
Salix Moon Apothecary Ltd

Swaminathan, Vengadan
Coty Manufacturing UK Limited

Swan, Brian Michael
Swanny's Ltd.

Swan, Eliot
Barony Universal Products PLC

Swan, Noi
Swanny's Ltd.

Sya, Kathia May Yin
Drops of Humanity Ltd

Symes, Becky Laura May
Holistica Skin Ltd

Takacs, Peter Laszlo
One Green Lab Ltd

Tanser, Mark James
11:11 Limited

Taylor, Christopher Mark
Eve Taylor (London) Limited

Taylor, Alan Leslie
Eve Taylor (London) Limited

Taylor OBE, Evelyn May
Eve Taylor (London) Limited

Taylor, Alan Leslie
Good Skin Care Co Ltd

Taylor, Callum John
Cactus Skincare Limited

Taylor, Christopher Mark
Good Skin Care Co Ltd

Taylor, Elizabeth Joanna
Fizzy Lizzy's Ltd

Taylor, Evelyn May
Good Skin Care Co Ltd

Taylor, Grant
Bear Head Grooming Products Ltd

Taylor, Jimmy
Bigben Healthcare Limited

Taylor, Krista Louise
Scence Ltd

Taylor, Paul Victor
Meiyume (UK) Limited

Taylor, Raymond Neil
Good Skin Care Co Ltd

Taylor, Robin Christopher Thomas
Corincraft Limited

Taylor, Sarah Upendo Hannah
Superfood Beauty Limited

Telford, Nathan Lee
Cool Gell Limited

Temofeh, Emmanuel Iretomi
D'lusso Collection Ltd

Teo, Kok SEN
Prosody London Limited

Thomas, Amanda Elizabeth
Chapel House Skincare Limited

Thomas, David
Skin Intuition Ltd

Thomas, Richard Jeremy
Fragrance Oils (International) Ltd

Thomas, Titty Pappachen
Heavenly Fragrance (UK) Ltd

Thompson, Leigh
LTSC Ltd

Thompson-Oloko, Manuel
Jaemae Ltd

Thorn, Julie Anne
Busy Bees Cosmetics Limited

Thorn, Kevin Barry
Busy Bees Cosmetics Limited

Tidy, Louisa
L & A Natural Limited

Tierney, Donna Marie
Marinical Limited

Tilbury, Charlotte Emma Bow
Islestarr Holdings Limited

Tiley, John Malcolm
Nutracrest Ltd

Tiley, Sandra Elizabeth
Nutracrest Ltd

Tipping, Linda Merrill
Garden Perfumers Ltd

Tischhauser, Christian Andre
Balmpots Limited

Tobias, James Mark
Clover Chemicals Limited

Tobitt, Stephen Henry
Neal's Yard (Natural Remedies) Ltd

Tong, Barry Keith
Raw Supremo Ltd

Tong, Katy
Raw Supremo Ltd

Tongomo, Ngongo Uyumbu Berekad
Uyumbu Limited

Tran, Kim Sec
Camblabs Ltd

Travis, Tracey Thomas
Make-Up Art Cosmetics (U.K.) Ltd

Trayling, Leon Keith
Ishga Ltd

Trevaskus, Amy Louise
Grace & Hartland Ltd

Bersch, Paulette
Geo. F. Trumper (Perfumer and Products)

Cherchi Bersch, Sebastian
Geo. F. Trumper (Perfumer and Products)

Tsavdaridis, Thomas
Monreale Limited

Tsekouras, Iraklis
Kisens Ltd

Tsuruta, Naoteru
Shinso Skin Care Limited

Turner, Alexandra Louise
Washworks Bodycare Limited

Turpin, Charles Edward
Sunshapers Limited

Tylko, Joanna
Gio Natura Ltd

Tzortzis, Akis Zafirios
Carzel Limited

Udo-Chijioke, Onyinyechi Chimamaka Adannaya, Dr
Onyii's Cosmetics Ltd

Ueber, Klaus Georg
Body Reform Limited
Gellure Ltd

Unavane, Mukund, Dr
Linden and Lime Limited

Usher, Deborah Frances
Pur-D Natural Skin Care Ltd

Usman, Godman
Maribella London Limited

Uvarova, Mariia
La Mu London Limited

V.David, Krisztin
Glamour Natural Cosmetics Ltd

V.David, Tamas
Glamour Natural Cosmetics Ltd

Vadher, Bharti
Sansuraya Limited

Vagnoni, Robert Julio
Ishga Ltd

Van Elkan, Amanda
TCJ Treatments Limited

Van Santvoort, Gerardus Arnoldus, Rev
Caldey Island Estate Co Ltd

Vasini, Lorenzo James
Vaunt Limited

Vaughan-Field, Laura
Squeaky Clean Queen Ltd

Verier, Alexander Peter
Blank Factory Limited

Vickers, Samuel William
Plant Department Ltd

Vieth, Christopher
Elemis Limited

Vijayam, Upendra Shenoy Umesh
Ayurveda Wellness Ltd

Vinogradoff, Paul
Prosody London Limited

Virk, Manjinder
4RM Ltd

Vleeming, Lauranne
Custom Skin Lab Limited

Von Pfefer, Alexis Rosalia
Lex Roris Ltd

Voorhees III, Kenneth Garretson
Ungerer Limited

Voorhees Jr, Kenneth Garretson
Ungerer Limited

Vorbach, Sarah
Face Boutique Limited

Vundum, Marina Emma Lucy
Essential Spirit Limited

Wagstaffe, Serina Claire
Bathroom Cosmetics Ltd

Walker, David Ian
Sensapeel Ltd

Walker, Donna
Aromatic Answers Ltd

Walker, Thomas Harry
Islestarr Holdings Limited

Walkling, Richard Jonothon
Buddy Direct Ltd

Walsh, Gary
Above Beyond Group Ltd

Walsh, Richard, Dr
Regis Personal Care Ltd

Walters, Emma Morag Dorothy
Coty Manufacturing UK Limited

Walters, Kathryn
Cybele UK Ltd

Walton, Wayne
Gelspa Limited

Wang, Lu
Potions & Possibilities Ltd

Want, Clare
Combe International Limited

Ward OBE, John Streeton
Sensa Personal Care Limited

Ward, Michael John
Solab Group Limited

Waring, David William
Scrubbingtons Limited

Waring, Karen
Scrubbingtons Limited

Waring, William Banks
Nectar International Limited

Warwick-Smith, Peter Timothy
Elsan Limited

Waterman, Gail Marie
Waterman Corporate Enterprises Ltd

Waterman, Matt Luca
Waterman Corporate Enterprises Ltd

Watson, Adam
Savage Alchemy Limited

Waud, George Edward Guilford
Islestarr Holdings Limited

Webb, Barbara
Q-Pack Limited

Webb, Roy
Q-Pack Limited

Weber, Kathleen Adams Kingsford
Sundarak Ltd

Wells, Susan Jane
Old Park Farm Estate Limited

Whall, Richard David
BCM Limited

Wheeldon, Rachael Louise
Tom's Garden Limited

White, Kevin
Juni Cosmetics Limited

White, Madeleine
Juni Cosmetics Limited

White, Paul Douglas
Escentric Molecules Limited
Kinski Limited
Project Renegades Ltd
This Wode Co Ltd
Vinculum Ltd

White, Suzanne
Juni Cosmetics Limited

Wibaux, Maxime Daniel Philippe
Toddle Born Wild Limited

Dunlop, Stephanie Renee
The Wild Bathing Co Ltd

Wild, Allison
AI Oxford Ltd
Protect Biosciences Ltd
Wild & Organic Bioactive Essentials

Wild, Fredrick
Splash Cosmetics Ltd

Wild, Hannah
Splash Cosmetics Ltd

Sorensen, Lars Soren
The Wildsmith Collection Ltd

Wilhelm, Daniel
Pandorra Ltd.

Wilkins, Stephen
Hypothesis One Ltd

Williams, Julia
Cocoa Twist Limited

Williams, Marie Ann
Reesoaps.co.uk Ltd

Williams, Stanley
Authenticus Ltd

Williams-Hamilton, Yvonne
Care By Jords Ltd

Willis, Susanne
Wilde Beauty Limited

Wilson, Dorothy
Ottimo Supplies Limited

Wilson, Harry Edward
Ottimo Supplies Limited

Wilson, Kate
Sundarak Ltd

Wilson, Matthew
Scots Mist Ltd

Wilson, Robert Douglas
United Beauty Products Limited

Wingate, James Paul
Eastwing Grooming Co. Limited

Winter, Susan Jane
Neal's Yard (Natural Remedies) Ltd

Winters, Joanne
Making Scents Ltd

Winwood, Amanda Jane Vivian
Spiezia Organics Limited

Winyard, Patricia
Sensa Personal Care Limited

Winyard, Simon Andrew
Sensa Personal Care Limited

Wittouck, Jozef Maria Jaak
Clover Chemicals Limited

Woerdenweber, Vivien
Whole International Limited

Wood, James Sebastian
Bearface Industries Limited

Wood, Josephine Alice
JWO Beauty Limited

Wood, Karen
30 Minute Tan Limited

Wood, Matthew
Bearface Industries Limited

Woodman, Cheryl Ruth
Honesty Skincare Limited

Wooi, Cheang Chin
Meiyume (UK) Limited

Workman, Joseph Bernard
Kao (UK) Limited

Wright, Daryl Olutoye
Scrummy U Health Ltd

Wright, Hilda
Scrummy U Health Ltd

Wright, Lee Steven
Wrimes Cosmetics Ltd

Wroot, Matthew Neil
Pot of Gold Cosmetics Limited

Wyn-Davies, Katherine
Elinor Sophia Limited

Yaneva, Asya
L & A Natural Limited

Yang, Chunxiang
Green Mass Limited

Yasir, Abdulla
Glamoessence Ltd

Yassin, Mohammed Fakhir Hashim
Omprus Limited

Fletcher, Jane
The Yellow Can Co Ltd

Gazzard, Matthew
The Yellow Can Co Ltd

Perman, Timothy James
The Yellow Can Co Ltd

Yilmaz, Husnu
Gillette U.K. Limited

Young, Andrew Stuart
Aroma Cosmetics Laboratory Ltd

Young, Anthony Kingsley
Lakeland Fragrances Limited

Young, Christopher John
Gillette U.K. Limited

Young, Valerie Elizabeth
Lakeland Fragrances Limited

Youri, Gloria Petrina
Berachah Consulting Limited

Yu, Aggie Him Yau
Eden in Valley Soapworks Ltd

Yu, Christopher
Ostens Limited

Zabari, Erez
E. Zabari Holdings UK Limited

Zartaloudi, Kyriaki
Sandine Zartaux Holding Ltd
Swiss Pharma Dynamic Ltd

Zatezic, Boris
Mulondon Limited

Zhao, Dongfang Daniel
Savillequinn Pty Ltd.

Zidi, Cendesse
Trees of Beauty Ltd

Standard Industrial Classification
excluding
Manufacture of perfumes and toilet preparations

01280 Growing of spices, aromatic, drug and pharmaceutical crops
Herbfarmacy Ltd
Scents of Nature Ltd
Seilich Limited

03210 Marine aquaculture
Ishga Ltd

08930 Extraction of salt
Anyki Ltd

08990 Other mining and quarrying n.e.c.
Ishga Ltd

10390 Other processing and preserving of fruit and vegetables
Elmbronze Limited
SE & SA Limited
Slavikk Ltd

10519 Manufacture of other milk products
Chuckling Goat Limited

10710 Manufacture of bread; manufacture of fresh pastry goods and cakes
Slavikk Ltd
Very Good Vegan Co Ltd

10821 Manufacture of cocoa and chocolate confectionery
Elinor Sophia Limited

10840 Manufacture of condiments and seasonings
Teknord Limited

10850 Manufacture of prepared meals and dishes
4RM Ltd

10860 Manufacture of homogenized food preparations and dietetic food
Cambridge Genefit Technologies Ltd
Haromatic Ltd

10890 Manufacture of other food products n.e.c. [28]
4RM Ltd
Ava Corporations Ltd
Ayurveda Pura Ltd
Benefit & Riley Healthcare Ltd
Bigben Healthcare Limited
Clarins & Felix Healthcare Ltd
Eifelcorp Consumer Care Ltd
Elie Consumer Care Ltd
Elliott Nutrition Ltd
Felix Medical Group Ltd
Flynn Group of Companies Ltd
Garnier & Hemo Healthcare Ltd
Hemo Bioscience Ltd
Jardins D'Eden Ltd
Julie's Natural Health Ltd
Lamer & Ava Healthcare Ltd
Nars & Elliott Healthcare Ltd
Nutracrest Ltd
Organic Stuff Limited
Phytacol Limited
Regis Personal Care Ltd
Revlon & Elie Healthcare Ltd
Riley & Sons Ltd
Rimmel & Flynn Healthcare Ltd
Stormfree Holdings Ltd
Terra Mater Ltd
Ungerer Limited
E. Zabari Holdings UK Limited

10920 Manufacture of prepared pet foods
Bespoke Natural Health Ltd

11010 Distilling, rectifying and blending of spirits
Linden and Lime Limited

11040 Manufacture of other non-distilled fermented beverages
Lese & Lista Ltd

11050 Manufacture of beer
Sloane Home Ltd

11070 Manufacture of soft drinks; production of mineral waters and other bottled waters
AA Group Holdings Ltd
Pharmaco Group Limited

13300 Finishing of textiles
Anyki Ltd
Ark Perfumeries Limited
Lucidly Ltd

13923 manufacture of household textiles
Organic Basics Ltd

13950 Manufacture of non-wovens and articles made from non-wovens, except apparel
Millicent and Snob Limited

13990 Manufacture of other textiles n.e.c.
Nobell Group Ltd

14131 Manufacture of other men's outerwear
Aswad P.S.S Ltd
Jaye O'Boye & Co Ltd

14132 Manufacture of other women's outerwear
Jaye O'Boye & Co Ltd

14190 Manufacture of other wearing apparel and accessories n.e.c.
4RM Ltd
Elmbronze Limited
Sophrina Gos Limited
Wild Bathing Co Ltd
Zaeda Alexia Limited

14390 Manufacture of other knitted and crocheted apparel
Ethical House Ltd

15120 Manufacture of luggage, handbags and the like, saddlery and harness
Ark Perfumeries Limited
Lucayan Limited
Jaye O'Boye & Co Ltd

16290 Manufacture of other products of wood; manufacture of articles of cork, straw and plaiting materials
Bill & Artisans Ltd

17220 Manufacture of household and sanitary goods and of toilet requisites [16]
Credo Felix Ltd
Divine Earth Ltd
Ekstaze London Limited
Es-Ssentially Yours Ltd
Evocativ Limited
Geltec Limited
Ginger & Vanilla Ltd
Green Mass Limited
Hanan Pacha Ltd
Lese & Lista Ltd
Lick Labs Limited
Luxurious Personal Care Ltd
Luxury Personal Care Ltd
Organic Basics Ltd
Pitt London Ltd
Sanofi International Biotech Co Ltd.

18201 Reproduction of sound recording
Baum of London Limited

20130 Manufacture of other inorganic basic chemicals
Bloom Aromatics Limited
Molton Brown Limited

20140 Manufacture of other organic basic chemicals
Bloom Aromatics Limited
Body Candy Ltd.
Lana-Rae Ltd Ltd

20200 Manufacture of pesticides and other agrochemical products
Emerald Kalama Chemical Ltd

20411 Manufacture of soap and detergents [112]

Anuvaayum Ltd
Anyki Ltd
Archem (N.I.) Ltd
Aromabar (Scotland) Ltd
Aromatherapy Infusions Ltd
Aromatic Scents Ltd
Aventual Ltd
Axwood Limited
Ayurveda Wellness Ltd
Berry Inc Ltd
Biologico Cosmetics Limited
Bloomtown Ltd
Body Candy Ltd.
Body Station Limited
CS Holistic Therapy Products Ltd
Caley's of Exeter Ltd
Carapoll Chemicals Ltd
Carzel Limited
Clover Chemicals Limited
Cocoa Lime Limited
Cosmetic Hooligans Ltd
Eco Earth Limited
Ed N' Grace Ltd
Eden Classics Limited
Elinor-UK Ltd
Essential Spirit Limited
Evans Vanodine International PLC
Evocativ Limited
Farasha-Cosmetics Ltd
Fillcare Limited
Freestyle Beauty Products Ltd
Freshorize Ltd
Fysifarm Limited
Gio Natura Ltd
Glamour Natural Cosmetics Ltd
Greatest of All Time Soapworks Ltd
Haromatic Ltd
Heavenly Fragrance (UK) Ltd
Highland Soap Co. Limited
Holistic Plant Technologies Ltd
Icilda's Ltd
Insensed Ltd
Sarah Ireland Perfumes Ltd
Itaconix (U.K.) Limited
Ko. Essentials Ltd.
LJSP Ltd
LU Aromatherapy Ltd
Lana-Rae Ltd Ltd
Lathersmith Ltd
Leum Skin Care Ltd
Lick Labs Limited
Little Green Beehive Ltd
Lofty Gardens Ltd
MWK Cosmetics (UK) Ltd
Madalyn and Rose Ltd
Magpie's Ocean Ltd
Making Scents Ltd
Maribella London Limited
Christina May Limited
Mbikudi Ltd
Robert McBride Ltd
Meadow Farm Friends Ltd
Molecula Ltd
Molton Brown Limited
Natural Soap Co Ltd
Naturali360 Limited
Nature B Limited
Old Park Farm Estate Limited
Orikii Naturals Ltd
Ottimo Supplies Limited
P & H Natural Skincare Ltd
Paisley Soap Co Ltd
Polka Lab Limited
Pretty Little Treat Company (Yorkshire)
Purdie's of Argyll Ltd
Quint Essence Lab Ltd
Reesoaps.co.uk Ltd
Relax Candle and Bath Co Ltd
Renbow Haircare Limited
Rustic Blends Limited
Rutherford Bambury Ltd
SE & SA Limited
Salopian Ltd
Saltaire Soap Ltd
Sanofi International Biotech Co Ltd.
Savage Alchemy Limited
Savon de V Ltd
Seilich Limited
Sheabynature Ltd
Shifting London Ltd
Sikania Ltd
Simply Ewe Limited
Smelliz Ltd
Soap Cellar Limited
Soap Legacy Ltd
Soap People Ltd
Soap Souk Ltd
Soapberries Ltd
Soapy Skin Limited
Spirit of The Isle Ltd.
Strathpeffer Spa Soap Co Ltd
Superfine Manufacturing Ltd
TAC Perfumes & Cosmetics (UK) Ltd
Thebubblebar Ltd
Tiger Lily Soapery Ltd
Travik Chemicals (UK) Limited
UK Pandora Fairy Skin Beautiyfying Co.,
Universal Chemicals Limited
Universal Toiletries Corporation Ltd
Very Good Vegan Co Ltd
Washworks Bodycare Limited
Yess Essentials Limited

20412 Manufacture of cleaning and polishing preparations [14]

Acheson & Acheson Limited
Archem (N.I.) Ltd
Carapoll Chemicals Ltd
Evans Vanodine International PLC
Evocativ Limited
Freshorize Ltd
Robert McBride Ltd
Old Park Farm Estate Limited
Organic Basics Ltd
Ottimo Supplies Limited
Qualkem Ltd
Sanofi International Biotech Co Ltd.
Tiger Lily Soapery Ltd
Travik Chemicals (UK) Limited

20530 Manufacture of essential oils [39]

Ark Perfumeries Limited
Aromatherapy Infusions Ltd
Aromatic Scents Ltd
B Luxury Scents Ltd
Bloom Aromatics Limited
Cocoa Lime Limited
Eco Labyrinth Limited
Eden Classics Limited
Emerald Kalama Chemical Ltd
Esensi Skincare Ltd
Freestyle Beauty Products Ltd
Freshorize Ltd
Good Skin Care Co Ltd
H H Formulations Ltd
Hands Organic Ltd
Haromatic Ltd
Heavenly Fragrance (UK) Ltd
Karaama Fragrances Ltd
Linden and Lime Limited
Lucayan Limited
Making Scents Ltd
Midnight Apothecary Limited
Millicent and Snob Limited
Nature Spirits Limited
Nova Extraction Ltd
Old Park Farm Estate Limited
Robertet (U.K.) Limited
Savillequinn Pty Ltd.
Scents of Nature Ltd
Seilich Limited
Soap Cellar Limited
H.E. Stringer (Perfurmery) Ltd
TAC Perfumes & Cosmetics (UK) Ltd
Eve Taylor (London) Limited
Thread and Co UK Limited
Tom's Garden Limited
Trees of Beauty Ltd
UK Pandora Fairy Skin Beautiyfying Co.,
Ungerer Limited

20590 Manufacture of other chemical products n.e.c. [19]

Archem (N.I.) Ltd
Aromatic Scents Ltd
B.S. Eurochem Limited
Brigantia Personal Care Ltd
Carapoll Chemicals Ltd
Clover Chemicals Limited
Eco Earth Limited
Elinor-UK Ltd
Evans Vanodine International PLC
Pierre Fabre Limited
Gio Natura Ltd
Glamour Natural Cosmetics Ltd
Green Mass Limited
Itaconix (U.K.) Limited
LJSP Ltd
Lucayan Limited
Qualkem Ltd
H.E. Stringer (Perfurmery) Ltd
Superfine Manufacturing Ltd

21100 Manufacture of basic pharmaceutical products [16]

Acarrier Limited
Cool Gell Limited
Dach Cosmeceutics Limited
Elemis Limited
Emerald Kalama Chemical Ltd
Pierre Fabre Limited
Farasha-Cosmetics Ltd
HBNatura Ltd
Little Green Beehive Ltd
Pharmaco Group Limited
Phytacol Limited
Sandine Zartaux Holding Ltd
Skin Defence Limited
H.E. Stringer (Perfurmery) Ltd
Swiss Pharma Dynamic Ltd
Thread and Co UK Limited

21200 Manufacture of pharmaceutical preparations
BCM Limited
Combe International Limited
Dermapharm Skincare Limited
Ferndale Pharmaceuticals Ltd
Pharmaco Group Limited
Sandine Zartaux Holding Ltd
Swiss Pharma Dynamic Ltd

22290 Manufacture of other plastic products
Perfair Limited
Sipro (UK) Ltd

23410 Manufacture of ceramic household and ornamental articles
Corincraft Limited
Perfair Limited

25710 Manufacture of cutlery
Kairn Holding Limited

25990 Manufacture of other fabricated metal products n.e.c.
D'Iusso Collection Ltd

26110 Manufacture of electronic components
Lily Her Limited

26400 Manufacture of consumer electronics
DBI Innovations Group Limited
Lily Her Limited
Perfair Limited

26520 Manufacture of watches and clocks
Bluhans Ltd

31090 Manufacture of other furniture
Bill & Artisans Ltd

32120 Manufacture of jewellery and related articles
Aswad P.S.S Ltd
Iam By Nature Ltd.
La Mu London Limited
Mbikudi Ltd
Missy D Collection Limited
Thomas Andy Ltd.

32990 Other manufacturing n.e.c. [25]
AA Group Holdings Ltd
Aroma Amour Ltd
Arriva Fragrances Limited
Beard Nature Limited
Black Gem Cosmetics Ltd
D'Iusso Collection Ltd
Daughters of Circe Ltd
Elmbronze Limited
Emily Victoria Candles Limited
Gillette U.K. Limited
LU Aromatherapy Ltd
Lana-Rae Ltd Ltd
Neal's Yard (Natural Remedies) Ltd
Nova Extraction Ltd
Perfance Limited
Pierre Precieuse Parfum UK Ltd
Potions & Possibilities Ltd
Prispens Limited
Since Six Ltd
So Skincare Limited
Tranquility Cosmetics Limited
UK Pandora Fairy Skin Beautiyfying Co.,
United Beauty Products Limited
Valencia Vanna Ltd.
Very Good Vegan Co Ltd

41100 Development of building projects
Cool Gell Limited

46160 Agents involved in the sale of textiles, clothing, fur, footwear and leather goods
Credo Felix Ltd
Precious Clothing & Beauty Ltd

46170 Agents involved in the sale of food, beverages and tobacco
SE & SA Limited

46180 Agents specialised in the sale of other particular products
Green Ladies N.I Ltd
Kairn Holding Limited
So Skincare Limited
Wild Bathing Co Ltd

46190 Agents involved in the sale of a variety of goods
Rasta Life Ltd
Universal Toiletries Corporation Ltd

46342 Wholesale of wine, beer, spirits and other alcoholic beverages
Sloane Home Ltd

46380 Wholesale of other food, including fish, crustaceans and molluscs
Honey Corn Limited

46390 Non-specialised wholesale of food, beverages and tobacco
House of 18 Ltd

46420 Wholesale of clothing and footwear
Cutelovelee Limited
Ethical House Ltd
Shifting London Ltd

46450 Wholesale of perfume and cosmetics [192]
11:11 Limited
A Natural Treat Limited
Adam Michaels Group Ltd
Ahwaz Ltd
Ajmal Perfume (UK) Limited
Al-Jazeera Perfumes Ltd
Alkaiser Perfumes Ltd
Arbar Ltd
Arizona Botaniq Limited
Aromabar (Scotland) Ltd
Askett & English Ltd
Aube Laboratories Ltd
Ava Corporations Ltd
B Luxury Scents Ltd
B. Silki Naturally Ltd
Beard Nature Limited
Beauty Alliance International Ltd
Bedeaux Ltd
Benefit & Riley Healthcare Ltd
Berry Inc Ltd
Bigben Healthcare Limited
Biologico Cosmetics Limited
Blank Factory Limited
Bloom Remedies Ltd
Bloomtown Ltd
Body Reform Limited
Andre Boyard Perfumes Limited
Bubble-Bubble Ltd
Clarins & Felix Healthcare Ltd
Contour and More London Ltd
Coriungo Limited
Cosmetic Hooligans Ltd
Cosmos Cosmetics Limited
Cutelovelee Limited
Dermafood Limited
Dermamaitre Ltd.
Designer Fragrances Limited
Dilecta Cosmetics Limited
Dr. Organic Limited
Dreamweave Products Ltd
Eabir Ltd
Eden's Legends Limited
Eifelcorp Consumer Care Ltd
Elan Skincare Ltd
Elegant Boss Ltd
Elequra Limited
Eleuthere Ltd
Elie Consumer Care Ltd
Elinor-UK Ltd
Elliott Nutrition Ltd
Ethical House Ltd
Evoiq International Ltd
Excel (GS) Limited
Face Boutique Limited
Fashion Fragrances & Cosmetics UK Ltd
Felix Medical Group Ltd
Flowery Whiff Limited
Flynn Group of Companies Ltd
Foad Wax Limited
Forte Organics Ltd
Fragrant Spa Limited
Freshly Whip'd Limited
Fysifarm Limited
G & G Skincare Ltd
Garnier & Hemo Healthcare Ltd
Glad Gent Ltd
Good By Nature Ltd
Good Skin Care Co Ltd
Gracetree Ltd
Green Jiva Ltd

Green Ladies N.I Ltd
Green Mass Limited
Hamiltons of Canterbury Ltd
Haych Cosmetics Limited
Heavenly Fragrance (UK) Ltd
Hemo Bioscience Ltd
Herc Ltd.
Highland Soap Co. Limited
Hoff Beards Limited
Holistic Plant Technologies Ltd
Honey Corn Limited
Iam By Nature Ltd.
Icebox Brands EU Limited
Icilda's Ltd
Image Hub Limited
Inovair Limited
Sarah Ireland Perfumes Ltd
Irregular Cosmetics Co Ltd
Jardins D'Eden Ltd
Jean Christian Perfumes Ltd
Jorum of Scotland Limited
Julie's Natural Health Ltd
Juni Cosmetics Limited
Karaama Fragrances Ltd
Kehal Ltd
Khali Min Limited
Khushi Skincare Limited
Kingdom Scotland Limited
Ko. Essentials Ltd.
Thomas Kosmala Parfums Ltd
LTSC Ltd
La Maison Hedonique Limited
Ladd Cosmetics Ltd
Lamer & Ava Healthcare Ltd
Lese & Lista Ltd
Lex Roris Ltd
Libhairation Ltd
Lola's Apothecary Ltd
Lumine Beauty Ltd
Lush Ltd.
Luxurious Personal Care Ltd
Luxury Personal Care Ltd
MWK Cosmetics (UK) Ltd
Madre Skincare Limited
Magpie's Ocean Ltd
Majestic Company London Ltd
Man Mask Ltd
Manhattan Group Ltd.
Mary Jean Limited
Maskologist Ltd
Mast - Art Group Limited
Mata Labs Cosmetics Ltd
Meadow Farm Friends Ltd
Meek and Mild Essentials Ltd
Doris Michaels Cosmetics Ltd
Mint Julip Ltd
Molecula Ltd
Mono Naturoils Ltd
Moyy Limited
Myroo Ltd
Nars & Elliott Healthcare Ltd
Natural Sheaness Ltd
Natural Skincare London Ltd
Neal's Yard (Natural Remedies) Ltd
Nectar International Limited
Neville Cut and Shave Limited
A W Oliver & Co Ltd
Oliver & Taylor Ltd
Omprus Limited
One Green Lab Ltd
Organic Stuff Limited
Orikii Naturals Ltd

Pandorra Ltd.
Penny Price Aromatherapy Ltd
Phyto Pharm Limited
Phyto Pharma Limited
Potions & Possibilities Ltd
Prispens Limited
Project Cosmetics Limited
Quint Essence Lab Ltd
Radiant Glow Beauty UK Ltd
Razias London Ltd
Regis Personal Care Ltd
Revlon & Elie Healthcare Ltd
Riley & Sons Ltd
Rimmel & Flynn Healthcare Ltd
Ring in Ring Ltd
Ru Si Lacquers Global Ltd.
Sandine Zartaux Holding Ltd
Scence Ltd
Sheabynature Ltd
Sikania Ltd
Sipro (UK) Ltd
Sloane Home Ltd
Soak Rochford Ltd
South West Aesthetics Ltd
Sphere 7 Lab Ltd
Splash Cosmetics Ltd
Stantondown Limited
Lauren Stone Limited
Sub Tropic Limited
Sweet Arabian Ltd
Swiss Pharma Dynamic Ltd
TAC Perfumes & Cosmetics (UK) Ltd
TWC Products Limited
Eve Taylor (London) Limited
TheManeCo Ltd
Three Organics Ltd
Trees of Beauty Ltd
Geo. F. Trumper (Perfumer and Products)
Twelve Beauty Ltd
Un Air D'Antan Limited
Universal Toiletries Corporation Ltd
Vetivert & Co Ltd
Villa Sauod Ltd
Waterman Corporate Enterprises Ltd
Wheesht Ltd
Wildsmith Collection Limited
Wonder and Wild Ltd
Wrimes Cosmetics Ltd
Zahrat Alqurashi Ltd
Zoe Lane Ltd

46460 Wholesale of pharmaceutical goods

Coriungo Limited
Mast - Art Group Limited

46480 Wholesale of watches and jewellery

Thomas Andy Ltd.

46499 Wholesale of household goods (other than musical instruments) n.e.c

Soak Rochford Ltd

46750 Wholesale of chemical products

Flo Ventures Ltd
Hair Systems Europe Limited
Ru Si Lacquers Global Ltd.
S.R.S.Aromatics Limited

46900 Non-specialised wholesale trade

Bubble-Bubble Ltd
Eastwing Grooming Co. Limited
Flo Ventures Ltd
MAC Professional Haircare Ltd
Macks Wax Ltd
Rasta Life Ltd

47190 Other retail sale in non-specialised stores [10]

Bedeaux Ltd
By Kathryn Ltd
Caldey Island Estate Co Ltd
L'Ocean Limited
Make-Up Art Cosmetics (U.K.) Ltd
Doris Michaels Cosmetics Ltd
Rasta Life Ltd
Un Air D'Antan Limited
Verde London Ltd.
Zaeda Alexia Limited

47240 Retail sale of bread, cakes, flour confectionery and sugar confectionery in specialised stores

Elinor Sophia Limited

47290 Other retail sale of food in specialised stores

Ayurveda Pura Ltd

47510 Retail sale of textiles in specialised stores

Manhattan Group Ltd.
Uncareditional Ltd

47710 Retail sale of clothing in specialised stores

Bloomtown Ltd
Psyche Com & Merch Ltd
Sophrina Gos Limited
Sphere 7 Lab Ltd

47721 Retail sale of footwear in specialised stores

Sophrina Gos Limited

47749 Retail sale of medical and orthopaedic goods in specialised stores (not incl. hearing aids) n.e.c.

South West Aesthetics Ltd

47750 Retail sale of cosmetic and toilet articles in specialised stores [143]

7 Virtues Beauty Ltd
AA Group Holdings Ltd
AD Fragrances Ltd
Affinity Organics Limited
Ahwaz Ltd
Almond & Avocado Ltd
Arbar Ltd
Arizona Botaniq Limited
B. Silki Naturally Ltd
Beard Armour Limited
Beauty Handmade Limited
Biologico Cosmetics Limited
Blank Factory Limited
Body Reform Limited
Cambridge Genefit Technologies Ltd
Charles Jordi Limited
Clay Club Skincare Limited
Claycoco Limited
Concept: Skin Limited
Contour and More London Ltd
Coriungo Limited
Cosmetics a la Carte Limited
Cosmos Cosmetics Limited
Daughters of Circe Ltd
Department Health & Beauty Ltd
Dilecta Cosmetics Limited
Liz Earle Beauty Co. Limited
Ekstaze London Limited
Elan Skincare Ltd
Elegant Boss Ltd
Eleuthere Ltd
Elibec Limited
Essancy Limited
Essentially Yours Limited
Fashion Fragrances & Cosmetics UK Ltd
Fikkerts Limited
First Natural Brands Ltd
Fizzy Thistle Ltd
Flowery Whiff Limited
Foad Wax Limited
Fragrance and Glamour Ltd
Fragrant Spa Limited
Freshly Whip'd Limited
Frosts of London Limited
Fysifarm Limited
G & G Skincare Ltd
Gagnon Essentials Limited
Gellure Ltd
Ginger & Vanilla Ltd
Glad Gent Ltd
Gracetree Ltd
Green Jiva Ltd
Hairs & Graces Cosmetics Ltd
Hamiltons of Canterbury Ltd
Haych Cosmetics Limited
Highland Soap Co. Limited
Hkka Limited
Hod Perfumes Limited
Holistica Skin Ltd
Honesty Skincare Limited
Honey Corn Limited
House of 18 Ltd
Icilda's Ltd
Sarah Ireland Perfumes Ltd
Ishga Ltd
Islestarr Holdings Limited
Jardins D'Eden Ltd
Juni Cosmetics Limited
Karma Cosmetics Co Ltd
Khali Min Limited
Kisens Ltd
LTSC Ltd
La Maison Hedonique Limited
La Parfumerie Anglaise Limited
Ladd Cosmetics Ltd
Lex Roris Ltd
Libhairation Ltd
Lum Lifestyle Ltd.
Luxurious Personal Care Ltd
Luxury Personal Care Ltd
M.C Skin Truth Ltd
MWK Cosmetics (UK) Ltd
Man Mask Ltd
Manhattan Group Ltd.
Maribella London Limited
Marinical Limited
Maskologist Ltd
Mast - Art Group Limited
Mata Labs Cosmetics Ltd
Mayen Velvaere Limited
Meadow Farm Friends Ltd
Midha Limited
Midnight Apothecary Limited
Milo and James Limited
Mono Naturoils Ltd
Moyy Limited
Nadarra Cosmetics Ltd
Natural Deodorant Co Limited
Natural Skincare London Ltd
Nature B Limited
Nature's Embrace Limited
Neal's Yard (Natural Remedies) Ltd
New Vistas Avant Garde Limited
Omprus Limited
Organic Stuff Limited
Orikii Naturals Ltd
Otte Limited
Paradoxical Solutions Limited
Penny Price Aromatherapy Ltd
Perfance Limited
Phyto Pharm Limited
Prispens Limited
Project Cosmetics Limited
Prophylaxis Ltd
Purdie's of Argyll Ltd
Purplelilac Ltd
Ru Si Lacquers Global Ltd.
Rustic Blends Limited
Savage Alchemy Limited
Savon de V Ltd
Scrummy U Health Ltd
Skin Nectar Ltd
Skyn Deep Ltd
South West Aesthetics Ltd
Sphere 7 Lab Ltd
Squeaky Clean Queen Ltd
Squires and Trelawny Ltd
Sundarak Ltd
Sweet Arabian Ltd
TheManeCo Ltd
Thebubblebar Ltd
Three Fizzy Pigs Ltd
Three Organics Ltd
Trees of Beauty Ltd
Tresaigh Ltd
Un Air D'Antan Limited
Uncareditional Ltd
Urban Nymph Limited
Urembo Naturally Ltd
Uyumbu Limited
Veloskin Limited
Vetivert & Co Ltd
Wonder and Wild Ltd

47770 Retail sale of watches and jewellery in specialised stores

Thomas Andy Ltd.

47820 Retail sale via stalls and markets of textiles, clothing and footwear

Ekstaze London Limited
Missy D Collection Limited

47890 Retail sale via stalls and markets of other goods [19]

Aroma Body Treats Limited
Beard Armour Limited
Blackbird and Rain Limited
CS Holistic Therapy Products Ltd
Claycoco Limited
Divine Earth Ltd
Elibec Limited
Hod Perfumes Limited
Insensed Ltd
Karma Cosmetics Co Ltd
Lola's Apothecary Ltd
MK Design & Art Direction Ltd
Macks Wax Ltd
Mary Jean Limited
Pure Ohana Limited
Saisha Marra Ltd.
Scence Ltd
Soap People Ltd
Umma Therapy Ltd.

47910 Retail sale via mail order houses or via Internet [84]

Almond & Avocado Ltd
Arizona Botaniq Limited
Aromabar (Scotland) Ltd
Askett & English Ltd
B. Silki Naturally Ltd
Bath Candy Ltd
Beard Armour Limited
Berry Inc Ltd
Blackbird and Rain Limited
By Kathryn Ltd
CS Holistic Therapy Products Ltd
Cactus Skincare Limited
Calibria Ltd
Cocobubble Ltd
Concept: Skin Limited
Contour and More London Ltd
Cosmos Cosmetics Limited
Credo Felix Ltd
D'lusso Collection Ltd
Department Health & Beauty Ltd
Dermamaitre Ltd.
Dreamweave Products Ltd
Eastwing Grooming Co. Limited
Eleuthere Ltd
Elinor Sophia Limited
Emily Victoria Candles Limited
Esensi Skincare Ltd
Flo Ventures Ltd
G & G Skincare Ltd
Good By Nature Ltd
Green Ladies N.I Ltd
Groomers Limited
HMMT Holdings Ltd.
Hod Perfumes Limited
Holistic Plant Technologies Ltd

The Top UK Perfume and Toilet Preparations Manufacturers

dellam

Hope and Rose Limited
Iam By Nature Ltd.
Insensed Ltd
Jogb Limited
Juni Cosmetics Limited
KD Trading (UK) Limited
Karma Cosmetics Co Ltd
Kisens Ltd
Ko. Essentials Ltd.
Kropp & Hem Ltd
LTSC Ltd
La Mu London Limited
Leum Skin Care Ltd
Lex Roris Ltd
Lola's Apothecary Ltd
Macks Wax Ltd
Madre Skincare Limited
Man Mask Ltd
Marinical Limited
Maskologist Ltd
Doris Michaels Cosmetics Ltd
Midnight Apothecary Limited
Milo and James Limited
Molecula Ltd
Myroo Ltd
Natural Skincare London Ltd
Neville Cut and Shave Limited
Ninni Ltd
Organic Alchemist Ltd
Perfance Limited
Phyto Pharm Limited
Potions & Possibilities Ltd
Pure Ohana Limited
Quint Essence Lab Ltd
Reesoaps.co.uk Ltd
Saisha Marra Ltd.
Scence Ltd
Scrummy U Health Ltd
Sensora Limited
Sikania Ltd
Soap People Ltd
Squires and Trelawny Ltd
Thebubblebar Ltd
Triblaz Limited
Umma Therapy Ltd.
Vetivert & Co Ltd
Wilde Beauty Limited
Wrimes Cosmetics Ltd
Yess Essentials Limited

47990 Other retail sale not in stores, stalls or markets
Claycoco Limited
Good Mela Ltd
Natural Sheaness Ltd
Organic Alchemist Ltd
Uncareditional Ltd

50100 Sea and coastal passenger water transport
Caldey Island Estate Co Ltd

51102 Non-scheduled passenger air transport
Andre Boyard Perfumes Limited

56290 Other food services [18]
Ava Corporations Ltd
Benefit & Riley Healthcare Ltd
Bigben Healthcare Limited
Clarins & Felix Healthcare Ltd
Eifelcorp Consumer Care Ltd
Elie Consumer Care Ltd
Elliott Nutrition Ltd
Felix Medical Group Ltd
Flynn Group of Companies Ltd
Garnier & Hemo Healthcare Ltd
Hemo Bioscience Ltd
Julie's Natural Health Ltd
Lamer & Ava Healthcare Ltd
Nars & Elliott Healthcare Ltd
Regis Personal Care Ltd
Revlon & Elie Healthcare Ltd
Riley & Sons Ltd
Rimmel & Flynn Healthcare Ltd

58141 Publishing of learned journals
Acarrier Limited

58190 Other publishing activities
Honesty Skincare Limited

59112 Video production activities
Storey Enterprises Limited

59200 Sound recording and music publishing activities
Baum of London Limited
Storey Enterprises Limited

62011 Ready-made interactive leisure and entertainment software development
Aswad P.S.S Ltd
XDC Limited

62012 Business and domestic software development
Gotvox Limited
IQ-Area Ltd
Storey Enterprises Limited
XDC Limited

62020 Information technology consultancy activities
Chaud Solutions Limited
Elibec Limited
Gotvox Limited
Paradoxical Solutions Limited
XDC Limited

62090 Other information technology service activities
MAC Professional Haircare Ltd

63110 Data processing, hosting and related activities
Aventual Ltd
Gotvox Limited

64204 Activities of distribution holding companies
Skin Nectar Ltd

68100 Buying and selling of own real estate
Christian Lincoln Enterprise Ltd
Sipro (UK) Ltd

68209 Other letting and operating of own or leased real estate
Caldey Island Estate Co Ltd
Christian Lincoln Enterprise Ltd

70100 Activities of head offices
IQ-Area Ltd
La Mu London Limited

70210 Public relations and communications activities
Psyche Com & Merch Ltd

70229 Management consultancy activities other than financial management
Dermapharm Skincare Limited
Midha Limited
Ninni Ltd
Renu Consultancy Ltd

72110 Research and experimental development on biotechnology
Acarrier Limited
Cambridge Genefit Technologies Ltd

72190 Other research and experimental development on natural sciences and engineering
Inovair Limited

73110 Advertising agencies
MK Design & Art Direction Ltd

74100 Specialised design activities
Geltec Limited
Hamiltons of Canterbury Ltd
MK Design & Art Direction Ltd

74300 Translation and interpretation activities
Aventual Ltd

74909 Other professional, scientific and technical activities n.e.c.
Astroscent Ltd
Organatural Ltd
Since Six Ltd

78300 Human resources provision and management of human resources functions
Berachah Consulting Limited
Eco Labyrinth Limited

79120 Tour operator activities
Ayurveda Wellness Ltd

80300 Investigation activities
Pandorra Ltd.

81100 Combined facilities support activities
Geltec Limited

82302 Activities of conference organisers
Muir Events Ltd

82920 Packaging activities
Laboratory Facilities Limited
Mata Labs Cosmetics Ltd
Pierre Precieuse Parfum UK Ltd

82990 Other business support service activities n.e.c.
Anuvaayum Ltd
Chaud Solutions Limited
IQ-Area Ltd
L A Partnership Limited
Marsh Organics Limited
Nobell Group Ltd
Scrummy U Health Ltd
Sheabynature Ltd
Yverman Ltd

84220 Defence activities
Pandorra Ltd.

85320 Technical and vocational secondary education
L'Ocean Limited

85410 Post-secondary non-tertiary education
Penny Price Aromatherapy Ltd

85520 Cultural education
Mbikudi Ltd

85590 Other education n.e.c.
Experimental Perfume Club Ltd
J2NR Ltd

85600 Educational support services
Christian Lincoln Enterprise Ltd

86900 Other human health activities
Ayurveda Wellness Ltd
Nature B Limited
Paradoxical Solutions Limited
Paz By Nature Ltd
Shaw & Company Business Ltd

90030 Artistic creation
Bedeaux Ltd
Experimental Perfume Club Ltd
Barbara Scott Aromatics Ltd
Sundarak Ltd

93210 Activities of amusement parks and theme parks
Eco Labyrinth Limited

93290 Other amusement and recreation activities n.e.c.
L'Ocean Limited

95250 Repair of watches, clocks and jewellery
Bluhans Ltd

96020 Hairdressing and other beauty treatment [19]
Advanced Aesthetics Training Academy
Almond & Avocado Ltd
Ayurveda Pura Ltd
Balance By Nora Limited
Bixie Group Ltd
Department Health & Beauty Ltd
Elegant Boss Ltd
Hart Enterprise Limited
Kylah K Skincare Ltd
Libhairation Ltd
Lumine Beauty Ltd
MAC Professional Haircare Ltd
Marinical Limited
Midha Limited
Neville Cut and Shave Limited
Skyn Deep Ltd
Soap Cellar Limited
Thread and Co UK Limited
Wheesht Ltd

96040 Physical well-being activities
Advanced Aesthetics Training Academy
Gagnon Essentials Limited
Hanan Pacha Ltd
Skyn Deep Ltd
Umma Therapy Ltd.

96090 Other service activities n.e.c.
Body & Face St. Cyrus Limited
Owen Drew Luxury Candles Ltd
Lum Lifestyle Ltd.
Pierre Precieuse Parfum UK Ltd
Sundarak Ltd

98000 Residents property management
Nobell Group Ltd

Printed in 8pt Nimbus Sans L

Designed by URW++ Design and Development GmbH

Dellam Publishing Limited

2 Heath Drive, Sutton, Surrey, SM2 5RP

Fax: 020 8770 7478   email: enquiries@dellam.com

SAN: 0177881   EAN/GLN: 5030670177882

www.ingramcontent.com/pod-product-compliance
Lightning Source LLC
Chambersburg PA
CBHW081117080526
44587CB00021B/3640